SPIES, LIES AND ALLIES

Praise for *Lady Doctors*

'Kavitha Rao's *Lady Doctors* is several things all at once: a richly satisfying read about a set of extraordinary women; a positively enlightening account of how ordinary girls, against the odds and through sheer—even painful—determination, became pathbreakers; and a much-needed reminder that Indian history is as much the story of understated, often forgotten pioneers as it is of our run-of-the-mill heroes. I learnt much from *Lady Doctors*, and drew great joy from its pages.' – Manu S. Pillai

'(A) riveting book on the trials, tribulations and triumphs of modern India's first women physicians' – *Mint*

'Detailed, extensively researched, told with sensitivity and nuance, it will nevertheless be remembered for delivering that distinct pleasure—of a richly satisfying and compelling read' – *Scroll.in*

'(A) clear-eyed and engrossing look back at six Indian medical pioneers ... The first aspect of this work that draws critical attention is the comprehensive sweep of Rao's research. This, in addition to the author's crisp world-building, transports the reader into the nineteenth and early twentieth centuries' India's in the space of a few words' – *The Asian Age*

'Rao has done a stellar job in documenting the journeys of these women ... Read it to your little ones or read it for yourself in a moment of extreme need for inspiration. *Lady Doctors* will not disappoint' – *The Telegraph*

'To Rao's credit is her indepth research' – *The Tribune*

'In this remarkable book, Rao paints a portrait of an India that was fighting for self-rule while simultaneously clinging to ultraconservative Hindu mores such as child marriage and sati. The fight to become a female doctor ran converse to Hindu society's desire for respectable, homebound women' – *Open The Magazine*

'It is shocking that this legion of extraordinary women has been relegated to the forgotten nooks and crannies of history. Rao deserves a medal for her painstaking efforts to scour through the scanty material available on their lives and deeds to reconstruct their magnificent deeds and phenomenal achievements' – *New Indian Express*

'Rao has done an excellent job of not merely documenting the stories of these women but also placing them in context so that the reader fully appreciates the force of their will to succeed in their goals' – *The Hindu*

KAVITHA RAO

SPIES, LIES AND ALLIES

THE EXTRAORDINARY LIVES OF CHATTO AND ROY

Published by Westland Non-Fiction, an imprint of Westland Books, a division of Nasadiya Technologies Private Limited, in 2025

No. 269/2B, First Floor, 'Irai Arul', Vimalraj Street, Nethaji Nagar, Alapakkam Main Road, Maduravoyal, Chennai 600095

Westland, the Westland logo, Westland Non-Fiction and the Westland Non-Fiction logo are the trademarks of Nasadiya Technologies Private Limited, or its affiliates.

ISBN: 9789360452070

10 9 8 7 6 5 4 3 2 1

Typeset by Ashutosh Jha

Printed at Thomson Press (India) Ltd

To the libraries that have sheltered me and the librarians that have guided me.

Contents

1

The Killing Fields

Death solves all problems. No man, no problem.

Joseph Stalin

Moscow, Stalin's Great Purge, 2 September 1937

AS NIGHT FELL, A SMALL, THIN MAN WITH PIERCING EYES AND A FIERCE moustache stood at the edge of a pit, facing a firing squad. At fifty-seven, Virendranath Chattopadhyaya—Chatto as he was popularly known—had run out of luck at last. Revolutionary, anarchist, spy, brother of Sarojini Naidu, friend of Nehru. Once described aptly and memorably by his lover Agnes Smedley as 'a revolutionary in a dozen different ways, a man of truly fine frenzy, nervous as a cat, always moving, never at rest'.[1]

The labels no longer mattered. What mattered was that he had been forced, finally, to come to rest, singled out for execution by a power-hungry dictator. As Chatto waited for his lonely death, what was he thinking about?

Perhaps of his tumultuous life, which had led him to this point, through England, France, Germany, Sweden and finally the Soviet Union, trying constantly to muster support for Indian independence. Perhaps of his homeland which he had not seen for thirty years. Perhaps of his happy childhood years, with his siblings and his progressive parents, debating with them over dinner in the large Chattopadhyay (which is how Chatto's family spelt their surname) house in Hyderabad.[2] Perhaps of the many women he had left behind in various countries–British, American and Russian. Perhaps of how he had evaded even the British secret service, but eventually ended up a victim of Stalin's paranoia, one of the estimated 700,000 people massacred in the Gulag system of labour camps by the 'man of steel'.

Or perhaps he thought enviously of his fellow revolutionary, the dashing and charismatic M.N. Roy. Seven years younger, Roy had done what Chatto had wanted to do but couldn't: won Lenin's friendship, founded one of the branches of the Communist Party of India, climbed to the top ranks of international communism, then cannily fled the Soviet Union in 1930, escaping Stalin's purge.

Chatto and Roy had been long-time bitter rivals, though they did not meet till 1920. But the world of the Indian revolutionary at the time was small and interconnected, and they had likely heard and speculated about each other despite being separated by vast distances. Chatto had spent most of his revolutionary career in Europe, while Roy travelled had through the Far East, the US and Mexico before calculating that the Soviet Union and Lenin's mentorship were India's best bet for freedom.

With the passage of time, we can see how similar Chatto and Roy were. Despite their diverse backgrounds, the two would lead parallel lives. But like parallel lines, they would never meet in agreement. Both would begin as revolutionaries–or as some called them, terrorists–then would become idealogues and communists. They would end up leading opposite factions of the communist movement, but then fall from grace. Roy would be summarily expelled from the Comintern (the international association of communist parties) and would eventually end up rejecting communism and founding his own philosophy: radical humanism. Chatto would be executed by the same communists he put his faith in.

Both were vagabonds who would travel the world to find arms and money for India's independence, always hotly pursued by

British intelligence. As Chatto would try to raise support for Indian revolutionary activities in Paris and Germany, Roy would be in Mexico where he would co-found the Mexican communist party. Both would live in near poverty for most of their lives, making a meagre and precarious income by writing and teaching. Chatto was a linguist, speaking several Indian and European languages, including Telugu, Bengali, Hindi, German, Swedish, Russian and French. Roy was more a man of action. Both would become deeply homesick and want to return to India but remain in exile for years for fear of being jailed on return.

Both would try desperately to win the support of Lenin—Roy would win this contest. Both would have complicated love lives, getting involved with revolutionary women who would pay a harsh price for loving them. Chatto would have a turbulent relationship with the radical American journalist and activist Agnes Smedley, who would later march with Mao and go down in history as one of the early women war correspondents. Roy would date and later marry an American journalist, Evelyn Trent, who would accompany him to Mexico and across the world. The quartet would have seething rivalries and intense jealousies. Roy would accuse Smedley of 'poisoning Chatto's mind' against him and call her an 'evil genius'.[3] Each man would move on from those women to other women and then yet more women.

While Chatto would face a firing squad, Roy would try to piece together his life after being expelled from the Comintern. He would rashly return to India in 1930 only to be imprisoned for six long years. He would emerge broken in health, but still battling for a new world.

Chatto's famous sister Sarojini Naidu would distance herself from him and his friend Nehru would eventually follow the Gandhian path. Roy would try to work with Gandhi but be advised to stay out of Indian politics and 'render mute service to the cause of Indian freedom'.[4] Gandhi's disapproval of Roy would see the former communist being completely excluded from the freedom movement and becoming a political pariah. Roy would eventually die in Dehradun in 1954 after a fall, while his beloved wife Ellen Gottschalk would later be brutally murdered.

Chatto's death would be covered up by the Soviet Union, his family left in the dark. India would cease to remember him. Despite his fondness for Chatto, Nehru, keen to develop a relationship with the Soviet Union, would not mention him after his sad end.

Roy would be described in his obituary by the *Anandabazar Patrika* as a 'lonely lion who roamed about the wilderness called the world'.[5] Chatto would not have an obituary at all since no one would know he was dead.

It made sense to me, given their parallel lives, to focus on these two mavericks among the many Indian revolutionaries of that period. 'But why would anyone want to read about failures?' asked a family member when I was writing this book. After all, no one could call them successes or household names, like Gandhi, Nehru, Patel or even Bose. Perhaps, because they failed so brilliantly and magnificently, with such flair, such courage, such passion and such individuality. Perhaps they could have been more 'successful' had they jettisoned their principles, but they did not. When Gandhi and Nehru were making mealy-mouthed compromises with the British and agreeing to dominion status for India, Chatto and Roy were battling for full independence, a stance they stuck to. They never gave up fighting for the worker and the peasant, and went to their graves believing India had cheated the masses.

One of Roy's many biographers, Samaren Roy, puts it pithily, 'At the superficial level, Roy had not been a successful man. Nor however did success bless a host of others, and that host included such illustrious names as Aurobindo Ghosh, Bipin Chandra Pal, Bal Gangadhar Tilak and Chittaranjan Das. Very few struggles have succeeded in a single generation.'[6]

Perhaps neither Chatto nor Roy cared much about success. Indeed, many political observers argue that it is 'misleading to regard the Indian revolutionary movement as powerless simply because it failed so completely in the end.' Instead, they say, the British hid the obstacles they faced because of Indian revolutionaries and 'deliberately underplayed its seriousness'.[7] The revolutionaries, including Roy and Chatto in their early years, did not see huge rewards, but with their activities across the globe in the US, UK, Germany, Sweden, Russia, Mexico and Switzerland, they caused plenty of fear amongst the British. Publicly, the British did not acknowledge the impact of the revolutionaries. In private, Home Department documents show they were full of alarm. So dangerous was Chatto that he narrowly escaped assassination at the hands of the British secret service. Later, Chatto would be immortalised as the revolutionary Chandra Lal in a Somerset Maugham story titled *Giulia Lazzari*. The story reveals the lengths to which the British went to defeat Indian revolutionaries through espionage.

The British downplayed the impact made by the revolutionaries of the First World War, and thus they succeeded in muffling their achievements. Then Gandhi's massively popular creed of non-violence ensured that the revolutionaries were forever erased from history. Information about them is hard to find because they moved from country to country, and much of the information available is in French, Russian or Swedish. Thus, they remain unknown and forgotten by most Indians.

That does not mean they should stay unknown and forgotten. Despite working in obscurity, their lives greatly impacted independent India. They were the first internationalists and cosmopolitans, even before the sophisticated and worldly Nehru emerged on the scene. Chatto and Roy were distrustful of narrow political constraints, and of religion and tradition. They mingled with nationalists from Russia, Egypt, Mexico, Germany, Sweden and China. Between them, they lived in ten countries, moving constantly to avoid being arrested. They met and befriended an impressive number of important figures, including Vladimir Lenin, Joseph Stalin, Leon Trotsky, Chiang Kai-shek, Sun Yat-Sen, Mao Tse-Tung and Ho Chi Minh.

Chatto was a passionate anti-imperialist who built a network of allies in Germany, the Soviet Union and Paris, and was one of the movers behind the League Against Imperialism (LAI). Later, Subhas Chandra Bose did the same, cultivating allies across the world without regard for geography or old alliances. The LAI was one of the first attempts towards anti-colonial global unity. Chatto urged Nehru towards the LAI, and the latter was appointed the official Indian National Congress (INC) representative. Later, the LAI acted as an unofficial blueprint for Nehru's darling: the anti-colonialist Non-Aligned Movement, though Chatto was not credited for his work.

Despite Roy's expulsion from the Comintern, his views and writings on communism influenced many communists and socialists in independent India, including Jayaprakash Narayan, V.B. Karnik and Maniben Kara. Roy was passionately in favour of trade unions, and his followers in newly independent India fought to unionise dock and railway workers. Defying his poor, patchy education, Roy wrote over a hundred books and pamphlets, produced several magazines and churned out huge quantities of influential literature.

They criticised Gandhi and Nehru savagely, which jeopardised their success. Other leaders, including Nehru and Patel, were forced to become protégés of Gandhi or else be politically isolated. But Chatto and Roy were not afraid to be isolated. They constantly picked battles, alienated friends and backed the wrong horses because of their convictions. Roy has been described as constantly pursuing 'one foredoomed cause after the next, and with combustible ferocity'.[8] The same could have been said of Chatto.

By 1929, Nehru had been sidelined by Gandhi, who had come to dominate the INC. At the time, Chatto wrote to Nehru, 'When the cunning Mahatmaji proposed your name for the Presidency of the Congress, it was obvious that it was a move to kill you and the opposition. Your hands will be completely tied.' When Nehru and Gandhi agreed to attend a conference to discuss dominion status for India, Chatto wrote to Nehru again, even more brutally, accusing him of surrendering to traitors, and urging him to resign. 'It is a fundamental error to think that unity in the Congress is more important than the vital interests of the masses.'[9]

He made things even worse by criticising his sister Sarojini. 'Mrs Naidu is a mere puppet who is placed in charge of the theatrical side of the campaign, while the wiser and cleverer heads are keeping their hands free for negotiations with the imperialist government.'[10] After that, he became persona non grata for the INC.

Roy was no less scathing about the icons of the freedom movement. He brutally described Nehru as a 'thoughtless, vain, egocentric, popularity hunting demagogue, who is popular amongst Congressmen with a modern outlook because his demagogy rationalises Gandhi's irrationalism, and supplies a pseudo-socialist veneer to reactionary nationalism'.[11]

They were flattened by the juggernaut that was Gandhi and the tidal wave of satyagraha. But they continued to follow their own paths rather than follow Gandhi's ideology like everyone else. Their reward was to be erased from Indian history and be forgotten. This book aims to unearth their stories.

The families and friends of the two men still survive, but sadly, they do not have any memories or letters to share. Instead, I have relied on archival sources: letters, newspaper reports, intelligence reports and the considerable number of books and pamphlets written by M.N. Roy and his many disciples. I have also relied extensively on M.N. Roy's frank and entertaining memoirs, despite them having no dates and being incomplete.

There have been many comprehensive biographies of Chatto and Roy already, which I have drawn on. I am particularly indebted to Professor Nirode K. Barooah's incredible biography of Chatto and Professor Sibnarayan Ray's biography of Roy. Anyone who wants to know more should read these. But most of these accounts are scholarly and inaccessible to lay readers. Some are out of print. I wanted to write a book that everyone could read and access.

Political theories are complicated and divisive. One could fill several books on the Marxist and Leninist theories that inspired Chatto and Roy, or indeed the subsequent theories that emerged. But again, I have decided to focus not so much on complex theories as on the people behind them, and show Chatto and Roy as the great but also the imperfect, vain and fallible men they were. This is not an exhaustive book and does not claim to be. It is merely a small snapshot of their lives. Many other fascinating anarchists, activists and possible spies worked alongside Chatto and Roy who have also been forgotten: M.P.T. Acharya, Har Dayal, V.V.S. Aiyar, Chempakaraman Pillai, Taraknath Das, Shapurji Saklatvala and A.C.N. Nambiar. Other foreign activists such as Rosa Luxemburg and Willi Münzenberg and trade unionists such as Philip Spratt and Lester Hutchinson probably deserve more space in this book. Massive world events such as the Russian Revolution and India's battle for independence could double, triple, even quadruple the size of this book if I include them. But I sought to focus only on the human side of Chatto and Roy. Two men who were two sides of the same coin but who remained rivals till the bitter end.

2

The Magnificent Failure

My father is a dreamer, a great dreamer, a great man whose life has been a magnificent failure. I suppose in the whole of India there are few men whose learning is greater than his, and I don't think there are many more beloved.

Sarojini Naidu

IN 1910, A VERY IMPORTANT LETTER REACHED THE LARGE AND chaotic Chattopadhyay house in Hyderabad. The letter was from Virendranath Chattopadhyaya to his sister Mrinalini. At the time, Chatto was being hunted by the British police. The CID learned of the letter through its spy network and surrounded the Chattopadhyay house. The notorious Sir Charles Tegart, the head of the Calcutta police, arrived to inspect the house. Chatto's father, the redoubtable Aghorenath Chattopadhyay, a distinguished academic and reformer, sat regally at a table, tranquilly allowing the search to happen.

As Aghorenath made polite small talk with Tegart, the police ransacked the house, even tearing up the children's dolls' house, to find the elusive letter. Meanwhile, Ranen, Chatto's younger brother, continued eating his lunch. The police were unsuccessful and left, deeply frustrated. A gently amused Aghorenath showed the fuming Sir Charles a photograph of Chatto and said, 'Tell them [the police constables], gentlemen, that my son Viren will bring them independence.'[1]

Once all the policemen had left, the eight-year-old Ranen solemnly spat out the remnants of his distinguished elder brother's letter, which he had been made to hide in his mouth.[2]

This was the unusual Chattopadhyay household, home to a large and opinionated brood, who lived in what Chatto's sister Sarojini called the 'Golden Threshold'. They did things differently, with artistry and panache, but above all with integrity.

Sarojini would describe her unusual father admiringly, 'My father is a dreamer, a great dreamer, a great man whose life has been a magnificent failure. I suppose in the whole of India there are few men whose learning is greater than his, and I don't think there are many more beloved. He has a great white beard and the profile of Homer, and a laugh that brings the roof down.'[3]

Naidu would go on to describe Aghorenath as something of a mad scientist. 'He has wasted all his money on two great objects, to help others and on alchemy. But this alchemy, as you know, was only the material counterpart of a poet's craving for beauty, the eternal beauty.'[4]

No wonder then that the eight Chattopadhyay children were glorious 'time wasters', seeking beauty themselves, roaming far and wide in their quest. The bubbly and witty Sarojini, the eldest girl, became the most famous, her fame somewhat overshadowing the rest. But all the Chattopadhyay women were formidable. Mrinalini, nicknamed Gunnu, studied modern sciences at Cambridge. She became a teacher and later, the principal of Girls College, Lahore. Middle sister Sunalini became an artiste and dancer. Youngest sister Suhasini married the mercurial A.C.N. Nambiar–who was rumoured to be a spy–and she was an ardent communist activist in her own right.

Virendranath was the eldest boy. Bhupendranath, the second brother, became the Assistant Accountant General of Hyderabad. Ranendranath was the third brother, though not much is known about him. And the baby of the family, Harindranath Chattopadhyay, became an award-winning poet, writer, dramatist and actor. But even in such an unusual family, Virendranath was something of a deviant.

Aghorenath's childhood had been adventurous too. According to Sarojini Naidu's biographer Padmini Sengupta, he grew up in an East Bengal village, making friends with the boatmen who would travel the rivers. 'In his wanderings, he fell in with some dacoits and made fast friends with them,' reports Sengupta, though thankfully he did not become a dacoit himself. On one of his trips down the river, he saw his future wife Varada Sundari Devi when she was only nine years old and fell in love. Apparently, his dacoit friends helped him meet her.[5]

As a young man, Aghorenath joined the Brahmo reformists of Calcutta, led by the dynamic Keshub Chandra Sen. Aghorenath formed his own group of reformists with his cousins, rescuing girls being forced by their parents to marry very old men. The girls were brought to Sen's school in Calcutta to be educated at the Banga Mahila Vidyalaya, of which Dwarkanath Ganguly was the headmaster. Ganguly later married India's first practising woman doctor, Kadambini Ganguly. When the community hit back, Aghorenath took shelter with the Brahmos.

Subsequently, the brilliant Aghorenath won a scholarship and travelled to the University of Edinburgh, where he earned a degree in physics in 1877, one of the earliest Indians to do so. He returned to India in 1878 and became a teacher in a Hyderabad school.

The Hyderabad that Aghorenath returned to was a city in churn. It had only recently got an organised system of government. Education, science and transport were all undergoing rapid change. The sixth Nizam of Hyderabad, Asaf Jah VI, also known as Sir Mir Mahboob Ali Khan Siddiqi Bayafandi, had ascended to the throne in 1866 when his father had died unexpectedly. At the time, he had only been two years old. Therefore, when Aghorenath arrived in the city, Hyderabad was being ruled by the experienced Diwan Salar Jung, who acted as the regent.

Salar Jung was a man who believed in reform, modernity, organisation and change. He was also a supporter of the British, with whom he had sided during the 1857 revolt. Salar Jung established a postal service, connected Hyderabad to a railway line, introduced a standard currency, organised a police force and began a campaign for education. He went on frequent tours to Europe, bringing new ideas back. The famous cartoonist Spy drew a caricature of the dapper and moustachioed Salar Jung for *Vanity Fair* in 1876, sitting in a chair, smiling widely, and titled it 'An Indian Statesman'.

Salar Jung employed some equally capable and reformist men. One of them was his private secretary, Syed Bilgrami, who was also a supporter of education. He scouted Aghorenath Chattopadhyay in 1887 to head the newly established Nizam College in Hyderabad as its first principal.

The Nizam, Mahbub Ali Khan, would grow up to become a great dandy with a huge collection of clothes and shoes, acquiring a reputation of never wearing the same outfit twice. But he would also become an equally passionate patron of the arts, music and the sciences.

Portraits of the previous Nizams showed portly old men, bedecked in jewellery and excessively ornate clothes, but the new Nizam had himself photographed as a slim, elegant figure in plain suits, his only indulgence being a bristling moustache and huge sideburns. He hired numerous photographers to capture his new image, until he eventually settled on Lala Deen Dayal.

By the 1880s, Hyderabad had become a centre for modern medicine, partly encouraged by the now grown-up Nizam. In 1888, at the request of his personal physician, the Scottish doctor Edward

Lawrie, the Nizam sponsored the first Hyderabad Chloroform Commission. The commission oversaw medical experiments to prove that the toxicity of chloroform first affected the respiratory system rather than the heart. The first commission's findings were published in *The Lancet*, a prestigious peer-reviewed medical journal.

A few years later, Hyderabad became the scene for a massive medical breakthrough when Ronald Ross discovered the malarial parasite on 20 August 1897 in a laboratory in the Begumpet area of the city. He infected the mosquito with blood purchased from a local patient for eight annas. The laboratory later became the Ronald Ross Institute of Parasitology, which still survives today. Ronald Ross was awarded the Nobel Prize.

It was into this febrile atmosphere that Chatto was born on 31 October 1880. New ideas, thoughts and movements were everywhere. Modern scientific ideas, education and reform were spreading like wildfire. And these were encouraged by Aghorenath, the classic Renaissance man, who dabbled in everything and anything.

Chatto did not write about his family life. But Harindranath—who was given to somewhat flowery language—wrote extensively about the household and described his parents thus, 'I realise that I was born under fortunate stars. They were not merely human parents, but rare spiritual beings, high points of evolution, two truly unworldly lights walking through the darkness of life, illumining it wherever they walked, casting hope and blessing on whoever they met on life's roadway.'[6]

The Chattopadhyay children were expected to be curious and inquisitive. Aghorenath would say with typical frankness, 'If my children cannot live by their wits, let them die.'[7] When his daughter Suhasini arrived home one day bragging about coming first in class, she was quickly put in her place. Said Aghorenath, 'Is that so, baby? What is the nature of the sun, do you know?' She answered, 'No.'

'What makes the rain? What is air?' On her saying that she did not know, he said, 'Broaden your knowledge. When you know many things, it is more important than being first.'[8]

The children would talk to each other in English but to their parents in Hindustani, while the parents talked to each other in Bengali. Chatto grew up to be an impressive linguist, learning Bengali, Telugu, Hindi, Urdu and English. He would later learn French, Russian, Dutch, Italian and Swedish as well.

Harindranath described the Chattopadhyay home as a cross between a museum and a zoo: 'A museum crowded with precious things of wisdom and culture, a zoo crowded with a medley of strange types—some even verging on the mythic, for our home was open to all alike. Our parents never made any invidious distinction between man and man.'[9] Probably influenced by this motley crowd, Chatto would associate with all types of people in his travels.

Aghorenath's influence on his children was profound. But so too was their mother Varada Sundari's. Harindranath wrote of the 'quality of my mother's eyes which were always brim-full of mercy, kindness and contemplation'.[10] Varada Devi was a singer—'a half angel, half bird'—as Harindranath lyrically described her.

Harindranath described his father as a 'veritable epoch' and an absolute stickler for the truth, so much so that hearing lies would make his 'hair stand up as quills upon the fretful porpentine'. On one occasion, Harindranath bought a rail ticket pretending to be under twelve to save some money. When he told Aghorenath, 'his eyes reddened like a sun set, his lips twitched in divine anger, his hair stood like sentinels on his hand guarding the tower of truth; his nose trembled with indignation and his voice almost choked when he raised it like thunder and said, "What, cheating the railway company?" I trembled like a leaf and felt that had father given me a good shoe beating for the lie to the ticket-collector, it would not have hurt as much as his single sentence.'[11] In another incident, where Aghorenath was offered a bribe of real gold ashrafis by a woman, he again became furious and called for the whipping of the woman who offered it.

Much was expected of the children and they measured up.

Aghorenath was apparently a 'walking encyclopaedia' as well. There was nothing he did not know. 'A morning walk for an hour would be enough to give one an insight into his interior stores of knowledge and information. Now, he would pick up a stone on the way and give a discourse on its formation and advance a calculation of years which took to shape it. He would raise it to dignity with a big, scientific name and would house it in a high-sounding category which would certainly dispel the fact that it was just an "ordinary" stone.'[12]

In one of her speeches, Sarojini Naidu summed up the secular Chattopadhyay family psyche, 'I was born in Bengal. I belong to the Madras Presidency. In a Mohammedan city I was brought up and married and there I live. Still, I am neither a Bengali, nor a Madrasi, nor a Hyderabadi, but I am an Indian; not a Brahmin not a Hindu, but an Indian to whom my Mohammedan brother is as dear and precious as my Hindu brother. My beloved father said, "Be not limited ever to Indians, but let it be your pride that you are a citizen of the world."'[13]

Harindranath too described the numerous interfaith celebrations that took place in the secular household. 'We never lost one opportunity of associating ourselves with celebrations of all kinds; festivals, whether they belonged to the Hindu or Muslim, the Christian or the Parsi, were all part of our yearly programme, and we knew them by heart. We were walking calendars.' During Moharram, the children were visited by men pretending to be tigers, with painted-on stripes, almost naked except for their loin cloths. The tigers were accompanied by drummers and buglers who created the atmosphere of a fight. The children's favourite tiger was their baker, who was brought in a cage and would perform a spectacular dance. His hands had tiger claws sewn on to bits of tiger skin and his head was covered by a cap of tiger skin.

'Brother Baker,' Harindranath wrote, 'What a tiger you made, and how deeply we respected you for your sheer mystery!'[14]

On one occasion, the then prime minister of Hyderabad, Sir Kishen Pershad, visited the 'Golden Threshold'. The young Harindranath sailed into the room in the middle of the conversation and performed a song and dance for the prime minister. Sir Kishen clapped enthusiastically. The next day a baby elephant was sent from the palace 'as a gift for the little artiste'. Harindranath was told that it had been a white elephant and that it had to be given away because of the expense of its upkeep. 'It was thus that I learned the meaning of the term "white elephant".'[15]

Despite the elephant being sent away, on Diwali, Kishen Pershad made it a point to send the household tray after tray of fireworks, carried by men who looked like they were out of the Arabian nights, including anars that leapt into magical trees of flames and 'scorpions' that would rush towards the children.[16]

The family would often be criticised by other Brahmos for exposing their children to theatre, dance and such other pastimes which were considered dissolute at the time, but they ignored the mutterings of the community.

Aghorenath is believed to have been the inspiration for the all-knowing character of the 'Man in the Train' in Rabindranath Tagore's *Kshudita Pashan* (*Hungry Stones*).[17] Tagore wrote, 'My kinsman and myself were returning to Calcutta from our Puja trip when we met the man in a train. The stranger could discourse on all subjects giving the impression that "The Disposer of All Things" never did anything without consulting him. Very soon the stranger was embarking on his extraordinary gift of make-believe, so quaintly interwoven with real life, so that one was always left with feeling of unreality after meeting him.'[18]

Along with song, dance and drama, Aghorenath held all-night addas in an unused gymnasium in Hyderabad, inviting students and teachers to debate modern ideas and theories. These probably influenced Chatto who would later become a keen debater himself, always ready for a good argument.

Aghorenath ended up paying a high price for his honesty and integrity. He was warned by his friends not to get involved in politics, but that proved impossible for one with his strong opinions and public spirit.

In 1883, Salar Jung died and the administration of Hyderabad passed on to a council consisting of prominent noblemen headed by the then Nizam. The council suggested investing in a controversial plan called the Chanda Railway Scheme. It suggested that an existing railway line be taken over by a British company and extended to Vijayawada on one side and Chanda on the other. The Hyderabad government would guarantee a certain interest and the railway would be known as the Nizam's guaranteed state railway. The details of the scheme were unclear and it came to be widely believed that it was financially unwise and would only end up in the state losing money.

The educated intellectuals of Hyderabad society, of whom Aghorenath was one, began to question the scheme. Aghorenath and his friend Mulla Abdul Qayum, a reformer and educationist, joined a committee to consider the railway scheme, which recommended that all the facts be placed before the public. The committee also asked why the scheme was being considered at all, a question that enraged the Nizam and the Council of Regency.

This resulted in Aghorenath being suspended from service and deported from Hyderabad on 20 May 1883. The papers reported it in detail, alleging that Aghorenath had been deported for agitating public feeling and causing unrest. The Hyderabad correspondent of the *Times of India* wrote, 'Dr Aghorenath Chatopadhya [sic], one of the leaders of the party opposed to the resolution of His Highness's Government against the railway scheme was deported last night in charge of the police beyond the limits of his Highness's territory, with an injunction that his return would be followed by apprehension and trial. By means of certain representations, an attempt has been made to arouse public feeling, and even Pathans and other bodies have, it is said, been tampered with.'[19]

But Aghorenath defended himself in a telegram sent from Sholapur, where he had gone into hiding. He blamed discontented officials vying for power and denied having sent a telegram to the viceroy with regard to the railway scheme. He admitted that the 'feeling in Hyderabad against the raising of a foreign loan is very strong. Designing persons, expecting large commissions, have it seems misrepresented matters to the Nizams and the British governments [sic]. They have given the movement, which is a peaceful one, the colour of a disturbance.'[20]

The actual deportation was swift and brutal. On the evening in question, Aghorenath was at his house with twenty or thirty members of the committee designated to petition the viceroy when a body of police appeared. Aghorenath was bareheaded and asked that he be allowed to get his turban, but was told there was no time for that. He was also told there was no time to see his wife Varada Sundari, who was seriously unwell, or say goodbye to his children. His friends were barred from travelling with him or saying goodbye.[21] He was forced into the train by eleven Arab military men and not allowed to buy a ticket. He spoke to the gathered crowd: 'Gentlemen, you will please bear witness that I do not enter the carriage willingly, but that I am compelled to do so.'[22]

A few years later, when the matter had blown over, both Aghorenath and Mulla Qayum were brought back to Hyderabad, and the former was again made the principal of Nizam College. Chatto was only three years old at the time of his father's deportation and would not have understood the implications of Aghorenath's courage. But the matter would likely have been talked about in the family and Chatto would have grown up expecting to question those in power.

While Chatto grew into boyhood, a wind of rebellion stirred through the land. By the late 1880s, a robust form of home-grown nationalism had begun to take shape across India, spearheaded by Bipin Chandra Pal and Aurobindo Ghose in Bengal, Bal Gangadhar Tilak in Maharashtra and Lala Lajpat Rai in Punjab. The trio of 'Lal Bal Pal' spread the message of Swadeshi across the land as British goods started being boycotted and burnt. Aghorenath reportedly supported many such meetings and risked his career.

Chatto's biographer Nirode Barooah describes Aghorenath's influence on his son thus: 'In his erudition and expertise in several languages—both Indian and foreign, in his cosmopolitanism and secularism, in his criticism of some of the backward Hindu religious and social practices including the caste system, in his interest in forming action groups of like-minded people for achieving common goals and above all, in his patriotism, Chatto seems to have inherited a great deal from his father.'[23]

But, eventually the golden years at the 'Golden Threshold' came to an end, as the money inevitably ran out. Aghorenath's lavish habits and endless generosity led to misfortune. By the time Harindranath grew out of boyhood, the household had fallen on hard times, which he says was due to 'the extreme generosity of his parents'. By then, Chatto had already left for the UK.

Varada Sundari was forced to rely on meagre household funds, and there was barely enough to feed the children. Those were frightening days, as the Chattopadhyays had not so much lived beyond their means as 'given away beyond their means'. 'Hard looking men came to attach our property, as Varada Sundari broke into a fit of sobbing. Father explained to mother that it was but the logical conclusion to their two pairs of hands that did not ever know how to withhold or stint.'[24]

Agorenath's botanical plates—his most treasured possession—the furniture, the carpets, the bookshelves, the chairs, were all taken away. But suddenly, as if by magic, a famous vendor of sweets called Ramnath, who adored and venerated Aghorenath, appeared and paid up all the debts. 'As if heaven had marvelled at father's patience and decided to grant him a prize,' said Harindranath.[25]

The family eventually broke up, the parents moving to Calcutta with Harindranath, with Suhasini left in Bhupendranath's care in a small house.

On a visit to Calcutta, Harindranath was given some stern advice by his father, advice that summed up the Chattopadhyay credo. 'Remember that I am leaving a great heritage for you. Not wealth, not houses, not lands. I am not leaving a penny for any of you—but I am leaving you a wonderful thing: a life of culture and a life of struggle. Thank God, I have been able to leave you with a brain, an intellect, knowledge and, I hope, a really honest and upright heart.'[26] Harindranath wept and shook and felt unworthy of being his son. 'My father seemed to me the picture of these lines, "I am the master of my fate. I am the captain of my soul".'[27]

A few years later, in January 1915, Aghorenath died. Harindranath wrote that his father's last discussion had been with a friend on the topic of life and death. 'They are one and the same, father is reported to have said. Then why not die, asked the friend. To which father replied, "I could at this instant, if I wanted." Twenty minutes later, the guests returned to find that my father had passed away, if perhaps only to prove that life and death were really one and the same.'[28] The only son present to carry out the last rites was Ranendranath.

By then, Chatto, who had grown up in a cosmopolitan and intellectual household, had embarked on his nomadic and uncertain path. Like Aghorenath, Chatto would dream—and dream big—of a free and equal India. Like his father, many would eventually think of him as a 'magnificent failure'.

3

The Bomb Maker

When, as a school boy of fourteen, I began my political life, which may end in nothing, I wanted to be free.

M.N. Roy

IN 1906, FRIGHTENED RESIDENTS OF KOYA VILLAGE IN RURAL WEST Bengal watched as Jatindranath Mukherjee grappled with a Royal Bengal tiger. Jatindranath (also known as Jyotindranath), had been summoned by the villagers to deal with this marauding big cat. He had arrived armed with a kukri or small knife, expecting to meet a small tiger. Now, he found himself locked in mortal combat with a huge man-eater instead.

Suddenly, the enraged tiger charged at him. Jatin caught hold of the creature by the neck and attacked it with the kukri. With its last roar, the tiger closed its jaws around Jatin's right knee and collapsed. Jatin lay immobile, his leg seriously injured. Someone eventually fired a rifle at the dead beast. Jatin chuckled and said, 'Useless. It won't move any more. Don't damage the skin!'[1]

Villagers started gathering from far and wide to pay their respects, thinking it might be Jatin's last day alive. He was taken to Calcutta to see a well-known surgeon. Jatin's legs were mauled badly, but he recovered under the care of the surgeon, who devoted himself to Jatin's care. Six months later, Jatin was able to walk without crutches. He was awarded a silver medal by the Government of Bengal and instantly became a hero. People started called him Bagha Jatin (Tiger Jatin). His particular brand of unapologetic, muscular Bengali nationalism influenced a whole generation of revolutionaries, including the fiery young M.N. Roy.

M.N. Roy grew up on the other side of India from Chatto, in a completely different world. While Chatto grew up attending intellectual addas with scientists, teachers and royals, Roy came of age attending a different type of gathering—one that made bombs.

Born Narendranath Bhattacharya on 21 March 1887, seven years after Chatto, Roy would later change his name to avoid arrest. I will refer to him as Narendranath in this chapter and the next few chapters because that is what he called himself in that period of his life. His father Dinabandhu Bhattacharya was the last of a line of priests from Midnapur, South Bengal. But Dinabandhu chose to become a Sanskrit teacher instead in Arbelia, a village near Calcutta. In 1899, he moved to Chingripota, a move that would have a significant effect on Roy.

What made the son of a respectable schoolteacher take to revolution and anarchy? It was a sign of the times. In the 1860s, Bengalis, mostly from the elite classes, had begun going abroad for study or work. Their tales of liberty, dissent and free speech had trickled back and stirred the imagination of all of Bengal. As historian Kris Manjapra explains, 'By the 1890s, in the prime colonial cosmopolis of Calcutta, it was common for individuals from diverse classes to have had some experiences of foreign travel, or to know someone with stories of life abroad, whether he be coolie, lascar, free labourer, haji pilgrim, student or bhadralok tourist.'[2]

Naren grew up with the heady scent of revolution in the air. Bengal was famous—notorious if you asked the British—for new ideas, social reform and rebellion. The reformist Brahmo Samaj was active here too, and was turning traditional Hindu culture on its head. The boy Naren was surrounded by dissent, revolution and an atmosphere of curiosity, much as the young Chatto was in Hyderabad.

By fourteen, Naren had become a revolutionary, heavily influenced by the Bengal revolutionaries of the time, especially those like Swami Vivekananda, Bankim Chandra Chatterjee, Aurobindo Ghose and Bipin Chandra Pal, who espoused a robust home-grown nationalism. Vivekananda was taking Indian philosophy and religion to the rest of the world, and the young Roy lapped it all up. At the time, he knew nothing about Marxism, but he was beginning to learn all there was to know about radical nationalism.

Later, he would write in his memoirs, 'When, as a school boy of fourteen, I began my political life, which may end in nothing, I wanted to be free. Independence, complete and absolute, is a new-fangled idea. The old-fashioned revolutionaries thought in terms of freedom. In those days, we had not read Marx. We did not know about the existence of the proletariat. Still, many spent their lives in jail and went to the gallows. There was no proletariat to propel them. They were not conscious of class struggle. They did not have the dream of Communism. But they had the human urge to revolt against the intolerable conditions of life. They did not know exactly how those conditions could be changed. But they tried to change them anyhow. I began my political life with that spirit, and I still draw my inspiration from that spirit than from the Three Volumes of Capital (Das Kapital) or three hundred volumes of Marx.'[3] Being free rather than tied to any ideology would define Roy's existence.

Naren began his life restless, and restless he remained to the end. His cousin Harikumar Chakravarty described him thus: 'He was constantly searching for something distant, something beyond and spent many nights in the cremation ground, which later became his favourite spot for secret meetings of his revolutionary group.' Roy would frequently walk thirty miles to the Belur Math, founded by Swami Vivekananda, in his quest for knowledge.[4]

In 1901, he met Sivnarain Swami, who had reportedly been one of the rebels in the Sepoy Mutiny of 1857, later called the

First War of Indian Independence. Sivnarain Swami, like many Bengali reformers of the time, believed that Hindu society had been weakened by caste divisions. He was looking for young men like Naren, who he could train in revolution but also those who would lead reforms in Hinduism. The swami told Naren inspiring tales of Bal Gangadhar Tilak, who had been charged with sedition in 1897, and the Chapekar brothers, who had become the face of revolution after they had protested the brutal anti-plague measures introduced in Pune.

The same tide of vigorous Bengali nationalism that had influenced Chatto now wholly consumed the young Naren. In some cases, the nationalism was both metaphorically and literally muscular. For example, the revolutionary activities of a nationalist secret society called Anushilan Samiti founded in 1902 included teaching young men to be physically fit and to focus on Indian sports like lathi, swordplay and wrestling. The well-known revolutionary brothers, Aurobindo Ghose and Barindra Ghose, both of whom were influenced by the fiery philosophy of Italian nationalists, Giuseppe Mazzini and Giuseppe Garibaldi, were closely associated with the Anushilan Samiti. By 1905, there were more than five hundred branches of the society in Bengal, Assam and Dhaka. In 1906, the Anushilan Samiti launched a newspaper called *Jugantar* or 'New Era'. Later, the newspaper lent its name to the West Bengal division of the Anushilan Samiti, which was being spearheaded by Jatindranath Mukherjee–the same Bagha Jatin we met earlier.

Jatindranath was the single biggest influence on young Naren. He embodied the qualities of Bengali revolutionaries of the time: a person deeply influenced by the teachings of Gita and Hinduism, but also muscular, physically impressive and charismatic, someone who would not hesitate to intervene if he saw British officers bullying the local population. 'Jyoti was a rare synthesis of the traditional Indian paths of action, devotion and knowledge: he believed that physical strength was to be acquired only on condition that simultaneously there would be an effort to realise the soul force. Thus, far from transforming an entire generation of Indians into violent rebels, he implanted the feeling of almost a sacred fervour of Mother India, a feeling in harmony with the essence of the Gita and enhanced by the vision of Bankim Chandra,'[5] wrote Naren of his idol.

There are legendary stories about Jatin. In 1905, the Prince of Wales (who later became King George V) visited Bengal. Jatin, along with a few friends, decided to wait for the prince at a road crossing, aiming to show him how much the British were detested in India. There he saw a hackney coach which had Bengali women sitting inside and a group of British solders sitting on the top, rudely swinging their legs in the ladies' faces. When Jatindranath politely requested the soldiers to move their legs, they refused. He then 'sprang to the hood of the coach, slapped the cheeks of the English offenders, and with quick footwork, kicked them off the coach among general cheers.'[6] This story demonstrated both his bravery and chivalry.

The then viceroy, Lord Curzon, took the decision to partition Bengal on 19 July 1905. Young Bengal erupted in anger at what they saw as an egregious application of the British policy of divide and rule. Bankim Chandra Chatterjee's rousing anthem *Bande Mataram* was sung for the first time at the 1896 session of the INC. And addressing the session was the stirring figure of Sister Nivedita, an Irish nationalist and follower of Swami Vivekananda. Sister Nivedita argued for political freedom for India instead of spiritual salvation. The same year, Aurobindo Ghose wrote the pamphlet *Bhawani Mandir*, laying down the ideals and methods of revolution.[7]

Meanwhile, *Jugantar* took a radical position. Its June 1906 issue argued, 'The foreigners manage by artifice to obtain and take away the wealth of the country and everything substantial in it, and throw the Indians, reduced by them to skeletons, into the horrid jaws of famine, pestilence and poverty. Is this to be called peace? War or a revolution is an infinitely better thing than the peace under which mortality is fast rising in India.'[8]

By 1907, *Jugantar* was calling for force to be used against the British, including bloodshed. On 3 March 1907, its issue said, 'The laws of the English are based on their brute force. If we want to liberate ourselves from those laws, it is brute force that is necessary for us to accumulate. You will inquire how, being weak, we can enter on a trial of strength with the powerful English. Be not afraid. Not very many listened to the young Mazzini on the day when wounded to his heart's core by the sufferings and poverty to Italy, he firmly resolved to free his country from bondage. Oh, sons of Bengal, worshippers of Sakti, will you be averse from that?'[9]

Naren could not resist this powerful appeal. He began attending anti-partition meetings in Calcutta, despite being warned not to do so. Around this time, Surendranath Banerjea, one of the early Indian nationalists, started travelling around Bengal, speaking against the partition. Roy asked the headmaster of his school for permission to host Banerjea, but he was refused. He then decided to organise a meeting outside of school hours. His participation in this peaceful procession led to him being promptly expelled from the school.

His cousin Harikumar described their new purpose: 'We had decided our course. Vivekananda's path was our path. Our god was our country. We had now before us the vision of Bankim Chandra's Mother that she would become.'

In 1905, when Naren's father died, the family moved to Calcutta. Naren and Harikumar joined the Anushilan Samiti in the same year and were sent to organise famine relief work in Orissa (now Odisha). However, despite being expelled from school, Naren's formal education had not yet ended, says his friend and protégé Sibnarayan Ray. Naren apparently passed the entrance exam of National College, an institution founded by Aurobindo Ghose, and was then admitted to Bengal Technical Institute, which included courses in chemistry. Ray claims that, in taking these courses, 'Naren might well have been largely motivated by the need for chemical knowledge in the manufacture of bombs.'[10]

An anecdote from this time shows how deeply a lonely Naren yearned for kindred spirits. One Dr Aswini Roy who also worked at the famine relief centre in Orissa narrated this incident, 'After all the volunteers had finished their meal in the evening, I saw Naren walking up to the top of the wall. And then he sat there in the posture of a yogi fixing his gaze on the full moon. His eyelids never moved. He sat there in that posture until the moon went down. When he came down, I asked him why he had done this. He would not say anything. After repeated urgings Naren said, "Ashwini, I am born in a poor family. There are so many great men in different parts of the world—I will never be able to meet them. So, I look at the moon on the night of the full moon, hoping that if these men also looked at the bright moon from other parts of the world, there might be some communication with them through the moon."'[11] Years later, Naren would meet and befriend some of the greatest men in the world: Vladimir Lenin, Lala Lajpat Rai, Sun Yat-Sen, Chiang Kai-Shek, Nehru and Gandhi among others.

In 1907, Naren met Bagha Jatin and was swept away by his charisma. 'All the dadas (gurus) practiced magnetism; only Jatin Mukherjee possessed it. Therefore, he was a puzzle and a despair for his rivals engaged in the game of *cheledhara.* He never cast out his nets; yet he was loved by all, even by the followers of other Dadas. Nor did he put on an air of condescending superiority. In what he said, there was no hint of an extensively ramified secret organisation accumulating vast quantities of arms and money for the day of liberation.'

Naren began committing dacoities to raise funds for nationalist activities—the first one at the Chingripota railway station in

December 1907. He was arrested shortly afterwards, while going to visit his sick mother and carrying a copy of Barin Ghosh's *Bartaman Rananiti* (*Blueprint for Present Day Warfare*). But he was let out on bail because he was still a student. Naren also wrote his first article on revolutionary practices in *Jugantar*. It was titled '*Bharater Raja Ke?*' (Who is India's ruler?). The answer, of course, was simple: the people of India.[12]

When he emerged from jail, Naren and Bagha Jatin began rebuilding Jugantar (the West Bengal division of the Anushilan Samiti) as an organisation. Many of the old guard, including Barin Ghosh, had been arrested and new blood was needed. Naren continued committing dacoities to raise money for the revolution. By now, members of Jugantar had also begun executing their plans for the assassination of police and judicial officers who had committed what they considered to be treason against the motherland.

In January 1908, Naren's mother died, leaving him free of all ties to family and responsibility. A few months later, in April 1908, an incident took place in Muzaffarpur that shocked and divided the nation. Two young Bengalis, Khudiram Bose and Prafulla Chaki, both members of the Anushilan Samiti, attempted to assassinate a British judge, Douglas Kingsford, by throwing a bomb at his carriage. However, Kingsford happened to be in another carriage at the time, and two British women—a mother and her daughter—were killed instead. Chaki killed himself after this incident, but Khudiram was hanged. He was just eighteen, which made him one of the youngest revolutionaries to be executed. Khudiram went to the gallows cheerful and smiling. Meanwhile, forty nationalists of the Anushilan Samiti were also arrested, including Aurobindo Ghose and his brother Barin, in what became known as the Alipore Conspiracy case. Aurobindo was eventually acquitted for lack of evidence, something that became a turning point in his life. Thereafter, he gave up bombs and turned to spirituality.

The revenge of the revolutionaries came swiftly. Nandalal Banerjee, the Intelligence Bureau officer responsible for catching Chaki, was assassinated by Shreeshchandra Pal, a member of a group allied to the Anushilan Samiti. Since Pal's nickname was also Naren, some accounts of the incident wrongly name Narendranath as the assassin.

After this, Bengal became notorious for 'terrorism' as the British called it, although the Anushilan Samiti saw it as a justified revolution. In 1908, there were eight dacoities, seven attempted murders and bomb explosions, eleven murders and two conspiracy cases in West Bengal. Though these cases do not seem excessive in number, the campaign demoralised the police force and seriously alarmed the British government. The government of Bengal informed the central government, 'It is easy to produce a reign of terror in Bengal. A few instances of successful action by the terrorists would confirm the impression that there is everything to fear from them and nothing either to hope or fear from the government.'[13]

Stringent laws were introduced to control the 'terrorists'. And soon, a formidable opponent arrived on the scene: Charles Tegart of the Imperial Indian Police, the man who would visit the faraway Chattopadhyay household in Hyderabad two years later. Tegart was an Irishman who had built up a huge network of informers and spies. For some time, he had even operated as a spy himself, though he could not pass for a Bengali. Tegart became a hated figure for Bengali revolutionaries because of his deep knowledge of Calcutta, his unorthodox policing and his ability to inspire loyalty in his juniors. He would survive several assassination attempts, but none would dent his confidence. Instead, he would drive freely and unafraid around Calcutta, his Staffordshire bull terrier sitting on the hood of his car.

Tegart's wife, Kathleen, later wrote: 'Tegart never once disguised himself as a Bengali. His features were strongly marked, he was tall and muscular, his eyes were dark blue, and his tan had a warm, reddish tinge. Whatever aids might be brought to disguise him, he could not appear other than a remarkable Bengali. At night wearing a puggaree, he could pass as a Sikh taxi-driver, but even in the daytime he could go unnoticed as a Kabuli or Pathan.'[14]

Jugantar was prosecuted for the sixth time in 1908 for an article it published, titled 'The Bengali's Bomb', which defended the perpetrators of the Muzaffarpur incident, but blamed the failure of the incident on their poor aim. 'Bengali boys have learnt to make bombs, but they have not yet learnt to throw them well. It is because they are yet unable to take proper aim and hit the mark that in the Muzaffarpur accident they killed persons other than him whom they intended to kill,'[15] said the article. The frankness of the article's tone surprised many.

In 1910, the revitalised police caught up with Naren at last. He, Jatin and forty-five others from the Anushilan Samiti were arrested for conspiring to commit the murder of Shamshul Islam, an intelligence officer who was investigating revolutionary groups. The case was called the Howrah Sibpur Conspiracy.

Naren was twenty-three at the time of his arrest. He was a striking young man, over six feet tall. His biographer Sibnarayan Ray described him as possessing 'thick wavy jet-black hair falling in abundant cascades on the well-built shoulders, the long slender throat reaching the curled beard and whiskers, the strong chin and full lips framed by the dark moustache, the straight noble nose, but most striking of all the high forehead and under it the large, pensive, magnetic eyes—together they convey the image of a young visionary whose life is fully committed to the pursuit of his vision.'[16]

Naren and Jatin were sentenced to a year's imprisonment. It did not deter them. When they emerged, Naren disguised himself as a sanyasi and travelled in the north, going to places like Varanasi, Allahabad and Agra, recruiting young men for revolution and distributing what arms they had.

By 1914, Bagha Jatin had begun to contact revolutionary groups in the US, Germany and Canada. The gregarious Naren, eager to travel, seemed the obvious candidate to act as a liaison to get ammunition and funds from revolutionary groups abroad. Indeed, Naren wanted to 'remake the map of the world through the agency of travel itself'.[17] Save for a brief return, Naren would not live in India for the next sixteen years. Travel would come to define him as a person and a revolutionary. In that, he and Chatto would be alike.

4

India House: Dying for Dharma

If it is anarchism to rise for the sanctity of our homes, the integrity of our life, and the honour of our God and our country, and to slay every individual tyrant, whether foreign or native, that continues the enslavement of our great noble people ... then we say cursed is the man who is not an anarchist!

Virendranath Chattopadhyaya

Highgate, London, 1905

A TALL, SQUARE-JAWED MAN STOOD BEFORE A GROUP OF ADMIRING young disciples, spitting out his words like bullets. First, he spoke in Hindi, then in English. 'Rise then, Hindustan rise! Die for dharma, while killing your enemies and win back Swarajya,' he boomed.[1]

The man was Veer Savarkar and the audience his core group of revolutionary vagabonds: men who moved from country to country, spreading the new message of complete independence for India. Not dominion status, no wishy-washy compromise. Nothing less than full independence, moderation be damned.

Today, the affluent London suburb of Highgate is full of expensive houses, leafy parks and posh shops frequented by film stars and footballers. But a tall, red-brick house in this neighbourhood, called the India House, was once the epicentre for a revolution against the British, grooming dozens of nationalists who carried the call to action to the US, Europe and Japan. Chatto was one of them. His journey to becoming a revolutionary took a few years, but the men he met at India House were key to his metamorphosis from an intellectual to a radical.

Around October 1901, the then twenty-year-old Chatto decided to leave India for his education. His brother Harindranath Chattopadhyay wrote vividly of his departure, 'My brother left India on his birthday for London for the ICS. I was hardly two years old when he left. My mother is said to have sobbed and said "My son, you are leaving on your birthday; and in our country we believe that he who leaves on his birthday for a country outside, never returns."' Superstition perhaps, but a coincidence as well, since Chatto never again returned to his motherland.[2]

The young Chatto arrived in London and appeared for the Indian Civil Service exam twice, unsuccessfully each time. Back then, the civil service was a popular career choice for young Indians. Chatto then joined the Middle Temple, one of the Inns of Court, in order to qualify as a barrister, but he never became one. Fate pulled him in a different direction.

Around this time, Chatto was often distracted by romantic interests, a penchant which would continue through his life. He developed a complicated love life, according to British intelligence officers. In 1903, he became involved with an Englishwoman, and they began living together as Mr and Mrs Chatterton. But in 1909, they parted ways, and Chatto cultivated a friendship with a Mrs Reynolds, who was acidly described as 'affluent enough to contribute to Mrs Chatterton's maintenance'.[3]

Still, Chatto's biographer Nirode Barooah says, he 'was not merely a playboy'.[4] At this time, Chatto continued his studies in languages and contributed to professional journals. He also began a slow journey towards radical nationalism, influenced by the inhabitants of India House.

India House was owned by the mysterious Shyamji Krishna Varma. Krishna Varma was a wealthy scholar, a former diwan of several Indian princely states, a graduate of Balliol College in

Oxford, and also a staunch revolutionary. He bought the house expressly to house radical nationalists. He also edited an English monthly called *The Indian Sociologist*, which called itself an organ of political, social and religious reform and carried articles supporting home rule for India. He also set up the Home Rule Society, which began to work for an independent India. In December 1905, he set up six lectureships of two thousand rupees each for authors, journalists and other Indians to enable them to visit Europe. Each applicant had to promise never to accept a post or service under the British government.

India House was opened on 1 July 1905 by the English author, socialist and politician Henry Hyndman. Amongst those in attendance were Dadabhai Naoroji and Madame Cama. We will hear more about the latter in this chapter. Lenin and Gandhi were amongst the many distinguished visitors. It could house twenty-five students at any given time. Scholarships were handed out by Krishna Varma to those deemed sufficiently nationalist, one of them being Savarkar. Chatto had not qualified for a scholarship because he was at the time a moderate, not extreme, nationalist.

Among the early guests at the house were the 'Lal Bal Pal' trio: Lala Lajpat Rai, Bal Gangadhar Tilak and Bipin Chandra Pal. They were joined by their lieutenants G.S. Khaparde and Vishnu Karandikar. Soon, young agitators started arriving from across India. These included Har Dayal from Punjab, M.P.T. Acharya and V.V.S. Aiyar from Madras and Basudev Bhattacharjee and Hemanto Kumar Ghose from Bengal. Of these, the highly educated and charismatic Har Dayal would travel to the US and become one of the founders of the Ghadar (Punjabi word for 'revolt') Party—a revolutionary party founded in the US by migrant Indians, which would later expand its influence to other parts of the world. But the fiercest and loudest of all of them was Veer Savarkar, who would, of course, go on to found the Hindu Mahasabha and become a key proponent of Hindutva.

Back in 1900, Savarkar believed in the religious unity of all Indians, his chief aim being to revolt against the British. Indeed, it is reported that Har Dayal appeared to be far more in favour of Hindu nationalism at the time. Har Dayal made a controversial speech to the inhabitants of the house, stating that he was working for only a Hindu India. If the Mohammedans wished to remain in India, he argued, they would have to worship Hindu gods. Savarkar is reported to have protested this and had suggested that Har Dayal ought to be reasoned with.[5] Today, a blue plaque on the house commemorates Savarkar's stay: 'Vinayak Damodar Savarkar, Indian patriot and philosopher, lived here'.

Chatto never actually lived in India House, according to his biographer, but its inhabitants had a profound effect on him, most importantly Savarkar. M.P.T. Acharya said of Savarkar, 'His charm was such that a mere handshake could convert men as V.V.S. Aiyar and Har Dayal—not only convert but bring out the best in them.'[6] For Chatto, the heated debates and exciting discussions between men from all over India must have brought back memories of his cosmopolitan childhood addas.

India House soon became a centre for intrigue against the British, with agitators of all stripes coming and going. An amusing criticism of Scotland Yard's inability to control conspiracy in India House was written by Lord Morley, the then Secretary of State: 'Experts from the Home Office and Scotland Yard pointed out that their men are wholly useless in the case of Indian conspirators. They have no sort of agency able to distinguish Indian from Mahomedan, or Verma from Varma. In short, both you and I can easily understand that the ordinary square toed English constable, even in the detective branch, would be rather clumsy in tracing your wily Asiatics.'[7]

The initial guests of India House—the Lal Bal Pal trio—believed in boycott and passive resistance. But when Savarkar arrived on the scene, the character of the house changed. A flood of energetic propaganda started pouring forth from India House, propelled by first Krishna Varma and then Savarkar. The mood changed from peaceful resistance to the support of violence if necessary. Savarkar used his considerable gifts of rhetoric and imagery—and his deep religious fervour—to write a passionate appeal to Indians to take up arms against the British. This was read out weekly in India House to an eager audience.

The partition of Bengal in 1905 angered many nationalists and there ensued a frenzied debate over British rule in India. Savarkar's brother Ganesh, an equally passionate advocate for independence, was sentenced to transportation for life for printing and distributing revolutionary pamphlets. This enraged Savarkar even further.

At around this time the bohemian writer David Garnett—a friend of Savarkar's and a member of the Bloomsbury Group—visited India House. He gives us a vivid eyewitness report: 'Soon after my arrival. I trooped into the dining room and Savarkar, after addressing the company in Hindi, stood up and began to read aloud. As I could not understand what he was saying, I looked about the room. The sight of those brown men, some sitting around a long table and others leaning against the wall, all listening to the staccato voice of the speaker was very strange to me.'

He adds, 'Meanwhile, how strange they looked, one older man near was bearded and wore a fez, the others were bare-headed with their black, oily ringlets and black eyes, some speaking with fun and life, others like dry, bare, olives.' But it was Savarkar who drew all eyes with his natural charisma.

Garnett further wrote: 'I looked at Savarkar and thought his was the most sensitive face in the room and yet the most powerful. He spat out his words with almost convulsive movements. And then I became aware that he was reading aloud in English, not Hindustani. I listened then attentively and made out that he was reading about a battle in which an Indian general called Tantia Tope had been defeated by English troops and Sikhs.'[8]

Garnett also met a 'Byronic youth' at India House, who turned out to be Madan Lal Dhingra, one of Savarkar's most passionate followers.

Why did so many Indian revolutionaries flock to London, to the very centre of the empire that was repressing, arresting and tormenting them back in India? Historian Nick Owen explains how the 'soft heart of the empire' came about: 'In India, there could be one rule for the Indians, and another for the British. This racial differentiation was harder to impose in London. Although it was known to the Indian authorities that the Indian radicals were plotting for an Indian revolution, almost nothing could be done legally to stop them.'[9] As Owen explains, Indian revolutionaries could freely travel to India and back because imperial subjects could not be barred from travelling in the empire. They could be deported only if they committed an offence. Indians could also travel easily to other European countries.

Besides, freedom of speech was mostly guaranteed in Britain. *The Times*, for instance, printed Krishna Varma's letters without changing them, even when they spoke of his support for political assassination. 'When Government ministers complained, the editor replied that it was the paper's policy to give even the devil fair play. Sedition law, which was used extensively in India to restrict even moderate criticism of the government, had effectively fallen into disuse. The India Office concluded that the Indian radicals could not be prosecuted for advocating violence, even though in India merely arguing that violence was bound to follow repression had earned Tilak a six-year sentence.'[10]

In 1907, the *Indian Sociologist* carried a passage stating, 'It seems that any agitation in India must be carried on secretly and that the only methods which can bring the English government to its senses are the Russian methods vigorously and incessantly applied.' In May 1908, the anniversary of the Indian Mutiny was observed at India House and the celebration was attended by over a hundred students. In June 1908, a lecture was given at India House demonstrating the making of bombs.

That said, even in this lax climate, Indian revolutionaries were sometimes prosecuted. In 1907, Lala Lajpat Rai was deported from the UK for sedition. Krishna Varma decided to flee to Paris when he got word that the British government planned action against him. Given a free hand to do what he wished, Savarkar began conducting bomb-making workshops and practising rifle shooting at India house.

Then on 1 July 1909, the tipping point occurred. High-ranking British official William Hutt Curzon Wyllie was shot point-blank at an event hosted by the National Indian Association, an organisation formed to improve the education of Indian women. Curzon Wylie was the head of the Secret Police and was trying to obtain information about Indian revolutionaries. The assassin was Madan Lal Dhingra. He came from a wealthy and privileged family, which disowned him as soon as they came to know of the assassination.

At his trial, Dhingra was unapologetic, refusing to acknowledge the authority of the court. His fiery speech held nothing back. 'If it is patriotic in an Englishman to fight against the Germans if they were to occupy this country, it is much more justifiable and patriotic in my case to fight against the English. I hold the English people responsible for the murder of 80 million of Indian people in the last fifty years, and they are also responsible for taking away £100,000,000 every year from India to this country ... it is perfectly justifiable on our part to kill the Englishman who is polluting our sacred land.'[11]

He was sentenced to death. After the judge announced the verdict, Dhingra is said to have retorted: 'I am proud to have the honour of laying down my life for my country. But remember, we shall have our time in the days to come.' Dhingra was hanged on 17 August 1909 at the Pentonville prison.

In India House, there was sorrow, but also great rejoicing at Dhingra's bravery. Three days after the assassination, there was a meeting of revolutionaries at India House, where V.V.S. Aiyar called the act 'glorious', while Savarkar unwisely blurted, 'There was one man to watch and guide the whole thing.' This was taken as a virtual admission by Savarkar that he had persuaded Dhingra to commit the act. It is not known if Chatto was present at this meeting, but we can assume that he was.

The courtly old guard of the Indian freedom movement condemned the assassination. Still in South Africa at the time, Gandhi regarded Dhingra's action as cowardly and thought he was incited by others. 'If I kill someone in my house without a warning–someone who has done me no harm–I cannot but be called a coward.' The general opinion was that Savarkar was the real brains behind the operation.

Gandhi continued to strongly emphasise that peaceful resistance was the only way forward. 'A man's courage consists in suffering deeply and over a long period. India can gather nothing from this rule of murders.'[12] Others of the old guard, like G.K. Gokhale, Madan Mohan Malaviya and the All India Congress Committee, also condemned the 'senseless' act. But the floodgates of revolutionary action had been opened and turned out to be difficult to close.

More assassinations followed. In February 1909, via a cook employed at India House, Savarkar sent twenty Browning pistols to India, concealed in a box with a false bottom. The pistols travelled all the way to Nasik. Arthur Tippetts Jackson, a British officer in the Indian Civil Service, was shot dead with one of these pistols on 21 December 1909 at a theatre in Nasik by seventeen-year-old Anant Laxman Kanhere. Jackson was a popular and well-liked officer, but he was reportedly shot for having sent Savarkar's brother Ganesh to jail in the Andamans.

Fearing arrest, Savarkar escaped to France and stayed in Paris for a while, but then he inexplicably returned to England despite being strongly advised not to do so by Chatto. Savarkar believed he would not be recognised, but as Harindranath Chattopadhyay colourfully put it, he 'walked into the mouth of treachery even as a deer walks right into the open mouth of a boa constrictor'.

On 13 March 1910, Savarkar was arrested at the Victoria station and sent to the Brixton prison. Between mid-March and June 1910, Chatto, who it was believed had not been involved in the assassination of Curzon Wylie,[13] reportedly visited Savarkar as many as fifteen times in Brixton.

Savarkar's return to India was ordered, and he was made to board a ship called the *SS Morea* on 1 July 1910. Harindranath described subsequent events as related to him by Chatto. Apparently when the ship had left Dover and was in the English Channel, Savarkar asked the guards to allow him to remove his handcuffs and take a bath. Incredibly, they agreed. 'Once inside the bath he locked the door, stripped himself bare, smeared himself well with soap until as slippery as an eel! Then in the wink of an eye, he squeezed himself through the porthole, and with the undaunted will of a Titan, slipping out right into the Channel swam towards France. Lord, he swam, but how! By a narrow shave, within an ace of being recaptured, Savarkar touched French Shores. Had Savarkar only known enough French to explain that he was a political refugee and had every right to French protection, he would surely have been saved those nightmarish after years of body rot and soul rust on the island beyond the black water, and the face of Indian history changed beyond recognition. But alas, Savarkar could not speak even one word of French. The British taking advantage of the situation shouted "Thief, thief!"'[14]

The French were alarmed by the sight of a half-naked man on their shores. The news spread to Paris, from where Chatto and his friends rushed to Savarkar's rescue, but by then the latter had been handed over to the British. Savarkar was tried by a special tribunal in what came to be known as the Nasik Conspiracy case and was convicted and sentenced to transportation for life to the Andamans in December 1910.

'Thus, sailed away to the Island of exiled patriots, the Andamans, Veer Savarkar, true-hearted hero, where he was about to undergo untold and unimaginable suffering, unrelieved and unmitigated torture,' wrote Harindranath. A desperate and broken Savarkar would later write several mercy petitions to the British, between 1911 and 1920, pleading to be released and expressing his willingness to give up political activity. After his release from the Andamans, Savarkar called upon Harindranath Chattopadhyay, who described him as 'quiet, weary and to some extent broken ... The Andamans had managed to tamper with his earlier zeal and temper the steel.'[15]

A clampdown was ordered on India House. Chatto was still trying to figure out his own political position at the time. Even though, initially, he believed that India would gradually achieve independence through dialogue, he did not sever his ties with Savarkar. His position in the UK was delicate. Be too outspoken and he might be arrested for sedition or have to flee like Krishna Varma. Say too little and he would be accused of being a British sycophant. Krishna Varma and Chatto now began an ideological debate on nationalism in the pages of *The Times*, each seeking to define what a nationalist was.

In February 1909, Krishna Varma, while living outside of England, had outraged observers by defending the death of the two innocent British ladies in Muzaffarpur in the august pages of *The Times*, calling it accidental and incidental. 'But supposing for argument's sake that they were killed deliberately, it would only prove that those who habitually live and associate with wrongdoers or robbers (and Indian nationalists regard all Englishmen in India as robbers) do so at their peril.'[16]

This was the beginning of a long battle between him and Chatto in the 'Letters' column of *The Times*. Chatto published a response saying that a true nationalist believed in peaceful resistance and a gradual move to home rule, not murder and assassination. 'The principles that enable a man to be called a nationalist have been very clearly laid down by such popular leaders as Bal Gangadhar Tilak, Bipin Chandra Pal, Lala Lajpat Rai and Aurobindo Ghosh. Mr Krishna Varma talks unmitigated nonsense when he says that Indians look upon Englishmen as "robbers" and that Englishmen submit to the "risks of war when they go out to India",' he wrote. Chatto went further, saying quite astonishingly, 'We are bound to accept historical facts as such, and there is no sane person who looks upon the British occupation as anything but a necessary phase in the advancement of our country.'[17] Nationalism, argued Chatto, was only justifiable if it did not exceed the limits of criminal law.

Krishna Varma responded with a brutal comeback, accurately surmising that Chatto had no choice but to conceal his real thoughts and suck up to the British. 'There are some Indian nationalists who are at heart really with me, but owing to their residence in British territory are obliged to say and do things quite contrary to their convictions ... But they deceive no one, and make themselves only ridiculous in the eyes of the English public.'[18]

This was the plain truth about Chatto's early political leanings. His hands were tied. In response, Chatto argued that while he believed that British rule in India must end, he did not believe in secret political assassinations as a method of achieving that. Rashly, he said, 'The day I feel convinced of the necessity of political assassination and underground work, I shall cease to write. I shall return to my country and put my theories into practice. But I shall certainly not seek a safe retreat within the hospitable walls of a European city.'[19] Brave words, but Chatto would live to regret them.

In only a few years, Chatto would do a complete about-face. Even in early 1910, Chatto was reported by the British authorities to have been making all sorts of libellous comments about the British rule in India. He was also described as preferring indirect and devious methods to achieve his aims. 'He says that he considers it right to meet strategy with strategy and diplomacy with diplomacy.'[20] In reality, Chatto had begun to adopt more extreme views.

Historian V.N. Datta explains the gradual radicalisation of the young men at India House, where they would start adopting British principles. 'It is natural that when Indians go abroad and live in England, their view of India politics is different. The free political institutions which they see the English enjoy around them bring to their mind the striking contrast between liberty on one side, and despotism on the other.'[21]

On 9 June 1910, Chatto fled to Paris, following in the steps of Krishna Varma. The scrutiny of the inhabitants of India House by the authorities had been making him nervous. Despite his fence-sitting, Chatto had already been expelled from the Middle Temple for stoking revolution, same as Krishna Varma. There was nothing to keep Chatto in England anymore. He had chosen a side at last and this decision would influence the rest of his life.

Soon after, India House closed down and the firebrand revolutionaries it once housed scattered all over the world. Despite their fervour and idealism, they did not have a cohesive plan or a united front and that would be a fatal lack of vision. Later, Gandhi's peaceful satyagraha would take over, and the idea of a violent struggle for freedom would be rejected by most of India.

* * *

The Paris Indian Society, 1907

A small Indian woman, her head covered, stood before the delegates of the International Socialist Conference being held in Stuttgart.

She held an unfamiliar flag with stripes of green, yellow and red. In the middle were written the words 'Vande Mataram' and on the sides, were displayed a crescent moon, a sun and eight lotuses. The woman was Bhikaji Rustom Cama, the first Indian to ever hold an Indian flag on foreign soil.

It was 22 August 1907. By this time, the Indian nationalists had grown tired of being moderate in the face of British repression. Chatto, visiting from England, was by Cama's side as she announced passionately, 'This flag is of Indian independence. Behold, it is born. It is already sanctioned by the blood of martyred Indian youths. In the name of this flag, I appeal to lovers of freedom all over the world to cooperate in freeing one fifth of the human race.'[22] This would have been considered treason at that time, but Cama was undeterred by the threat of arrest.

The Flag of Indian Independence as it was called is now on display at the Kesari-Maratha library in Pune. The green colour represented Islam, the yellow Hinduism and the red Buddhism. The lotuses represented the eight provinces of British India.

Paris at the time was a meeting place for nationalists and revolutionaries from across the world, including those from Egypt. It was here that Chatto and his friends regrouped in 1910, under the leadership of Madame Cama as she was known.

Cama was a very unusual figure, one of the few women who were a part of the macho Indian nationalist movement. Born into a wealthy Parsi family in Bombay in 1861, she married the solicitor Rustom Cama. But as she started travelling and reading extensively, she grew ever more nationalistic and unconventional. Her marriage had become suffocating and claustrophobic, and she would spent most of her time away from her husband, reading, talking and meeting other nationalists.

In 1901, Cama fell ill and was sent to London for medical treatment. She arrived in London around the same time as Chatto, then travelled to Germany, Scotland and Paris. Immediately, she threw herself into the revolutionary movement. In 1905, Cama fled London for Paris, because she feared arrest by the British. There she started the Paris Indian Society with Sardarsinh Ravajibhai Rana, another revolutionary.

By 1907, when many Indian nationalists were still talking about dominion status, Cama had started preaching revolution. Her history sheet prepared by the Criminal Intelligence Office makes for interesting reading. At Stuttgart, she made a speech dedicated to the 'dumb millions of Hindustan, who are undergoing terrible tyranny under the English capitalists and the British government'.[23] Thirty-five million pounds were being drained annually from India to England without return, said Cama, and thus half a million people died of poverty in India every month.

It was one of the most extreme early speeches by an Indian nationalist. The intrepid Cama did not stop there. On 28 October 1907, she addressed the members of the Minerva Club at the Waldorf Astoria Hotel in New York, saying, 'The people here know about the conditions in Russia, but I don't think they know anything about the conditions in India. Our best men are deported or sent to prison like criminals, and there they are flogged. We are peaceful, we do not want a bloody revolution, but we do want to teach the people their rights and to throw off despotism.'[24]

Not content, Cama started a paper called *Bande Mataram*. In its first issue, it declared that three stages have to be passed for independence: 'The first of educating the people, the second war, and the third reconstruction. Virtue and wisdom first, then war, finally independence.'[25] In Paris, Madame Cama asked Chatto to start another paper, *Talvar*, which was every bit as radical as *Bande Mataram*. These papers full of revolutionary ideas were spread across the world by the society.

In the second issue of *Talvar*, published in December 1909, Chatto passionately defended the anarchist movement: 'But if it is anarchism to be thoroughly ashamed of being ruled by a handful of vile alien vandals, if it is anarchism to wish to exterminate them with the noble desire of establishing our national freedom upon the basis of popular sovereignty, of justice, of mercy, of righteousness, and of humanity, if it is anarchism to rise for the sanctity of our homes, the integrity of our life, and the honour of our God and our country, and to slay every individual tyrant, whether foreign or native, that continues the enslavement of our great noble people, if it is anarchism to conspire ceaselessly to take human life with the only object of emancipating our beloved Motherland, then we say cursed is the man who is not an anarchist.'[26]

It is likely Cama's influence that led to Chatto's communist leanings and his ties with Russia in his later life. Cama had a wide circle of friends, that included Russian revolutionaries. Indeed, the Russian writer Maxim Gorky, a close friend of Lenin, wrote to her in 1912, asking her to write to him about the condition of Indian women and their role in the freedom struggle.[27] Nothing seems to have come of that, but Cama is reported to have been greatly moved by Gorky's revolutionary poem *Song of the Falcon*.[28]

In a 1934 speech he gave in Leningrad, Chatto acknowledged Bhikaji Cama's influence on his political views and said, 'Bhikaji Cama used to tell us about Lenin and the Russian social democrats and of their attitude towards the questions of war and the right of self-determination of nations.'[29]

Meanwhile, the Indian contingent in Paris began to make connections with other peoples fighting for independence, including Egyptian nationalists. In 1910, Boutros Ghali Pasha, the Egyptian prime minister, was assassinated by a nationalist, Ibrahim Nassif al-Wardani, who had just returned from Britain. Madan Lal Dhingra and Wardani were both praised by an Egyptian nationalist poet, Ali Al-Ghayati for their revolutionary actions. These were the first stirrings of a common sympathy amongst colonised countries.[30]

By now, Madame Cama had set up a National Fund Scheme with 5,000 francs to provide financial aid to help Veer Savarkar in particular, and the revolutionary movement outside India in general. Apparently, the fund was used only for Indians who 'performed' well overseas in the service of revolution.

In September 1910, Madame Cama's name surfaced again in official records. The Indian and Egyptian extremists held a meeting at the Palais hotel, where Cama called for a general rising of all Indians against the English and the throwing of bombs at English officials in India. The Scottish nationalist and Labour MP Keir Hardie, who was an ardent critic of the British Raj, was also present at this meeting and declared that Madame Cama's statements had been completely out of order.[31] At this time, Chatto's name too began to crop up in official records because of his many visits to Cama's house. He was described as working to 'promote unity between the Indians (Hindus and Mohammedans) and also between the Indian and the Egyptian nationalists'.[32]

However, soon after, cracks began to appear in the solidarity of the Paris coterie. By the end of December 1911, 'things had come to so bad a pass that Chattopadhyaya, finding Madame Cama's dictatorial behaviour intolerable, addressed some of the other members of the society with a view to her removal from the council'.[33] The Paris Indians constantly argued between themselves over money, with different factions of the group frequently accusing each other of appropriating scarce funds.

The British police, who kept a close watch on the revolutionaries, found Cama to be quarrelsome and vain. 'Like many of the so-called leaders, she had a very exaggerated idea of her own importance, and was constantly quarrelling with Krishna Varma, Chattopadhyaya and others of her party.'[34] They didn't have a high opinion of the young Chatto either. 'He is full of imagination, like many Bengalis, and was continually propounding elaborate schemes for revolution which were not of the slightest practical value, as Madame Cama sometimes said of him, he was "all talk and no work".'[35]

By 1914, Chatto was comically reported by British intelligence to 'be so engrossed in his private affairs as to give Cama and Rana very little help'. In 1911, Chatto's paramour, Mrs Reynolds, would sometimes visit him in Paris 'disguised as a boy'. In 1912, when Chatto reportedly got married to her, he was considered somewhat 'lost to the revolutionary movement'. But two years later, they broke up, and 'Chattopadhyaya was again thrown upon his own resources'.[36]

Meanwhile, Chatto's sister Sarojini had become an ardent Gandhian. A meeting with Gandhi in London on 8 August 1914 had changed her life. She met him one day when Gandhi was organising an ambulance unit to contribute to the First World war effort. He later wrote in his autobiography, 'The Lyceum, a Ladies club, undertook to make as many clothes for the soldiers as they could. Shrimati Sarojini Naidu was a member of this club, and threw herself wholeheartedly into the work. This was my first acquaintance with her.'

Sarojini Naidu had a different, more colourful account of their meeting. 'I went wandering in search of his lodging in an obscure part of Kensington and climbed the steep stairs of an old, unfashionable house to find an open door, framing a living picture of a little man with a shaven head, seated on the floor on a black prison blanket and eating a messy meal of squashed tomatoes and olive oil out of a wooden prison bowl. Around him were ranged some battered tins of parched groundnuts and tasteless biscuits of dried plantain flour. I burst instinctively into happy laughter at this amusing and unexpected vision of a famous leader, whose name had already become a household word in our country. He lifted his eyes and laughed back at me, saying "Ah, you must be Mrs Naidu! Who else dare be so irreverent?" Come in, said he and share my meal. "No thanks," I replied, sniffing. "What an abominable mess this is." In this way and at my instance commenced our friendship.'[37]

Years later, in 1968, Chatto's sister Mrinalini would recall the widening chasm between Chatto and Sarojini, one devoted to violent anarchy, the other to Gandhian ahimsa. Apparently, as Chatto's revolutionary activities began to increase, Sarojini was warned by Sir Akbar Hydari, a top civil servant and later the prime minister of Hyderabad state, to disown her brother. In response, she impulsively wrote a letter to Hydari distancing herself from Chatto and his deeds. But when the letter was published, an outraged Aghorenath—forever loyal to his son—refused to allow Sarojini to enter the Chattopadhyay family home.[38]

By 1914, the Paris group had broken up, decimated and demoralised by both the infighting and the strong government suppression. The ravages of time had affected Madame Cama as well. Some years later, in 1927, Chatto's brother Harindranath would write about meeting Madame Cama in Paris around this time. He described her as an 'old wrinkled woman, with a face which seemed obviously a history of Indian revolution. Every line traced upon it was a sentence which expressed a determination to help to set India free.' He wrote that Cama had vowed to him that she would go back to India only when the country was free. She had also asked Harindranath to give Chatto her blessings.

Jawaharlal Nehru had also met her a year earlier and described the encounter thus: 'In Paris we saw old Madame Cama, rather fierce and terrifying as she came up to you and peered into your face, and, pointing at you, asked abruptly who you were. The answer made no difference (probably she was too deaf to hear it) for she formed her own impressions and stuck to them, despite facts to the contrary.'[39]

Madame Cama remained in exile in Europe for many long and lonely years. In 1935, weary, humiliated and sick, Cama petitioned the British that she be allowed to return to India, agreeing to give up her anarchist activities. In August 1936, she died in Mumbai aged seventy-four, never tasting the freedom for which she had fought so valiantly.

5

In Search of the Golden Fleece

'Tell me young friend, do you really believe that you will be able to rule your country without foreign advice and help?' asked the German ambassador.
I snapped, 'Well, don't you think that the privilege of helping us in future should be earned by helping us win freedom?'

M.N. Roy

ON THE OTHER SIDE OF THE WORLD, STILL WAITING IMPATIENTLY IN India, the young Narendranath was at an impasse. The Anushilan Samiti had inspired him to fight for independence, but they did not have the necessary arms and weapons to do so, and the British had cut off many of their options. Then came the First World War and the possibility of a new ally in Germany, which seemed to be the only great power that would be able to stand up to Britain.

The German government promised to give the Indians arms and weapons, sourced from the US. It was too risky to travel to Germany to get them, so it was proposed that the arms be delivered to a neutral third-party country. Java (now in Indonesia) was suggested as a possible location for delivery. An elaborate plan to get the weapons to India was devised by Irish republicans, German agitators and Indian revolutionaries in the US, all of whom had a common enemy: the British. By January 1915, 8,080 Springfield rifles, 410 repeating rifles, 2,400 carbines, 500 Colt revolvers and a supply of cartridges had been amassed at San Diego. The plan was that, in March 1915, the ship *Annie Larsen* would carry the secret cargo and pass it on to another ship called *Maverick*, which would then transport it to Java. Naren was asked by the organisation Jugantar to go to Java in April 1915 to collect the arms and then deliver them to the coast of north-eastern Orissa. The arms were to be used for surprise terror attacks within the country.[1]

In the end, it all came to nothing. *Annie Larsen* waited for the *Maverick* to turn up, but the British authorities had got wind of the plan and had stopped the *Maverick* from leaving port. With worsening weather conditions, *Annie Larsen* was forced to travel to Hoquiam in Washington, where her cargo was seized. The plan ended up being nothing more than a wild goose chase.

Naren would go on many such chases to acquire arms, all of which came to nothing, mostly because of the efficiency of the British authorities. In 1915, he left India again to chase what he called 'The Golden Fleece', the name he gave for the money and arms that were needed to equip Indian revolutionaries. He would not return to India for the next sixteen years.

Like Jason and his Argonauts searching for the Golden Fleece, Naren would move ceaselessly around the world, trying to muster support for an armed insurrection in India. At the same time, his pacifist counterpart Gandhi was urging Indians to join the British army and fight in the war, in the hope that the country would be given more freedom in exchange for this support.

The next few years were disappointing for the youthful and idealistic Naren. Ally after ally would let him down. From Java he went to Japan, where he met Rash Behari Bose in 1915, a fascinating figure who deserves a whole book to himself. He was about the same age as Naren and came from a similar background of having grown up in revolutionary Bengal. He, too, was a disciple of Jatin Mukherjee and an early follower of the Ghadar movement, which had spread across the west coast of the US.

Rash Behari Bose had been plotting to assassinate the then Viceroy of India Lord Hardinge. On 23 December 1912, a homemade bomb was thrown into the viceroy's howdah as his procession moved through Chandni Chowk in Delhi. Bose, while not the thrower, had been the mastermind behind the plot. Hardinge was injured, but survived. Rash Behari evaded capture for nearly three years, but finally fled to Japan in 1915. The thrower of the bomb, Basanta Kumar Biswas, was eventually hanged.

Such a man might have been expected to be supportive of Naren. But when Naren met Bose in 1915, he found Bose to be totally enthralled by Japan. Bose had come to believe that the liberation of India could only be spearheaded by Japan. Even this liberation, he believed, could come only after Japan had fulfilled its mission to free the rest of Asia from white powers. This had puzzled Naren, who said, 'I could not forget that Japan was Britain's ally. How could we rely upon her?' To which, Bose had replied, 'We must have faith in the leader of Asia, and wait patiently for our chance.'[2] But Naren wasn't willing to wait for Japan to make a choice. 'How could we leave in the lurch the comrades, who were waiting neither safe nor comfortable, somewhere in the tribal regions of the Indo-Chinese frontier?' he thought.

Bose would go on to marry a Japanese woman, becoming an adopted son of Japan. Many years later, he became one of the key founders of the Indian National Army headed by Subhas Chandra Bose. And in 1943, his adopted country, Japan, honoured him with its highest title, the Order of the Rising Sun.

But back in 1915, Naren did not believe Bose when the latter said that Japan was a good ally. Japan had close ties with the British colonial empire, Naren thought. He began to look elsewhere for help, specifically to the Chinese nationalist leader Sun Yat-Sen of the Kuomintang party (KMT), who became the first provisional president of the Republic of China in 1912. He was a much-admired figure in India and was in exile in Japan after the failure of the Kuomintang party's 1913 revolution against Yuan Shi-Kai, the dictatorial second provisional president and later Emperor of China.

Sun too believed that India, like the rest of Asia, ought to wait to be liberated by Japan, which was then the most powerful power in the region. His argument was to let Japan drive the Europeans out; after which China and Japan could come to an agreement on the basis of the unity of race and culture. 'It appealed to my nationalist prejudice but was a little jarring to common sense,' wrote Naren later. Also, Sun was a fervent and evangelical Christian. Naren described himself as a heretic. He wrote drolly, 'Face to face with him, I found it difficult to go down on my knees humbly. The prejudice of hero-worship was challenged by the native intelligence of a born heretic.'[3]

This was the first time Naren realised, to his shock, that others did not respect or admire Indian revolutionaries the way he did. Indeed, most supposed allies he ended up meeting did not agree that Indians deserved independence, or that they were capable of winning it. Finding true allies was proving to be a difficult task.

By 1915, the Chinese provinces of Yunan and Szechuan were in revolt against the then Chinese emperor, Yuan Shi-Kai. Sun Yat-Sen was on the side of the rebels and made an interesting suggestion to Naren. He suggested that Naren approach the German ambassador in China with a request for US $5 million to purchase arms and ammunition from rebels in Yunan and Szechuan. If the ambassador agreed, Sun would use it to purchase the support of Yuan Shi-Kai's allies and bring about his downfall through a Third Revolution. The remaining arms would then be handed over to Naren for his own war in India. A sort of 'I scratch your back, you scratch mine' strategy, which depended entirely on the German hatred of the British.

The plan was hare-brained and risky, but it appealed to the young, rash Naren. He called it grandiose himself, but he could not let go of his long-cherished dream of 'appearing on the frontiers of India with arms enough to raise an army'. Besides, he was already being tailed in Tokyo by the police, so he needed to come to a quick decision. Rash Behari Bose had told Naren that he might be served with a notice to leave Japan in twenty-four hours or be arrested, but offered no help at all. Therefore, Naren thought it best to leave Japan as soon as possible.

To shake off his hounds, he employed a clever strategy. He went to the biggest department store in Japan. 'Even there, foreigners had to take off their shoes at the entrance in return for cloth shoes, so that the dirt from their streets did not soil the spotless matting,' wrote Naren. 'I did not return to recover my shoes, went out by another entrance and straight to the railway station. It seemed that I had succeeded in getting the four sleuths off the track.'[4]

Naren crossed quietly into Pusan (now Busan), South Korea. He had planned a circuitous voyage to Peking, his final destination, changing routes several times to shake off British police and their allies. Finally, he took a ship across the Yellow Sea, heading for Shanghai. But on a local train on the way to Shanghai, he was accosted by an Englishman, a 'typical colonial tough of the pre-war days'. This man addressed Naren as 'Mr White', which had been his assumed name in Japan. Naren tried to pass by, but the Englishman asked him very politely, 'Before you go to your destination, would you mind accompanying me for a few minutes?' Naren asked where the man wanted him to go to. 'To the police station. I am the chief of the British police,'[5] was the response. In a desperate attempt to evade him, Naren replied that he would rather go to a good hotel, but the man refused to take no for an answer. In the police station, Naren was told he would have to spend the night there as they were expecting some information from Japan. Then he was put in the lock-up.

The next morning, Naren was presented before the British consul-general in China and bombarded with questions. Naren explained that he had wanted to go to England to study, but the war had prevented it so he had gone to Japan as he had been eager to go abroad. On the boat, a fellow passenger had given him an address in Tokyo to call at in case he ever needed any help. But soon thereafter, Naren continued, he had realised that he had made a mistake. Now all he wanted to do was to return home to India.

The consul-general likely did not believe a word of this far-fetched story, but the expected information had not come from Japan. Naren was saved by what he called the 'British sense of justice', which would not allow the consul general to keep him locked up with no evidence. Instead, he was merely admonished, 'There are many revolutions in these parts. Stay away from them.'[6] He did not, of course, intend to follow that advice.

In fact, the ever-cheeky Naren could not resist a last plea before the consul-general. He asked for a passport so he could travel easily. This was the very definition of chutzpah. The old gentleman stiffened a little. 'No, I cannot do that; I don't know that you are a British subject.' Naren replied immediately, 'If I was not a British subject how could your police arrest and detain me, sir?' The old man was visibly rattled. 'Oh, these are delicate points of law,' he said.[7]

Naren continued his journey, again giving his tails the slip. He went to Peking with a concrete agreement from the Yunan rebel leader for arms to be delivered across the frontier to North East Assam, enough to equip an Indian revolutionary army of thousands. Naren thought the situation in India was perfect to start an armed uprising using German money and Yunan arms. But tragically, the wavering Germans failed to keep their promise. The German ambassador said that he was unable to earmark such a large sum of money for activities in India since he was not confident of their success.

At this Naren lost his temper. Once again, he had come up against racial prejudice and the commonly held notion that Indians were incapable of governing themselves. 'What was the cost of winning such a battle in Europe?' he asked the German ambassador. The ambassador was astonished at this question. 'The patronising junker did not expect such insolence from a youngster belonging to a non-white race,' thought Naren to himself. Aloud, he said that if the British lost India, they would also lose the war against Germany. 'Was 5 million dollars too much to win the possibly decisive battle?' he asked. But Naren's arguments were useless. The Germans simply did not have enough faith in Indian revolutionaries, a pattern that would repeat itself over the years.

A frustrated Naren then blurted out that he would win the battle for India with or without Germany. The ambassador was astonished at Naren's confidence. While saying his goodbyes to Naren, he asked, 'Tell me young friend, do you really believe that you will be able to rule your country without foreign advice and help?' Naren snapped, 'Well, don't you think that the privilege of helping us in future should be earned by helping us win freedom?'[8] The ambassador laughed and then asked, 'How many young men like the one I have just met are there in India?' Naren replied, 'I am the solitary representative of a very large party of such revolutionaries.' Thus ended Naren's attempt at getting money from Germany. All his youthful oratory could not defeat the Germans' belief that Indians were weak, divided and not capable of ruling their own country.

In September 1915, came shocking news from home. Naren's mentor, Bagha Jatin, had been killed in a bloody shoot-out with police in Balasore. He had lived and died by his tenet, '*Amra morbo, jagat jagbe*' (We shall die to awaken the nation). Even Jatin's sworn enemy Charles Tegart, the then police commissioner of Bengal, paid grudging tribute to the man: 'He was the first Bengali to have died fighting from a trench.'[9]

His death had a deep effect on Naren. 'I could not forget the injunction of the only man I ever obeyed almost blindly. Jatin Da's heroic death must be avenged. The corollary to that realisation was that Jatin Da's death would be avenged if I worked for the ideal of establishing a social order in which the best in man could be manifest.'

Naren was now twenty-nine. And where was he in his journey? Taking stock, he realised that while he had gained much revolutionary experience, it had all come to nothing. He had begun to realise that armed insurrection was likely to remain a pipe dream and dimly sensed that he should be working for a social revolution rather than a violent uprising.

Even Naren's close friend and biographer Sibnarayan Ray admitted to the former's many faults. 'Although Jatin was his model, he had little of Jatin's warmth, compassion and tolerance. Recognising the supreme importance of joint effort, he had single-mindedly devoted himself to the organisation of Jugantar, but his relationship with the leaders of the federated groups was rarely very close.'[10]

Naren had begun to show signs of his future inability to work with a team or get along with others. His memoirs suggest that he did not get along with Rash Behari Bose. His later harsh observations on Sun Yat-Sen, Bhagwan Singh and Herambalal Gupta, even if partly justified, also indicated his 'intolerance of weakness in others whose revolutionary passion might not have been matched by an equal[11] measure of integrity and intelligence. On the whole, he was more admired than loved.'[12]

'More admired than loved' would become Naren's epitaph. His vagabond life had shaped him, but also hardened him. He had lost contact with his family. With the police constantly in pursuit, he had to always be on the move. He had no time for romantic entanglements, being what Sibnarayan Ray called 'a political brahmachari'.[13]

But if Naren was something of a lone wolf rather than a team player, with no softer side to him, he had other qualities. His presence of mind, single-minded dedication and faith in himself were considered arrogance by some but served him well. Sibnarayan Ray has described an incident in which Charles Tegart visited Naren's room. 'There were two stolen Mauser pistols lying on the table. Naren simply covered them with a newspaper and talked with Tegart for thirty minutes, convincing him that they were two innocent young men with no interest in politics.'[14]

By this time, Naren had become friendless and rootless. He now had to make his own way in the world. He contemplated going to Germany for another attempt at getting arms, but had no more faith in Germany's support for Indians. Meanwhile, Jatin's death had made him realise that he had to look beyond revolution, and instead attempt to change the entire political system. Where better to do so than America, the land of the free and the home of the brave, where many Indians had sought shelter?

But before Naren could find shelter for himself, he needed to cross the Pacific, which was no easy feat as he had no visa for the US. In Shanghai, he was luckily taken on board a German gunboat that was on its way to the US. Much to his dismay, on the boat he met Bhagwan Singh—one of the leaders of the Ghadar Party—who was returning to America. They did not get along. Naren described Singh uncharitably as a heavily built man of about fifty 'who had picked up many vulgarities of the American "He-man" without losing any of the equally objectionable native characteristics'. Bhagwan Singh was apparently a man who loved his food, and in typical Punjabi style, had arranged for a long list of goodies and several cases of beer to be placed on board, hoping to 'eat, drink and be merry'.[15]

The two men were squashed under the sailors' bunks in a tiny cabin. But when the ship set sail, the British police came aboard to search it. The men were forced to hide in 'the pitch-dark entrails of the ship' for what seemed like an age, until the ship was well on its way to the US.

Eventually, they were let out, and Bhagwan Singh immediately began eating and drinking. But once again, the men were forced to rush to their hiding place because a British battleship had signalled the boat to stop. Within a short time, a number of men came down the stairs into the small sailors' cabin. Naren later wrote, 'Someone in a very imperious voice said: "I know for certain that those chaps are on board; damn it! Where can they be?" The remark was emphasised by stamping with a heavily booted foot on the plank right over our heads. At the same time, I heard a pitiable whisper: "*Babuji, ab to pakraya.*" With difficulty could I resist the impulse to laugh aloud in disgust when almost instantaneously my clothes were soaked in an invisible trickle of some warm fluid. I had to remain in that filthy condition still for quite some time, wondering if the revolutionary hero had fainted out of fear.' Bhagwan Singh had wet himself in his fear, but neither man could move a muscle.[16]

The sailors on the ship were grilled by the colonial police officers, but they did not divulge any information about the two men. The ship was thoroughly searched and every piece of cargo moved, which took hours. But when nothing came of it, the British officers deboarded. Eventually, the men were let out and Bhagwan Singh once again fell upon the food, drinking many bottles of beer. Naren restricted himself to bread and cheese.

By now, Naren was determined to escape the unpleasant company of his fellow stowaway on their month-long voyage. In Kobe, their ship was to stay overnight. 'I made a tempting proposal to my companion,' wrote Naren later. '"Let us go ashore in one of these boats and have a good time in the city." He was very enthusiastic: "Yes, it would be a pity to go away from Japan without a last look at the geisha quarters."'[17]

The two men were let down by a rope ladder and told to return only in the dark. Naren then came up with an excuse to not return, saying he wanted to go to Tokyo to meet Rash Behari Bose. Having given Bhagwan Singh the slip, Naren rushed to the railway station to catch the train to Tokyo, in order to embark on the next stage of his journey. Ever the solitary traveller, he preferred to make his way in the world alone and unaided.

6

Archaeology and Jihad in Berlin

Our consuls in Turkey and India must get a conflagration going throughout the whole Mohammedan world against this hated, unscrupulous, dishonest nation of shopkeepers (Britain)–since if we are going to bleed to death, England must at least lose India.

Kaiser Wilhelm II, German Emperor

IN 1899, A GERMAN DIPLOMAT, ORIENTALIST AND AMATEUR archaeologist called Baron Max von Oppenheim was travelling through Aleppo (in present day Syria). Local villagers told him unbelievable stories about mysterious stone idols buried in the sand. He decided to dig and fantastic treasures emerged. A majestic seated mother goddess. Winged creatures of ancient myth and legend. Mythical birds and sphinxes. Bearded and stately kings, adorned with ornate jewellery. But Oppenheim didn't have a legal permit to excavate, so he reburied the statues until he could return. It took him over a decade.

Oppenheim came from a wealthy Jewish banking dynasty of Cologne that was involved in many social and philanthropic ventures. The Oppenheim family had set up Sal Oppenheim, a German bank, in 1789. This later became a subsidiary of Deutsche Bank. They had also set up zoos, music schools and horticultural societies. The young Oppenheim grew up in a 'magnificent Louis XIV style palais with an outstanding collection of paintings including works by Van Dyck, Hans Holbein, Rembrandt, Rubens and Velasquez'.[1]

As Oppenheim grew older, he developed a deep and enduring interest in the Middle East. Encouraged by travellers like George Sadler, Richard Burton, T.E. Lawrence (later known as Lawrence of Arabia) and Gertrude Bell, by the end of the nineteenth century, interest in the Middle East, Arabia and Africa had become common. At a young age, Max had become a passionate nationalist, whose chief aim was to promote Germany's well-being and progress in archaeology and everywhere else. 'If I could promote Germany's national interests in any way, it would be my most fervent wish to do so,'[2] he wrote.

In 1892, Oppenheim travelled from Morocco, went across North Africa, reached Cairo and spent seven months there. He 'lived exactly as the local Muslims did' in order to become fluent in Arabic and to learn their customs. In 1893, he went to Damascus. He wrote about how he had come to 'love the wild unconstrained life of the sons of the desert',[3] and adopted many of their customs, such as eating with his hands. It is also possible that the pure racial make-up of the Bedouins appealed to him.

On his way back to Germany, he passed through India and the Persian Gulf. He established connections with many Muslim rulers, including the Sultan of Turkey. In 1896, he ended up in Cairo, where he lived almost like a sultan himself, entertaining the rich and famous and becoming a hugely popular host. He even took a harem of mistresses, one of whom was killed by her husband when her affair with Oppenheim was discovered.[4]

Oppenheim had always wanted to be a diplomat. But he was rejected several times, because he was a Jew. He was not told this outright, but in a private letter, the then Secretary for Foreign Affairs, Herbert von Bismarck (son of Otto von Bismarck) explained that he was against having Jews in the diplomatic service because 'Jews, even when they are gifted, always become tactless and pushy as soon as they get into positions of privilege. The other members of our diplomatic corps would not be happy to have a Jew boy added to their ranks just because his father had been crafty enough to make a lot of money.'[5]

'Jew boy'. Oppenheim would be called this ugly slur his whole life and have to battle for respect as a member of the German diplomatic service. Consequently, he would also go the extra mile to prove his patriotism. By 1896, Oppenheim had managed to be assigned to the Middle East as a quasi-diplomat, though he had also acquired a reputation for 'pushiness, talkativeness, servility, lavish expenditures and general reputation for deviousness'.[6] Perhaps this was his natural response to the bigotry he faced.

Even though he was not officially part of the German diplomatic service, Oppenheim became the unofficial 'eyes and ears' of the German government from his base in Cairo. His assignment was to make the 'most strenuous efforts to obtain news of all events covering Muslims in every part of the world'.[7] He would often exaggerate his own power and influence and once referred to himself, when doing a tour of the United States, as 'Dr Baron Max Von Oppenheim, former German Minister Plenipotentiary'.[8]

His house in Cairo was often full of Egyptian and Muslim leaders, politicians and anti-British nationalists. His new friends and activities made the British secret service name him 'The Kaiser's spy'. He also entertained celebrities including Crown Prince Wilhelm of Germany and American millionaires John Jacob Astor and Mrs Cornelius Vanderbilt.[9]

By the late 1890s, his dispatches to the German government stressed the growing influence of pan-Islamism, a movement intended to unite all Muslims under one banner to defend Islam against the predations of the West. One dispatch, in particular, drew the attention of the Kaiser. Entitled 'Die Panislaische Bewegung', the report said that anti-European Sufi brotherhoods were at work in North Africa and Arabia, and messianic movements were inflaming many tribes with 'a fanaticism bordering on madness'.[10]

If Muslims could be prepared and motivated to start a holy war, suggested Oppenheim, jihad would attract volunteers and money from all over the Muslim world, but especially from Britain, France and Russia. Oppenheim compared a possible future jihad to the Turkish sultan's fierce war against Russia in 1877, which had drawn support from Muslims everywhere, including India. Entirely convinced, the Kaiser promptly gave a speech in which he declared himself the eternal friend of the three hundred million Muslims around the world.[11] This drew the attention of the British government, who began to monitor Oppenheim's activities thereafter.

In 1910, Oppenheim was dismissed from his unofficial position with the German government for his off-duty activities. Unperturbed, he returned to Aleppo in 1911 with money from his indulgent father to excavate the statues he had left behind eleven years earlier. With a team of five archaeologists and five hundred residents, Oppenheim began a massive digging campaign. Substantial equipment was imported, including a small steam train. The costs totalled a whopping 750,000 marks. On their arrival, the archaeologists discovered that, since 1899, locals had uncovered some of the idols and heavily damaged them—in part out of superstition, in part to gain valuable building material. Nevertheless, Oppenheim unearthed the ruins of the town of Guzana, dating from 2000 BCE. Huge statues, reliefs and tombs were discovered, belonging to a palace of King Kapara. Neolithic pottery from around 6000 BCE was also discovered, which was the oldest painted pottery that had ever been unearthed. The site became known as Tell Halaf and the discovery made Oppenheim famous. Agatha Christie, then travelling in the region with her archaeologist husband Max Mallowan, also visited the spot. Oppenheim would describe his most striking find to her—a female statue with curly locks and a refined nose—as 'my Venus'.[12]

The Kaiser's Spy

Oppenheim would go down in history as the discoverer of Tell Halaf, much to his deep satisfaction. But he would be equally well-known as a German agent skilled in fomenting unrest against the British. Only three years after his archaeological discovery, the Kaiser's spy would become the chief organiser of a proposed Muslim jihad against Britain, France and Russia.

And he would be aided in this unlikely jihad by Chatto and other Indian agitators.

It was in 1914 that the worlds of Chatto, the Indian revolutionary, and Oppenheim, the fervent German nationalist, collided. By then, like many Indian agitators, Chatto had been forced to flee to Berlin. At the time, Berlin was an important centre for anti-British activity, with Germany actively providing anti-colonial forces across the world with financial, military and foreign policy aid against its First World War enemies England, France and Russia.

By 1914, the Germans had found a new ally: pan-Islamism. Indian Muslims had begun to fear Hindu domination of the nationalist movement. Influenced by the Ottoman empire in Turkey, they too wanted to be included in the fight against British imperialism.

Kaiser Wilhelm II was greatly excited by these developments and began to talk about revolutionising Muslims. In 1914, he wrote, 'Now our job is to show up the whole business ruthlessly and tear away the mask of Christian peacemaking and put the pharisiacal hypocrisy about peace in the pillory. And our consuls in Turkey and India must get a conflagration going throughout the whole Mohammedan world against this hated, unscrupulous, dishonest nation of shopkeepers–since if we are going to bleed to death, England must at least lose India.'[13]

Cometh the hour, cometh the man. Luckily for the Kaiser, Oppenheim, with his deep knowledge of the Middle East, was on the scene. On 18 August 1914, Oppenheim wrote to the German Foreign Office: 'Britain knows that if she is pushed out of India, she may never get India back again. If there were deeper unrest in India, Britain would be forced to send a major portion of her fleet to Indian waters.'[14] Oppenheim now began to make efforts to increase that unrest.

Meanwhile, another key player arrived on the scene, the peripatetic Har Dayal, who was evading arrest by US police. As we read earlier, after working with Chatto in London, Har Dayal had moved to the US, where he had become one of the founders of the Ghadar nationalist movement (of which more later). He'd then had to flee to Germany for refuge.

In Germany, Chatto had got himself enrolled as a student at the University of Halle, his cover for revolutionary activity. He and others travelled around Germany and Switzerland to gather sympathetic Indians. Eventually they would end up with the nucleus of an organisation, comprising Indians from across the country, that included Har Dayal, Chempakaraman Pillai, Mansur Ahmed, Abder Rahman, J.C. Dasgupta, A. Siddiqui and M.R. Prabhakaran.

Oppenheim, aided by other German officials, would act as a sort of liaison between the Indians and the German Foreign Office. He was expected to coordinate the activities of the Indians in Berlin, which included propaganda work, sending news from Europe for circulation in India, sending weapons and explosives to India and collecting information from India to be used by what he called 'The Information Service of the Orient'.[15]

Together, the Indians and Germans formed the Indian Independence Committee, also called the Berlin India Committee.

Their first goal was ambitious: to organise a mission to Afghanistan and seek the then Emir's permission to use Afghan territory to launch an attack on India with a battalion of armed men. Their second was to launch a propaganda campaign amongst the British Indian soldiers in the Persian Gulf and the Suez Canal area and recruit other Indian nationals in the area to invade India. Their third was to ship arms and ammunition to India for an armed rebellion.[16]

Oppenheim began well, sending up to 10,000 marks to various revolutionaries in India, even as he tried to send larger sums. But just as things were beginning to fall into place, the unpredictable Har Dayal, who was spearheading these activities, deserted the movement. Har Dayal had been staying in Constantinople to help start an uprising with the help of Afghan soldiers who he believed hated Britain and Russia. He was hoping Germany would help Afghanistan, Persia and the Indian nationalists with arms, bombs and ammunition. Suddenly, however, without any warning Har Dayal left for Geneva.

Har Dayal, who had a very good opinion of himself and did not take kindly to being directed, had been having trouble getting along with the German officials. His views were shared by many of the Berlin Indians, who felt that they had no control in framing strategy or policy. Later, Har Dayal, fickle to the last, would write a book praising the British empire and be completely exiled from the circle of Berlin Indians.

Eventually, the Berlin India Committee would fail, due to both its reliance on unreliable men and Oppenheim's overconfidence in the Arabs, who did not embrace the idea of jihad with as much enthusiasm as he had expected. On 14 December 1917, Chatto would write sadly, 'This use of untried men has led to various misfortunes. These men have been enthusiastic in their work, but when arrested, betrayed much of what they know. Much of the misfortune is due to men picked up in a haphazard fashion for the work.'[17]

M.N. Roy, who was a distant observer of these events, did not have a high opinion of the Berlin Indians. He recounted an incident in his memoirs that summed up their ham-handed attempt to win over Afghanistan in 1915. The German foreign office planned to set up a provisional government of independent India in Kabul, which would then call upon the Indian people to revolt. German experts thought, for some bizarre and inexplicable reason, that this government should be headed by an Indian prince or someone from a royal family. Chatto, with his wide range of contacts and resourcefulness, found one Raja Mahendra Pratap of Hathras who was then touring Europe. Pratap agreed to come to Berlin if he could be received by the Kaiser himself. As it happened, the Kaiser did not turn up. Instead, Pratap was received by the crown prince and accepted this as his consolation prize. When the Indo-German mission eventually reached Kabul, they found that the Emir of Afghanistan had been replaced by his son Amanullah. He welcomed them and allowed the establishment of the provisional government of independent India with Raja Mahendra Pratap as its president and Maulana Ubaidullah, a recent arrival from India, as the prime minister.

However, Amanullah could not rid himself of British influence and pressure, and eventually he ended up expelling the German mission from Afghanistan, although he continued to tolerate the Indians. Despite this, the grandly named new provisional government could not exert any influence inside India. Its activities remained confined to the borders, and even there, only to the frontier tribes.

Roy wrote of how this failure gave the Bolsheviks a low opinion of the Berlin Indians. Later, he received a first-hand report from Lenin that showed just how badly the plan had been put together. 'It seems that, from his youth, Mahendra Pratap was obsessed with the belief that he was a prophet. While at Kabul, he had written a tract on what he called the Religion of Love. He presented a copy to Lenin with the remark that unless the latter guided the new regime in Russia according to the principles formulated therein, the Revolution would fail. Lenin promised to read the tract and see its author again to give his opinion. In the second interview, he advised the prophet of the religion of love to go to England and preach his gospel there. In addition, he remarked that the Bolsheviks did not believe in God; they would listen to the admonition of the prophet only when the latter had accomplished in his country what they had done in theirs.'[18]

Jawaharlal Nehru also had a poor opinion of the Berlin Indian Committee, writing in his autobiography that the Berlin Indians had become important because 'importance had been thrust upon them by the German Government, who were, naturally, anxious to exploit all anti-British feelings'. But as Nehru pointed out, 'This sudden importance, thrust on a small group, consisting mainly of inexperienced young men, went to the heads of some of them. They felt that they were playing a historic role, that they were involved in great and epoch-making undertakings. Many of them had exciting adventures, hair-breadth escapes. In the later stages of the war, their importance visibly lessened, and they began to be ignored.'[19]

The German journalist Harry Stuermer wrote savagely about the many charlatans who tricked Oppenheim. 'The reality is that the Young Turks are themselves exploiting Pan-Islamist sympathies and Muslim religious feeling as cynically, for their own political ends, as the Germans are. Our government's costly, unscrupulous, thoroughly unmoral efforts against European civilization in Mohammedan countries have resulted in the terrific counter-stroke of the defection of the Arabs and the foundation of a purely Arabian Caliphate under English protection. It was a miserable farce, or rather a tragicomedy.'[20]

Stuermer tellingly exposed the shady adventurers who duped Oppenheim despite the latter's long years of experience. 'Many of the individuals, who claiming to be devout Muslims, offered their services and received funding, were simply crooks who milked the German government–and Oppenheim himself, since he was helping to finance the program with his own money–for all they were worth!'[21]

In the end, Oppenheim himself, looking back on the jihad plan and his propaganda efforts, admitted that they had been a washout. '*Ein schlag ins wasser.*'[22] It was a huge waste of money and resources, and a complete debacle for all involved.

But Chatto continued to live in Berlin, a safe refuge for agitators and spies. And over the next few decades, several of Chatto's family members visited him.

His younger sister Suhasini was by then already married to the Indian journalist and alleged spy A.C.N. Nambiar, who was a close friend of Chatto. In 1924, Chatto helped Suhasini and her husband move to Berlin. Nambiar was a well-connected person in his own right, being a member of the All India Congress Committee and also a correspondent for the nationalist paper *Free Press Journal*. He had helped Chatto publish *The Industrial and Trade Review* to be circulated within India, but this ended up being banned by the British. Nambiar eked out a precarious living by working for the *Bombay Chronicle*, *Amrita Bazar Patrika* and the *Hindu*. Suhasini taught at a local university as an English teacher.

Senior intelligence officer Vappala Balachandran described the exciting atmosphere of mid-twenties Berlin thus, 'Regardless of whether one was an intellectual, a writer, journalist, student or teacher, everyone seemed connected to a dense web of politics and intrigue. Who indeed was a spy and for whom, given the rapidly shifting political climate, seems more a question in hindsight.'[23] But by the time Nambiar arrived in Berlin, the Berlin Indians had become scattered. Only Chatto, Chempakaraman Pillai and

Tarachand Roy remained. Roy too visited from Moscow, but as mentioned earlier, he had deep differences with the Berlin Indians and they would never fully reconcile.

Still, there were enough Indians in Berlin to make Nambiar feel at home. Many of them went on to reach high positions in India—a future President of India and the future founder of Cipla. One of Berlin's prominent Indians then was Shahid Suhrawardy, a fascinating man who was a witness to important events in world history. Nambiar remembered how Chatto's house in Berlin had acted as a refuge for the Indians there, most of whom lived precariously and near poverty. They would gather at Chatto's house to share their scarce resources and cook together. 'Once Suhrawardy told me in his customary half joking and half serious way: I will sell my religion, philosophy and art for Indian food. He mentioned this in the flat of Chattopadhyaya in Berlin, when Indian food was being cooked for lunch by Abdul Hameed, then a student in Berlin, and who some years later founded the chemical concern of Cipla in Bombay. The company assembled in Chatto's flat also included Zakir [Husain], the future president of India. Shahid came with a small packet of powerful curry powder in his pocket. After this performance, executed with skill, he came to me and said "Nanu, succeeded. It is done. No one will eat much of those dishes. They will find them hot. My portion is secure for two or three meals."'[24]

While attempting to correct the generally orientalist view of India, Nambiar had a memorable tussle with John Hagenbeck, a writer and businessman. Hagenbeck was a half-brother of the notorious Carl Hagenbeck, the father of the modern zoo and also one of the early pioneers of 'human zoos' that brought Inuit and Nubian peoples to Europe to exhibit them as 'savages'. John Hagenbeck followed in Carl's footsteps and in 1926, brought some Indian tribals to Berlin and exhibited them along with birds and animals.

Nambiar wanted him stopped. The Berlin Indian Committee wrote a letter to the Chancellor of Germany: 'We beg to point out that only the people of India and Africa, who have been reduced to political and economic slavery by the European imperialist powers, are brought to Europe for such so called cultural shows.' Nambiar himself wrote scathingly, 'The only effective way to reply to such acts would seem to be some enterprising Indian Hagenbeck coming to Europe and taking over similar specimens from the country and quartering them in Indian zoos.'[25]

The Berlin Indians tried their best, despite their crumbling numbers, to speak out on behalf of India and against imperialism. But their best was never quite good enough.

7

California Dreaming

When she (Evelyn Trent) met the refugee stranger from a distant land–tall with long slim expressive hands and black-white eyes that flashed frequent wrath out of a dark face–who had been for years in the centre of a revolutionary movement, she found in him the embodiment of all her vague radical aspirations, and decided to link her life with his in open defiance of her father and his clan.

Sibnarayan Ray writing about the meeting between
M.N. Roy and his first wife

IT WAS 1916 AND THE GOOD SHIP *NIPPON MARU* WAS ON A TWO-WEEK voyage from Yokohama to San Francisco. On board was a somewhat dubious character. He claimed to be a priest from Pondicherry and called himself Charles Allen Martin, but other passengers had already found holes in his story. One Tamil Christian girl wanted to know why Martin did not speak Tamil. A Unitarian man of the cloth found that Martin would fumble every time he explained why he wore a cross. The suspicious priest was the intrepid Naren Bhattacharya in disguise. He described the journey as 'skating on thin ice', which was a typical understatement by him.

The ship was crammed full of missionaries from China, Japan and India. Wrote Naren dryly, 'One could imagine how very difficult it was for a heathen to simulate the learned Christian theologian or a meek novice aspiring for the sacred frock.' And yet, carrying 'a Morocco bound copy of the Holy Bible beautifully printed on rice paper', Naren gamely weathered cross examination from the curious passengers.[1]

To his credit, young Naren put on a good act. He did not know the differences between various denominations of Christianity, so he stuck to a basic reply when asked why he wore a cross: Christ had died on the cross. In one instance, the Unitarian priest from America began to cross-examine him. Did he, the American asked, really believe that Christ had lived and died on the cross? Naren managed to wriggle out of the situation by saying he wore the cross because it was an emblem of sacrifice and idealism.

'The linguistic diversity of the cultural unity of Mother India helped me explain why,' said Naren of his meeting with the Tamilian girl who wanted to know why he didn't speak Tamil if he came from Pondicherry. He resourcefully passed himself off as a native of Chandernagore, a Bengali territory of the French, and one who had lived in Pondicherry only a few years.

Naren may have fooled some of his fellow passengers, but he did not fool the American press. The day after he landed, *The Daily News* of San Francisco reported, 'When the *Nippon Maru* touched port today from Hong Kong, it carried a man of mystery. He is Chas. A. Martin, who despite his name is a Hindu and a high caste brahmin. Martin declared that he boarded the boat at a French-Indian port and that he was en route to Paris to study. Passengers however declared that he did not board the ship at such a point, and believed him to be either a revolutionary leader or an emissary of the British government.'[2]

Thanks to *The Daily News*, immediately after landing in San Francisco, Naren was forced to flee again. He went to Palo Alto, where he sought refuge with Dhan Gopal Mukerji, once an anarchist but now a respectable professor at Stanford University. It was at Dhan Gopal's suggestion that Naren gave up his name to evade arrest. From then on, he adopted the name Manabendranath Roy, or M.N. Roy. The name was significant, says biographer Sibnarayan Ray. 'It was not a caste name, as was Bhattacharya, though many Brahmins used it. "Roy" was symbolic of a break with orthodoxy, though at that time the significance might have been submerged under considerations of expediency–the need to cover up his trail as an exile.'[3] (From here on in the book, I will refer to Naren by his new name: M.N. Roy.)

Dhan Gopal also tried to persuade Naren to give up his anarchist ways and take the path of a philosopher or a thinker. Roy was not averse to this new direction, and after lying low for two months, he went to New York, to 'celebrate his rebirth spiritually, as well as politically'. However, he still had hopes of an alliance with Germany and of making it there in the future. Roy explained his new avatar thus. 'I had come to America as an emissary of revolutionary nationalism actually in alliance with Germany in the fight against British imperialism. Walking in the footsteps of the future Netaji, nearly a quarter of a century ahead of time, I was on the way to Germany.'[4]

In New York, Roy found a teeming nest of Indian revolutionaries. America's interest in India and its civilisation had begun in 1893, when a self-assured Swami Vivekananda had arrived to address the Parliament of the World's Religions in Chicago. Vivekananda had emphasised religion as a tool for political progress and had established a branch of the Vedanta Society in New York in 1895. Vivekananda's brother, Bhupendranath Datta, editor of *Jugantar*, had arrived in America in 1908 to escape arrest in India for sedition. Many Indian revolutionaries in America had links with Irish insurgents, who were also fighting for their independence and were always ready to take up arms against the British. New York in fact was a febrile mass of discontented agitators–Indians,

Irish, Germans and even American socialists–who found common ground in the city.

The mercurial Har Dayal had arrived on the scene in 1911, using his considerable academic and persuasive gifts to befriend professors of Eastern philosophy at the University of Berkeley, California. In June 1913, he gave a well-attended lecture at Astoria in Oregon, decrying the British empire's waste of money. 'The Delhi durbar for King George "whatever number that fellow is" cost 5 million dollars, while the people went hungry,'[5] he pointed out.

By 1913, Har Dayal had founded the Ghadar movement, which had been started by disgruntled Punjabis who had immigrated to the US West Coast and Canada, including Sohan Singh Bhakna, Bhagwan Singh Thind, Kartar Singh Sarabha and many others. Between 1903 and 1913, nearly ten thousand Indians had entered North America, mostly farmers from the Punjab desperate for work. The US and Canadian government had restricted the rights of immigrants with a series of discriminatory laws. New immigrants faced widespread racial prejudice and suspicion from the locals, which had led to the emergence of the Ghadar movement.

The Ghadar movement had a chequered and bumpy history. By 1913, educated men like Har Dayal and Taraknath Das had taken over the movement and begun to organise themselves. The party was officially founded on 15 July 1913. Many members were students at UC Berkeley, including Har Dayal, Taraknath Das, V.G. Pingle, Kartar Singh Sarabha and Mullah Barkatullah.

From the very beginning, Ghadar was a militant, not moderate, party. The party had a weekly paper with the caption '*Angrezi Raj Ka Dushman* (Enemy of British Rule)'. Subsequent events made them even more militant. In 1914, Gurdit Singh, a Sikh businessman, chartered a ship called the *Komagata Maru* at Hong Kong to help poor farming Sikhs and other Indians migrate to Canada. The ship set off from Hong Kong on 4 April 1914, carrying 376 Indian passengers—340 Sikhs, 24 Muslims and 12 Hindus. Over a month later, on 22 May, the *Komagata Maru* arrived on the coast of British Columbia. There the passengers found a hostile crowd. They were denied permission to land or even access their funds. The *Komagata Maru* was sent back to India on 26 September 1914. British authorities, believing that the passengers were revolutionaries, shot at the ship without warning. Twenty-two passengers died and two hundred imprisoned. Gurdit Singh was forced to go into hiding. This incident shocked both Indians and Canadians, and further inflamed passions. (In 2016, Canadian Prime Minister Justin Trudeau would formally apologise for the *Komagata Maru* incident in the House of Commons after years of lobbying from Indian immigrants in Canada.)

Another incident that enraged the Ghadar party was the brazen discrimination that Bhagwan Singh Thind faced while attempting to get a US citizenship. Between 1918 and 1923, he fought a series of cases to gain US citizenship, which eventually ended with the US Supreme Court denying citizenship to all Indians, on the ground that they could not be classed as 'white'. Only white people, the court ruled, could be US citizens. (Thind would eventually get citizenship, twenty years later, on the basis of being a US army veteran.)

When the First World War broke out, Ghadar members, like other radicals, argued for complete independence for India and refused to support Britain in the war effort. Meanwhile, Gandhi, Motilal Nehru, Annie Besant and other moderate Congress leaders decided to support Britain in the war, in the hope that their cooperation would eventually lead to home rule status for India. As it turned out, they were completely wrong. India got no concessions for its support of Britain in the war.

But by 1915, there was constant infighting amongst Indian revolutionaries in New York, something that alarmed Roy. The fight for German patronage had increased the divide between various figures. Har Dayal, leader of the Ghadar movement, had been put aside. A man called Chandra Kant Chakravarty, the nominee of the German government in New York, had been put in charge of secret Indian operations in America. The unpopular Chakravarty was corrupt and slippery, described by Roy in his usual sarcastic style as 'the oily leader of the oily revolution'. He conned the Germans out of large sums of money and lived in luxury in a house in New York, doing nothing to help the revolutionary movement.[6]

As per Roy, while the revolutionaries in New York, including Lala Lajpat Rai and members of the Ghadar movement, had been successful in carrying out a propaganda campaign against British rule, they had 'not been very discriminating in seeking support and alliance'. Seeking help from Germany had backfired. In the feverish years of the First World War, Indian revolutionaries were thought to be German sympathisers. From the perspective of the colonisers, if someone was not for the British, they were German allies. The result, explained Roy, was that 'anti-German hysteria reached the fever heat; in that hectic atmosphere, the anti-British propaganda of the Indian nationalists was naturally condemned as pro-Germanism. Indian nationalists in America were suspected as German agents, arrested en masse and tried as such immediately after the USA joined the war.'[7]

In the autumn of 1916, Roy met the grand old man of the Punjab, Lala Lajpat Rai, who had arrived in the US on a lecture tour. With his magnificent oratory he had won much sympathy for India's independence, but he could not return to India because he was wanted by the British there. Roy and Lajpat Rai became friends. A homesick Rai would ask Roy to cook Indian food for him. 'One day he asked if I could prepare rasgollas. Proud of Bengali culture influencing Punjabi taste, I set about the task. Chhana of course was not available in the land of civilised barbarism. It had to be made at home by applying some acid to boiled milk. To make the long story short, I was myself surprised when the experiment succeeded and the old man behaved like a child.'[8]

The real basis for their friendship, however, was their common disappointment and frustration with the efforts for Indian independence. 'He [Lajpat Rai] longed to return home and address one mass meeting before his death, I to go to Germany in quest of help for raising an army to liberate India,' wrote Roy.[9] They consoled each other as best they could.

But while waiting in New York for his fortunes to change, Roy met someone who would deeply affect his life, even mould it. And he, too, would completely shape her life, though not for the better. This was a radical American woman called Evelyn Trent, who fell in love at first sight with Roy, as she would tell Roy's biographer Sibnarayan Ray forty years later.

Trent was a young graduate student at Stanford University, and she harboured a deep loathing for capitalism as well as an interest in socialism. She was the youngest of eight, and had been alienated from her small-town family because of their conservative, fussy outlook. On the other hand, the exotic, passionate, articulate Roy was like no one she had ever met. Indeed, by then, Roy was being described as a man 'steeped in crime' and 'the most dangerous Indian still at large on the American subcontinent'.[10] How could Evelyn resist this dashing exile? She didn't even try.

Writes Sibnarayan Ray of their first meeting, 'When she met the refugee stranger from a distant land—tall with long slim expressive hands and black-white eyes that flashed frequent wrath out of a dark face—who had been for years in the centre of a revolutionary movement, she found in him the embodiment of all her vague radical aspirations, and decided to link her life with his in open defiance of her father and his clan.'[11] Trent would tell Sibnarayan Ray that Roy, who at that time was still called Charles Martin, struck her at first sight as 'a revolutionary John the Baptist coming out of the wilderness bringing some fiery message'.[12]

Evelyn's father, a conventional and conservative engineer, tried to get the couple arrested. But they quickly got married to escape the law. They had no money, no house, and no way of acquiring either. It was the kindly and avuncular Lala Lajpat Rai, ever the patron saint of young anarchists, who came to their rescue. He opened his house to them and hired them for some secretarial and research work to help them make ends meet. Rai wrote of their meeting, 'The Hindu boys in New York including Chakraborty [Chandra Kant Chakravarty] were disposed to consider M.N. Roy as a traitor to the cause in so far as he had fallen in love with the girl and consequently impaired his usefulness to the country. Roy was in dire need and I gave him in all 350 dollars, out of which 50 were earned by Mrs Roy in doing some work for me.'[13]

In his own memoirs, Roy does not refer to Evelyn even once, an omission that biographers have called 'inexplicable'.[14] Perhaps it was because he did not want to hurt the feelings of his second wife, Ellen Gottschalk. Perhaps it was just Roy's intensely private nature. One of his biographers has written, 'If he was possessive of any one thing, it was his sentiments. He did his best to keep them away from public gaze. He nourished them within himself, and ultimately carried his secrets with him to his samadhi at 13 Mohini Road.'[15] Or perhaps his relationship with Evelyn Trent had not been as equal as she had believed it was and he thought far less about her than she did of him. Evelyn was a good writer and an activist in her own right, but her own achievements would be completely erased and overshadowed by the flamboyant Roy.

Roy attended Lajpat Rai's meetings and made many new friends as he tried to find his ideological moorings. He met socialists, anarchists, syndicalists and pacifists. Slowly, he began to see the holes in Lajpat Rai's ideology. After one meeting he remarked, 'The audience was small; but the greater part of oratory is the love to hear one's own voice. Lajpat Rai was an orator; I was not, having been a conspirator all my political life until then.'[16]

One day, Roy had an epiphany. At a meeting where Rai carried on his usual anti-British tirade, blaming the British for the poverty of the Indian masses, someone in the back of the hall got up to ask a question. 'What difference would it make to the Indian masses if they were exploited by native capitalists instead of foreign imperialists?' Hearing this, Lalaji flew into a towering rage and retorted, 'It does make a great difference whether one is kicked by his brother or by a foreign robber.'

Roy was astonished by this incident and the scales suddenly fell from his eyes. All at once, nothing made sense. 'In the beginning, I shared Lalaji's indignation at the cheekiness of the hoboes (a derogatory designation for the extreme left wingers in the American labour movement) but I also felt uncomfortable; there was something wrong in our case. Suddenly, a light flashed through my mind; it was a new light.'[17] He realised that independence for India might only mean a change of master for the working class, who would continue to be exploited, this time by rich Indian businessmen instead of the British.

To make sense of his mental confusion, Roy began to look at other philosophies. He visited the New York public library daily and read the works of Karl Marx, to which he had never been exposed before. This was the beginning of his long overdue education. The school dropout had much to learn and finally he had access to libraries. He began to learn about socialism and realised that the liberation of India from the British would not solve the problems of the common peasant. Instead, what India needed was a whole different order.

This change in Roy did not happen overnight. His close friend and protégé, the socialist and trade union leader V.B. Karnik, described Roy's evolution thus, 'The revolution that he visualised after his conversion to socialism was basically different from the revolution that he worked for as a militant nationalist. One visualised a new social order, while the other was restricted only to the overthrow of the British rule. One was to be the result of well-planned activities of large masses, while the other was to be brought about by a small band of brave revolutionaries. One was based on the operation of economic forces, while the other did not insist on any change in the mental and social outlook of the revolutionaries.'[18]

But before Roy could further develop his new ideology, he was arrested in 1917 while attending a meeting addressed by Lala Lajpat Rai at the Columbia University campus. The arrest was a result of his alleged involvement with the Ghadar revolutionaries in what came to be called the Hindu-German Conspiracy trial. Since Ghadar activities along with that of their German allies had begun to alarm American authorities, a mass arrest of seventeen Ghadar members, including Taraknath Das, Ram Chandra, Bhagwan Singh, Gopal Singh and Chandra Kant Chakravarty, plus nine German citizens and several Americans also took place. Their sensational trial began on 20 November 1917, with plenty of press coverage. The defendants were variously described as 'Hindoos' who gave 'dark glances' and were 'turbaned'.

The British government had been arguing for some time that by allowing Indians to conspire with the Germans, the US was shedding the neutrality it had promised to follow in the war. This had led to the arrests of the defendants. Roy too was arrested and charged with 'violating American neutrality laws by participating in a nationwide conspiracy, financed by the Kaiser and promulgated through the German Foreign Office, to foment rebellion in India'.[19]

The arrest was not like the polite arrests of the Japanese, wrote Roy later, or the inefficiency of the Chinese. This was the real thing, tough, efficient, brusque. 'Half a dozen hefty fellows pounced on me out of the darkness, a couple of pistols were actually pointed at me. Presumably they apprehended that the Hindu revolutionary was a walking arsenal, and did not want to take any chance. Taken by surprise, I asked what was the matter, the reply was a rather violent prod, with the exclamation "Pronto".'[20]

Roy was dragged into a car and delivered to the District Attorney of New York. Back then, US District Attorneys would try to wear out suspects by incessant questioning, eventually luring them into making contradictory statements. Undertrials were held for months in a dank, hellish prison called 'The Tomb'.

Roy described the interrogation as 'interesting, not quite excruciating. I was still young, in the early twenties, and with nerves steeled by years of terrorist activities'. The process began jovially, with the district attorney offering him a cigar. Roy refused, and the attorney hissed at him, 'How did you enter this country?'[21] But Roy had encountered the third degree before and apparently the treatment 'did not intimidate one accustomed to similar encounters with the Tegarts of the Imperial Indian police. My answer "Across the sea" infuriated the modern inquisitor.' Roy could not resist adding cheekily, as he always had to have the last word, 'I thought America was the land of liberty.'[22]

Roy was then marched downstairs to the bowels of the Tomb, where he was shown a door, behind which crouched a small human figure; one could not tell whether he was dead or alive. The guards jeered. 'Look here, boy, [this] lily-livered fellow has vomited the whole yarn.'[23] It was Chakravarty.

Roy was taken back up and indicted for violating immigration laws. He was released on personal bail, but before he could be brought to trial, he escaped to Mexico with Evelyn.

On the other hand, the trial of his fellow detainees lasted a hundred and fifty-five days. It had a scandalous ending when

Ram Chandra, a Ghadar Party leader, was shot dead in court by a disgruntled associate, Ram Singh, who was in turn shot dead on the spot by a police officer. *The New York Times* described the shocking incident: 'Ram Chandra arose and started across the room. Ram Singh also arose. He raised his revolver and began firing. Ram Chandra staggered forward and fell dead before the witness chair, with a bullet in his heart and two others in his body! While Singh still pressed the trigger of his automatic pistol, he, too, was shot and killed by United States Marshal James H. Holohan, who fired across the room over the heads of attorneys.'[24] Eventually, twenty-nine people were convicted, including fourteen Indian nationalists.

It had been clear to Roy that he could expect no help from either the Germans in the US or the Indian revolutionaries, so he had decided to flee. The Hindu-German conspiracy trial had shown him that he could also not expect any mercy. Mexico, a land of constant revolution, seemed more promising. Roy did not know anyone in Mexico, but he had to get out of the United States and the choice was between Canada and Mexico, since crossing the Atlantic would have been difficult. Canada was under British rule, so Mexico was the easy choice.

Just before escaping the US, Roy wrote an essay in English titled 'An Open Letter to Woodrow Wilson, President of the United States'. (A year later in Mexico, he had it translated into Spanish and published it as '*La Voz De la India*', The Voice of India.) The letter opened by appealing to Wilson to not be misled by British propaganda that the Indian nationalist movement was the product of a German plot. Instead, the letter argued, India had possessed an advanced civilisation long before the coming of the British, and England's industrial supremacy originated from its plunder of India's wealth. It reminded the president that, in fighting for independence, India was only repeating the history of the American revolution, and in seeking German help, the Indian revolutionaries were doing nothing very different from what the rebellious American colonies had done in seeking help from France. At this stage, Roy made no mention of socialism or Marxism, and his thoughts followed the trend set by previous nationalists.

While trying to flee without detection, Roy and Evelyn resorted to a scramble familiar to Roy: going into various restaurants to shake off the police and moving about in crowds. Eventually, Roy was 'over the Rio Grande, laughing heartily for having called the American bluff'.[25] He would not return to the land of the free in his lifetime.

8

A Dagger, a Revolver and a Bottle of Chloroform

*'He is the most dangerous conspirator in or out of India.
You know that there's a gang of these Indians in Berlin; well, he's the brains of it. I've been trying to catch him for a year. But by now at last I've got a chance and by God, I am going to take it.'
'And what will you do then?'
R chuckled grimly. 'Shoot him and shoot him damn quick.'*[1]

Somerset Maugham describing Chandra Lal, a fictional spy inspired by Chatto

BY 1915, ON THE OTHER SIDE OF THE WORLD FROM ROY, CHATTO HAD become such a thorn in the side of the British secret service that they had decided to send a special envoy to kill him by any means possible. Donald Gullick, a British secret service agent, lured Chatto to Switzerland. According to Chatto, Gullick arrived in Switzerland with a dagger, a revolver, a bottle of chloroform, £5,000 and instructions to dispatch Chatto.

The entire unbelievable—even comic—incident was later described with a multitude of exclamation points by the excitable Harindranath Chattopadhyay, who had met Chatto in 1927 and been given this version of events. Apparently, Chatto had got a telephone call from an unknown person who had wanted to discuss providing a shipload of guns and ammunition to India. A credulous

Chatto had not suspected a trap. Instead, wrote Harindranath, he had 'jumped with joy at the prospect which held out for him such high hope for his poor enslaved country smarting under the Imperialist yoke for over a century and a half! Whenever anybody started on the subject of guns for India, Viren was all enthusiasm and had the sorry knack of immediately conjuring up the vision of a final struggle against the insolent white man who had no right to be in his country. His optimism was immense and unshakeable.'[2]

That optimism had been his undoing. Harin wrote of Chatto's exciting journey. 'Off went Viren, his heartbeats competing, in all the way, with his footsteps in speed and excitement. Guns for my country! Hurrah!'[3] When Chatto had reached the meeting place, two men had greeted him with smiles, and while extending their hands to shake, had gripped him, gagged him, chloroformed him and bundled him into a car. Luckily, the Swiss government, steadfastly neutral, had got wind of the assassination attempt and caught the car on its way to the border. The gendarmes had patted Chatto patronisingly on the back and advised him not to trust strange phone calls ever again. Chatto had then gone into hiding to escape further assassination attempts, moving around Switzerland and sleeping in humble country cottages. Eventually, he had paused his travels and resigned himself to being forever hunted.

This incredible turn of events inspired the British author Somerset Maugham, who had himself worked as an agent for the British secret service in Geneva during the First World War, to write a short story. Maugham had been writing a series of autobiographical stories about a writer named Ashenden, based on his own experiences. In the rather orientalist story titled *Guila Lazzari*, Ashenden, now an agent for the British secret service, travels to Paris where he is given the details of a dangerous agitator, Chandra Lal, a character based on Chatto. Chandra Lal is described thus by a British intelligence officer code-named R:

> 'He is the most dangerous conspirator in or out of India. He's done more harm than all the rest of them put together. You know that there's a gang of these Indians in Berlin; well, he's the brains of it. If he could be got out the way, I could afford to ignore these others. I've been trying to catch him for a year. I thought there wasn't a hope. But by now at last I've got a chance and by God, I am going to take it.'
>
> 'And what will you do then?'
>
> R chuckled grimly. 'Shoot him and shoot him damn quick.'[4]

In the story, Chandra Lal falls in love with Giulia Lazzari, an Italian dancer and Mata Hari-like figure who is under Ashenden's control. (Here again, the plot echoed Chatto's numerous love affairs.) Ashenden forces her to lure Chandra to a meeting place nearby. Eventually, Chandra commits suicide by taking poison to avoid being arrested and tried. The story ends with Giulia telling Ashenden that Chandra always carried poison on him so that 'the English would never take him alive'.

Fleeing from the British secret service, Chatto and his friend M.P.T. Acharya were forced to take shelter in yet another country. This time, it was the neutral haven of Sweden. They arrived in Stockholm on 13 May 1917, at a time of great churn for Sweden. The conservative King Gustav V was on the throne, but the winds of change had started blowing. The Social Democrats, a socialist party, were pressuring the government to introduce universal suffrage, including women's suffrage, and a more parliamentary system. A majority of Swedish men had been given the right to vote in 1908. The women, too, demanded the vote. There was opposition, so the Swedish suffragettes collected 351,454 signatures in favour of votes for women in 1913.

In October 1917, five months after Chatto and Acharya arrived, the social democrat leader Nils Eden took over as prime minister. He ushered Sweden into a long period of liberal democracy, helping introduce universal suffrage and laying the foundation for the country that exists today. Women finally got the vote in 1921.

Meanwhile, Sweden stayed resolutely neutral in the war. This meant the city of Stockholm teemed with international revolutionaries, socialists, anarchists and enemies of the British empire, all looking for one thing: safe harbour.

Chatto and Acharya were there to help arrange and attend the international socialist conference in Stockholm. But Chatto's main aim was to use Sweden as a base for propaganda against the British. Could the Indian socialists represent themselves at the conference? Apparently not, because only countries had representation, therefore India would be represented by the British government. This, of course, was anathema to Chatto and the other Indian nationalists.

The climate of the times was such that, just as Roy had found in New York, any propaganda against British colonial rule was assumed to be pro-German. Chatto found himself walking a tightrope. The socialists attending the conference simply did not believe in self-determination for India and the African nations. They were keen to give them socialism, but not necessarily independence. 'The Indian question', as the knotty question of Indian independence was called, was constantly swept under the carpet.

Chatto and Acharya met the organising Dutch-Scandinavian Committee in July 1917, arguing India's case for independence, but they were mostly ignored. The Dutch socialist Pieter Jelles Troelstra noted that 'the Indian question is important, but it is a distraction from the peace negotiations'.[5] Eventually, the grand socialist conference simply did not take place because British and French socialists did not arrive. The question of Indian independence was shelved.

But Chatto did not give up. He began to do what little he could. On 7 July 1917, an Indian propaganda office was opened in

Stockholm, which was called the European Central Committee of Indian Nationalists, also known as the Indian National Committee in Sweden. It was funded by the Germans, but its aim was quite simply to send a 'telegraphic contradiction of English lies'.[6] Chatto funded himself by teaching Hindi at a nearby school, and by doing odd jobs of translation and journalism.

Chatto had gradually drifted away from Germany because the Germans did not officially support India. Now, he began to move towards the Bolsheviks, who had captured the imagination of many colonial subjects. Lenin, in particular, had stirred many Indians to the core. Had he inspired Chatto? Chatto was a pragmatist. He believed, above all, in militant nationalism and he was ready to cleave to whoever might give India support. For the time being, that was Russia. Chatto, after all 'had no political ideology, only a political goal, which was the independence of India'.[7]

Meanwhile, Chatto and M.P.T. Acharya began to churn out propaganda. Their main aim was to publicise the question of Indian independence, which in those days was considered unimportant on the world stage. They began by collecting the opinions of British and American socialists on Indian independence. The first brochure, 'Opinions of English Socialist Leaders on British Rule in India', contained excerpts from articles and manifestos written by such prominent socialists as H.M. Hyndman, Keir Hardie and Ramsay MacDonald. Another brochure, titled 'Some American Opinions on British Rule in India', contained savage criticisms of the British Empire by Americans such as William Randolph Hearst, Andrew Carnegie and even Mark Twain.

A flood of brochures followed, with dramatic titles such as 'England's Perfidy in India: A Chronology of Broken Treaties and Wanton Confiscation'.[8] Many focused on the plunder of India by Britain, the extravagance of the Raj, the denial of civil liberties and the suffering of peasants and farmers. One pamphlet carried the face of Rabindranath Tagore, who in 1913 had won the Nobel Prize for Literature and been knighted in 1915 (Tagore would return his knighthood in 1919, after the Jallianwala Bagh massacre). In a 1917 essay titled 'The Great and the Small', Tagore praised the 'great Britons' who ruled in their homeland but sent 'little Britons' to rule in India. He blamed the 'little Britons' for handing over Indian youth to the secret police. To introduce Tagore to the Swedes, who were unfamiliar with the Indian litterateur, Chatto had 'The Great and the Small' published in several Swedish newspapers in 1918. The headline was 'Nobel Prize winner Tagore about Britain in India'.[9]

This flood of propaganda alarmed the British. They decided to fight back with their own version of events—better still, conveyed by a convincing Indian, a 'useful idiot' as it were. The Indian they picked to give Chatto a taste of his own medicine was Abdullah Yusuf Ali.

In his own way, Ali was every bit as brilliant as Chatto, but he was his polar opposite, a man in deep thrall to the British empire. At the time of the invitation, Ali was a Hindi professor at the School of Oriental and African Studies (SOAS). Ali had been born into the Bohra community of traders in Surat on 4 April 1872. He had an excellent academic record, having graduated from Wilson College at fourteen. He received a first class BA from Bombay University in 1891. That became his ticket to the UK. He was awarded a scholarship to study in England. He arrived still a teenager and studied law at Cambridge. Then he capped it all by passing the tough Indian Civil Service exams—which Chatto had failed twice—with top marks.

Yusuf Ali was a committed Anglophile who wanted nothing more than to bridge the gap between British and Indian societies. He demonstrated this by marrying a British woman, Teresa Shalders, in 1900. He was posted to the United Provinces (now called Uttar Pradesh) as part of his ICS duties and Teresa joined him there. A rapid succession of children followed, three boys and a girl. In his professional life, he had risen to the top. In his personal life, he was miserable.

In 1907, Yusuf Ali was invited to give a series of lectures at the Passmore Edwards Institute, London. There, he portrayed India as an ancient civilisation, one that had been corrupted by religion and evil practices. 'One of the most marked tendencies of Indian social life is that all forms of institutions making for order and joint action are getting disintegrated or undermined,' he said.[10] At around that time, he was described by the *Times* as a 'very talented member of the Indian Civil Service and a representative of the great Muhammadan community'.[11]

But Ali's subservience to the British was also noted. Even his own biographer acknowledged it. 'Abdullah Yusuf Ali belonged to the group of Indian Muslims from professional families who were concerned with rank and status. In pursuit of his aspiration for influence, deference, if not outright obsequiousness, became a central feature of his relationship with the British. He was particularly impressed by the apparently genteel behaviour and cordiality of those with whom he associated, and, as a result, became an incorrigible Anglophile.'[12]

Meanwhile, his marriage was crumbling. Teresa had an affair in 1908 and the couple divorced. Yusuf Ali asked for custody of his four children, all under the age of ten, eventually leaving them in England under the charge of an English governess. He wrote in 1934, 'A man's life is subject to inner storms far more devastating than those in the physical world around him. Such a storm in the bitter anguish of personal sorrow which nearly unseated my reason and made life seem meaningless.'[13]

In 1914, Ali left the ICS and returned to England, partly to look after his children but also to find a new job for himself: as a publicist for Britain and the empire. The First World War had begun and there was much debate going on about whether India should support Britain in the war. Yusuf Ali gave an incredibly servile speech in London in November 1914, in which he urged Indian soldiers to fight for their beloved 'Sovereign'. The sovereign, of course, was George V. 'India salutes and falls in, ready to die for country, Padishah flag and Empire,' assured Ali, despite no one authorising him to do so.[14]

Over the next four years, he wrote several more articles proclaiming his devotion to the Emperor, and he received a CBE for his efforts in 1917. Yusuf Ali hoped, like many, that India would be rewarded with dominion status if it supported Britain in the war. To be fair, even Gandhi believed that India supporting Britain in the war would lead to India getting independence sooner. Not so Chatto and his friends, who remained strongly resolute against the empire in general and India's support of Britain in the war in particular.

By now, Yusuf Ali had earned the reputation of being a useful soldier for the empire. When the British Foreign Office heard about Chatto's propaganda, they decided to 'arrange a counter campaign of lectures against the enemy activities now having their centre at Stockholm'.[15] Yusuf Ali was chosen to give the lectures and was paid for them.

Ali arrived in Stockholm in July 1918 and immediately began to hit back at Chatto. In an interview to the Stockholm-based *Tidningen*, he said that all Indian political organisations, except for a few anarchists, were loyal to Britain. India, he claimed, had willingly contributed £100 million to the British war campaign and Indians had voluntarily joined the army in great numbers.[16]

Ali also lost no time in giving a series of lectures in English on Indian culture and religion in Stockholm, Copenhagen, Oslo and Uppsala. They were translated into Danish and published as *Træk af Indiens Kultur* (*Features of Indian Culture*) in 1918. 'In the Foreword, Ali conceded that the lectures were not intended to be published in book form, but "valuable friends" persuaded him to do so. What

Ali did not admit was that these "valuable friends" were the British Foreign Office (FO).'[17]

Chatto did not take this shameless public relations campaign lying down. He pointed out that Madan Mohan Malaviya, a member of the Indian Legislative Council, had specified that the Indian financial contribution to the war meant an annual increase of £6 million in tax for the next thirty years for the poor Indian peasant. Three hundred thousand Indian soldiers had joined the army not out of loyalty to the empire, but because they had no choice, and were starving, he argued.[18]

Chatto also did not spare Indian political parties. He divided them into three camps: a small minority of 'cowards and job hunters' (the implication was that Ali was one of these), the moderate nationalists of the Indian National Congress and the Muslim League, and the revolutionaries. Chatto was not prepared to be called an 'anarchist'. He preferred to be called a revolutionary or a nationalist, and argued that it was because of him—and others like him—that the situation of the moderates had improved. According to Chatto, people like Gandhi and Nehru only took a moderate line because they believed that, given the war, there was no possibility of escape from the British rule.[19]

The war of words escalated. Ali hit back in another Swedish newspaper, alleging that the Indian National Committee in Sweden consisted of only two anarchists, Chatto and Acharya, without any kind of popular support. The *Times* in the UK supported his argument, calling Chatto and Acharya 'bogus' and not representative of India.[20]

Chatto responded in kind in a letter to the Swedish paper *Aftontidning*. He wrote bitingly, 'The Swedish public learns from your paper that Mr Yusuf Ali is a politician and a patriot. In his own lectures and speeches, he makes it appear that he is commissioned by some body as the Indian National Congress or the All India Muslim League to speak on behalf of India. We challenge him to show how he is justified in calling himself a politician, and whether any political organisation in India commissioned him to come to Sweden and make the false statement to the Swedish people that India is happy, flourishing and satisfied under England's sceptre, and to mention a single organisation or a single leading politician in India who maintains anything of the sort. And we protest most emphatically against the word "patriot" being used for a man who during his whole life has only furthered the interests of India's Foreign Government.'[21]

After this salvo from Chatto, Ali returned to London and the furious war of words came to an end. Ali would get no recognition for his service to the Foreign Office as the war ended. Towards the end of his life, he would be found sitting bewildered on the steps of a house in Westminster, which was not his own. He died in 1953, estranged from his children. His body was unclaimed and no funeral was arranged by his family. Eventually, he was buried in the Islamic section of Brookwood cemetery, Surrey. Small thanks for a man who worked so hard for his adopted country.

By 1920, as the fallout of the Russian Revolution started to be felt, many colonised people began to look to Vladimir Ilyich Lenin and the Bolsheviks for salvation, fed up of pointlessly appealing to Western socialists. Chatto was no exception. British intelligence reported that he was receiving Bolshevik money, though found himself 'often short of funds'.[22]

British intelligence also reported that Har Dayal, despite being accused by many of his disgruntled peers of spying for the British, was actually a secret Bolshevik in close touch with Russian Bolsheviks in Stockholm. 'Being a Delhi man he is able to exercise power and influence equally between Hindu and Mohammedan students—he would use Russia, or Germany, or England to gain his object.'[23]

All roads, it seemed, led to Moscow in 1920, and to the brave new world offered by Lenin.

9

Al Companero Indio: The Indian Comrade in Mexico

Mexico was the land of my rebirth. It is true that before coming there I had begun to feel dissatisfied with the ideas and ideals of my earlier life. But it was during my stay in Mexico that the new vision became clear.

M.N. Roy

A YOUNG MAN STOOD GAZING WITH FASCINATION AT THE DISTANT snow-covered peak of Ixtaccíhuatl (popularly called the Sleeping Woman) near Mexico City. He described it excitedly: 'The peak looks like a woman lying on her back. It being perpetually snow covered, she is white, and to lie there still, she must be sleeping.'[1] It was 1917, the man was M.N. Roy, and his newly adopted home would change him forever.

The striking image of the peak would stay with him in the years to come and even many decades later, when tired and weary, he would still talk about his great admiration for Mexico. 'I was fascinated by the "Sleeping Woman", and still feel a strong attraction for the simplicity, wildness, barbarism, cruelty and kindness of Mexico and her people. Both may have changed during the last thirty years; but I feel that they can never change beyond recognition. Therefore, if I ever shall have to live elsewhere, I shall go to Mexico. Everything may have changed; but the "Sleeping Woman" is still there.'

Roy arrived a friendless, directionless and gauche young man in 1917, with only Evelyn accompanying him. Two and a half years later, he would leave as a man with a plan.

For the first time in a long time, he stayed at one place and had his own home, instead of constantly having to dodge the police. He had a loving companion in Evelyn who smoothed his way in Mexico. He had left India with a distrust and suspicion of Western ideas and a belief in nationalism. But in Mexico, as his biographer Sibnarayan Ray put it, 'he learnt to appreciate all the good things in life, not only good food and wine, but also music, the fine arts and literature, the beauty of the landscape, and the delights of refined recreational activities'.[2]

The influence of other Indian revolutionaries on M.N. Roy waned, and he made friends mostly with American bohemians and radicals–writers, artists, cartoonists, socialists, many of whom had moved to Mexico to avoid being drafted for the war. The gregarious Evelyn helped him enter this society. He was free of the heavy burden of Indian expectations and of the promises he had made as a young man.

He gave up his vegetarian diet, even ordering a beef steak when he found he could hardly get any authentic Mexican food that did not come in a tin. Persuaded by the Americans, he also began drinking. As one of his biographers wrote, 'Only one Indian had mixed with western writers and artists before Roy. That was Rabindranath Tagore, but not on his first visit to Europe.'[3] Besides, Tagore had mingled only with artists. Roy was everyone's friend and he was in his element.

He wrote, 'Mexico was the land of my rebirth. It is true that before coming there I had begun to feel dissatisfied with the ideas and ideals of my earlier life. But it was during my stay in Mexico that the new vision became clear, and the dissatisfaction with a sterile past was replaced by a conviction to guide me in a more promising future.' This was the birth of a true cosmopolitan. From then on, Roy would subscribe to no national boundaries and would feel free to borrow ideas from across the world.

Mexico, like all Latin American countries, had thrown off the yoke of Spanish rule, achieving independence in 1821. But it continued to be a nation in turmoil. Power was in the hands of the Catholic church, feudal landlords and military dictators. But the biggest problem of all was its powerful neighbour, the United States, which wanted to bring Mexico under its rule. Mexico had already been forced to cede Texas to the US in 1845 and to endure a long war.

When Roy arrived in Mexico, the country was emerging from a long period of dictatorship under the regime of autocratic leader Porfirio Diaz who had ruled the country for thirty-five years. Under Diaz, Mexico, as Roy described it, was a 'happy hunting ground'[4] for mostly the rich elite. Diaz had given free rein to big commercial planters while ignoring the concerns of the poor. The gap between Mexico's haves and have-nots was huge.

There were no political parties in Mexico, just various groups and factions led by mostly military men, all vying for power. The poverty of the peasants and the constant unemployment of the labourers made 'soldiering an attractive profession', as Roy noticed. 'Consequently, any movement against the established regime took the form of a military rebellion.'[5] The middle classes had distanced themselves from politics and as Roy put it, much like the Indian people, 'the disgust and apathy of the bulk of the educated middle-class precluded the rise of any political party'.[6] There could be no better place for a young man interested in socialism to make his mark.

Diaz's rule had been halted by the Mexican Revolution in 1910, seven years before the Russian Revolution. It was spearheaded by the political reformer Francisco Madero, who called upon the Mexican people to rise against Diaz's tyranny. His army was made up of poor peasants and workers as well as middle-class liberals and intellectuals. The peasants in Madero's army hoped that he would reward their sacrifices by giving them back their lost lands, guaranteeing workers a fair wage and introducing social reforms. But their hope would be misplaced.

Other rebels joined the battle against Diaz. Local guerrilla leaders Pancho Villa and Emiliano Zapata stormed haciendas, clashed with federal troops and mustered their own rag-tag armies of peasants, cowboys and mine workers. Pancho Villa, a fiery bandit turned Robin Hood of sorts seized haciendas commanded by big sugar farmers and turned them over to the peasants and workers. A skilled rider and a crack shot, Villa's charisma inspired thousands to join the cause. By 25 May 1911, Porfirio Diaz submitted his resignation, fleeing to Paris. He would die four years later, one of the very few Mexican leaders to die peacefully in his bed.

But the revolution was far from over. Madero wanted political changes, not land reform. Indeed, as Diaz remarked when he left, 'Madero has unleashed a tiger. Now let's see if he can control it.'[7]

Madero excluded populist leaders like Zapata and Villa from key positions. The Mexican peasantry was deeply disappointed by Madero's reluctance to redistribute land and enact meaningful land reform. Zapata issued his own Plan of Ayala, demanding Madero's overthrow and suggesting a radical land reform programme. The next two years were divisive and violent. In February 1913, Madero was dragged from his car and shot execution-style by General Victoriano Huerta. Huerta was called El Chacal—the jackal—for his brutality and wanted to establish a dictatorship backed by big business. But he had not accounted for Zapata and Villa, who continued their rebellions and attacks against federal outposts.

By 1914, all of Mexico was under the control of various rebels. A series of unstable governments had collapsed, leaving the country in charge of General Venustiano Carranza, a wealthy and highly educated Spanish landowner. Carranza's cabinet was full of intellectuals, the educated and the elite. But Carranza had his hands full with problems and unrest. He attempted to placate the peasants by introducing a constitution in 1917 which was radical for the times. It abolished the privileges of the church, voided previous concessions to foreign governments, established state control over water and minerals, and provided for the redistribution of land to the actual farmers.

Roy arrived in the middle of Carranza's term. The country was in chaos, with many players jostling for power. By then, Roy was sceptical of armed struggle and had distanced himself from revolution. He believed only in political reform, which is why he stayed away from the Zapatistas and the Villistas and gravitated towards Carranza, who at least had the advantage of having established a constitutional regime. Indeed, despite his own 'terrorist' past, Roy did not have a great opinion of the Zapatistas and Villistas. He described Pancho Villa acidly: 'After the failure of his nearly successful bid for the Presidency, Pancho Villa degenerated into sheer banditry. Nevertheless, he maintained his hold on two northern States by pretending to play the Robin Hood. That role is bound to be very popular in a country where riches are monopolised by a small minority and the vast bulk of the people is submerged in abject poverty.'[8]

Roy's opinion of Zapata was slightly better. 'He was not a mere bandit. He had a social base. Because he was a son of the people and did not have the chance of going away far from them towards the corrupting atmosphere of governmental power, Zapata never lost the halo of medieval heroism.' But later, Roy changed his mind. He heard of Zapata's savage cruelty from a former Zapatista, the anarchist lawyer who had drafted the Carranza constitution. By then, aided by their sympathisers, Zapatistas had begun to roam around plundering Mexico City. In turn, they were hunted by Carranzistas. Roy made an unsuccessful attempt to meet Zapata, but he was discouraged by the lawyer. He, along with the lawyer, did attempt to meet certain Zapatista followers who lived nearby, but when he arrived at the spot, he saw several dead Zapatistas dangling from trees as a warning.

Left-wing politics was equally disorganised and chaotic, and Roy found it hard to enter the scene. But he had a stroke of luck immediately upon his arrival in Mexico. Roy had in his possession a letter of introduction to one General Alvarado and that letter drew the attention of President Carranza. So, he was summoned to meet the Minister of Defence, who happened to be Carranza's son-in-law. When they met, the minister assured him he was very welcome and safe in the Republic of Mexico, though apparently they had already received some advance information about him (likely from the US police).

The next day, Roy was invited to meet the editor of a prominent newspaper, *El Pueblo*. In his memoirs, Roy wrote of the meeting: '"You are a guest in my country, and we Mexicans are a hospitable people, although they say," the editor added, rather in irony than in bitterness, "that we are backward." The editor went on to say unexpectedly, "We are also Indians, you know!"'

Roy was quick to respond to this expression of sympathy. 'I took up the cue and replied "Well, Sir, we are in the same boat, my country is similarly stigmatised by the arrogant imperialism of the White race."' The two were simpatico.[9]

Roy managed to meet Ignazio Santibanez, the leader of the tiny socialist party. Then he was invited to meet the other members of the socialist party. He also met Don Manuel, the socialist president of the Chamber of Deputies. Roy suggested that a proper socialist party be founded, with representatives from other countries.

In spite of his overtures to socialism, Roy never gave up on the idea of allying with the Germans; after all India and Germany shared a common enemy: Britain. Germany still remained the centre of anti-colonial activity. Roy even chose to study German rather than Spanish even when he was in Mexico, and he would eventually achieve near native-level fluency in both written and spoken German.

Mexico was where the raw young Roy developed into a sophisticated and well-read person. He learnt to play chess from the Mexican national champion. He learnt to ride horses. He attended ballet and opera performances, and became acquainted with Western dress, though he never wore a morning coat or dinner jacket, because he believed men 'looked like monkeys' in them. Instead, he stuck to grey flannel pants and a brown jacket.

One anecdote is especially amusing. Roy received an invitation to attend a meeting of the executive committee of the Socialist Party. He later described the mysterious letter thus: 'It was written in red ink on an old typewriter, and concluded not with any of the usual conventional expression, but with the exclamation: Soludoy Revolucion Social (Greetings and Revolution). The signature of the person who so hailed me through the postal service was evidently not meant to be read, though it was extremely decorative—with several artistic flourishes trailing down to the lower edge of the sheet. My "secretary" was very much distressed by the nakedness (as he said) of my signature. He actually tried to teach me to embellish it with at least a few loops and rings, so that it looked like the signature of a distinguished person.'

Along with all these enjoyable pursuits, Roy also met with many fascinating characters who helped him crystallise his thoughts on colonialism, race and other important subjects. In Mexico, Roy lost his innocence and idealism, but gained a larger perspective of the world.

One of these fascinating characters was the American boxer Jack Johnson who became the first black heavyweight champion in the world. His crushing 1910 defeat of a white man had triggered race riots across the US. In 1912, he was arrested for dating and later marrying a white woman, Lucille Cameron, which was against the law at the time. He had to flee the US, and went on to live in exile in Europe, South America and eventually Mexico.

Roy first encountered Johnson at his favourite hangout place, the fashionable drug store Sanborn's, which was famous for its ice cream and coffee. Johnson came in with his wife and was ignored by the waitresses. He eventually left, amongst titters and smirking from some of the staff. This surprised Roy because the Mexicans were well known for their tolerance and 'racial Catholicism'. But a few minutes later, just as Roy was rising to leave, determined never to return to Sanborn's, Johnson returned with the police. The manager of Sanborn's was summoned and told to personally wait on Johnson, much to the manager's dismay and humiliation. When he hesitated, wrote Roy delightedly, 'he was reminded that he was in Mexico where the black man was as good as the whitest of the white'. All this deeply impressed Roy, but what happened next impressed him even more. Johnson got up, shook the hand of 'the insolent white man' and said, 'Pardon me for all the trouble'. As he left, a cheering crowd greeted him and carried him on their shoulders.

Later, Roy and a friend met Johnson and asked him to donate to the Russian Revolution, which he was happy to do. About thirty years later, in 1946, Jack Johnson would once again be refused entry at a segregated diner in North Carolina. But this time there would not be such a joyous result. Johnson would drive away in a fury, exhausted after years of this kind of treatment, and crash his car against a telegraph pole, dying at the age of sixty-eight. In 2018, he would finally get some measure of justice when President Donald Trump, at the urging of many black people, including Mike Tyson, would issue him a presidential pardon for his crime of marrying a white woman.[10]

In December 1918, the first meeting of the Socialist Party of Mexico was convened, with Roy and his friend Charlie Shipman as the chief representatives. Thus, it was 'an assimilated Jew and an Indian Brahmin' who came to represent early Mexican socialism.[11] Also in attendance were several hundred delegates from Mexico: mostly workers from oil fields, textile mills, mines, docks and railways. There were also leaders from other Central and South American countries, but these were mostly lawyers, teachers and journalists. They were inspired by Lenin's October Revolution and the Bolshevik overthrow of the Czar, which had astonished and shocked the world only a year earlier. The conference opened with great enthusiasm, but as Roy pointed out, the hall was reserved for 'bourgeois politicians' and working-class peasants were excluded. Roy was referred to as 'Al Companero Indio'.[12]

But as Roy had made sure, those gathered 'did not propose to play Hamlet without the Prince of Denmark'. Suddenly all the delegates rushed out into the street for a mass demonstration. 'Behind a huge picture of Lenin, held high in front, there was a forest of red flags and festoons. Slogans written of course in Spanish on the latter were striking: "Down with Yankee Imperialism!", "Petroleum Belongs to the Mexican People", "Long Live Revolutionary Alliance of Latin America Republics", "Long Live the Soviet Republic of Mexico",' Roy wrote. The children of the poor were brought to the mass protest.[13]

The scene was stirring: 'To the north stood the magnificent old cathedral built by the slave labour of countless pagan Mexican peons to satisfy the vanity of conquering Christianity; and to the east, the rambling ugly structure of the Palacio National, once the gilded residence of proud Spanish Viceroys, now seat of the Republican government.' The meeting was addressed by speakers that included Charlie Phillips, an American deserter from the army who would later organise revolutionary movements throughout Latin America. Then, by previous arrangement, President Carranza appeared on the balcony of the Palacio National to greet the crowd and to declare that the voice of the people being the voice of God, he would obey it. Slogans followed: 'Long Live Lenin' and 'Long Live the October Revolution'.

While inclined to socialism, Roy was by no means entirely taken in by these theatrics. Indeed, he wrote cynically, 'A new god and a new religion demanded the devotion of the revolutionary proletariat. I joined the ranks of the faithful in quest of the utopia.'[14] The crowds began to sing the *Internationale*. Everyone joined in except Roy, who was an unmusical person. Ten years later, he could still not sing the communist anthem. The conference concluded with the naming of the new party and the election of the office bearers. Roy was elected general secretary and the party was named the Partido Socialista Obrero, the Socialist Workers Party.

Soon, another fascinating character arrived in Mexico, a real-life Bolshevik from Russia called Borodin, who caused much excitement amongst the radical American community, which called him the 'First Bolshevik'. A man described later by the British artist Claire Sheridan as 'having shaggy black hair brushed back from his forehead, a Napoleonic beard, deep set eyes, and a face like a mask, speaking abrupt American English'. She added, 'Borodin mystifies me, I cannot make out, when all his questions have been answered, what he thinks.'[15] He was an inscrutable man, one who would go on to do great things and influence Roy deeply and, indeed, change the trajectory of his life.

Borodin's original name was Mikhail Markovich Gruzenberg. Born into a Jewish family, he had joined the Bolsheviks in 1903. Fearing arrest by the Romanovs for his revolutionary activities, he had fled to the US. There, he had attended university, started a family and lived in Chicago for years. When the October Revolution blazed through Russia in 1917, Borodin had returned to his home country and soon become a close confidante and aide of Lenin.

In 1919, he was sent to the US with the Czarist crown jewels. Only a year earlier, on 17 July 1918, the Bolsheviks had brutally executed the last imperial family of Russia—Czar Nicholas II, his wife and his five children. They had been shot at first and stabbed with bayonets, after which their bodies had been burnt, soaked with acid and thrown down a mineshaft. Czar Nicholas's four daughters had reportedly been wearing over a kilo of gold and diamonds under their dresses, which had deflected the bullets.[16] Their jewels were snatched to fund the revolution.

Roy wrote in his memoirs, 'The mission was to smuggle crown jewels worth a million roubles (approximately 500,000 dollars at the then prevailing rate of exchange). The precious stones were sewn into the sides of two stout leather suitcases.'[17]

Borodin travelled through Europe under various false names until he reached Amsterdam. In Vienna, he made friends with an Austrian sympathiser. The two boarded a Dutch ship for the West Indies, but suspicious American customs officers stopped the ship in Haiti. A flustered Borodin entrusted the two suitcases to the unsuspecting Austrian man, asking for them to be delivered to his wife in Chicago. Borodin was expected to secretly sell the jewels in New York.

But the jewels did not arrive. Immediately on arriving in New York, Borodin was arrested, because of which he could not make enquiries about the jewels. With the help of skilful lawyers, he was eventually released on bail, after which he fled to Mexico. Roy helped Borodin send a reliable messenger and die-hard anarchist to Haiti to enquire if the suitcases were still there. It turned out that the Austrian aristocrat was still in Haiti but had become a hermit of sorts and had left behind the two suitcases as containing useless possessions for his new way of life.

By this time, the messenger sent to recover the suitcases had put two and two together and realised that no one would go to such lengths to recover ordinary suitcases. Since the suitcases were lying unguarded, the messenger took possession of them and took the first ship to an American port.[18]

When Borodin and Roy reached Moscow a year later, a terrified Borodin was asked to account for the jewels. Roy testified to Borodin's honesty and integrity. Luckily, at around the same time, the suitcases reached Borodin's wife with the contents intact, saving him from the wrath of the revolutionaries. Roy took credit for this, perhaps somewhat arrogantly. 'My second contribution to the cause of revolution was his life. In those days, revolutionary justice was swift and cruel.' No more would be heard of the jewels and what happened to them.

Roy and Borodin became close friends. They would stay up at night reading Marx and discussing revolutionary ideas. It was Borodin who convinced Roy that political freedom for India would be pointless without social justice and liberation from feudal landlords. It was also Borodin who made Roy a true internationalist, one who believed that revolution had to be international and not just limited to India. No longer would Roy take up arms. Now he wanted to spread ideas to bring about an ideological revolution. He started looking outward to the world, overcoming the attachment to his homeland. 'The new ideal of freedom was not to be attained within national or geographical boundaries.'[19]

In 1919, less than two years after arriving in Mexico, Roy decided to leave. The situation in the country had once again deteriorated and civil war appeared likely. Roy believed, rather foolishly, that the middle class was now invested in the political future of the country and had given up its political apathy. Borodin convinced Roy to go to Moscow and meet Lenin, who had been well-briefed on Roy's potential.

Before leaving, Roy met the beleaguered Carranza. He detected a 'touch of dejection and sadness in the Spartan proud old aristocrat.

Yet, he must see it through until the bitter end, and alas, the end was indeed bitter. Whatever little I did in Mexico could not save the old man, but it did make some contribution to the crystallisation of social forces which before long freed the country from the curse of the civil war.'[20] In retrospect, Roy was being ludicrously arrogant in thinking he had changed Mexico in any way at all.

As they parted, Carranza put a hand on Roy's shoulder, and said in a voice choked with emotion, 'You are still very young. Don't gamble with fate. I wish you a long, successful life.'[21] Then he walked away.

Carranza, Zapata and Villa would all be devoured by Mexico's bloody politics. By 1923, all three would have been killed by unknown gunmen, one after the other, like every single icon of the Mexican revolution. Even Pancho Villa, Mexico's beloved bandit and icon of the poor, who was living quietly in semi-retirement and had laid down his arms, could not escape this fate. On the morning of 23 July 1923, he was peppered with bullets by a group of eight gunmen. The gunmen went scot-free. None of them were ever charged.

In the end, Mexico may have changed Roy, but he was not able to change Mexico's brutal politics. He had tried to gain control of the Mexican Socialist party and convert it into a communist organisation. But he was only able to persuade a few people to join him, leading a contemporary to describe his new party as consisting of only six members and a calico cat.[22] This tiny party, nevertheless, was the first communist party outside of Soviet Russia. In fact, Roy would attend the 1920 Communist International (Comintern) as a representative of the Mexican party.

Meanwhile, the angry young man had grown up. Roy had lost faith in bombs and assassinations and was now focused on proper ideological change. Perhaps he had seen enough violence in Mexico and was weary of guns and bombs. He summed it up thus, 'I still believed in the necessity of armed insurrection. But I had also learned to attach greater importance to an intelligent understanding of the idea of revolution. The propagation of that idea is more important than arms.'[23] With that, Roy left Mexico for Berlin, to wait for word from his mentor Borodin about when he could enter the Soviet Union.

Chaos in Berlin

Berlin, 1919

A woman wrote a letter, '*Order reigns in Berlin! You stupid henchmen! Your "order" is built on sand. Tomorrow the revolution will already "raise itself with a rattle" and announce with fanfare, to your terror: I was, I am, I will be!*'

Those were the last words she wrote. And that woman was the fearless Polish-born socialist revolutionary Rosa Luxemburg. She would be clubbed over the head and shot; her nameless body then dumped in an icy river.

The post-war Berlin that M.N. Roy went to for refuge in 1919, passing himself off as a Mexican, was a chaotic, feverish, struggling city. Germany, a once-proud country, had been humiliated by the Allies and forced to accept harsh conditions in peacetime. Roy described the streets when he arrived: 'The most striking spectacle was the large number of street beggars in frayed military uniforms, men with mutilated limbs, faces disfigured beyond recognition, many of them suffering from "shell-shock" as evidenced by the various symptoms of a shattered nervous system. They simply sat, lining the streets like a mute monument to the gruesome experience of war.'

The average German chafed at these restrictions. The Social Democratic party was in power, with Friedrich Ebert at its head. Ebert needed to keep control of the peace, so he allied himself with nationalistic armies, including the right-wing Freikorps, an army of renegades. The typical Freikorp member 'hated the revolution, hated the new German Republic, hated the Socialists who led it and the Communists trying to replace them'. Indeed, he hated civilians in general. He believed that Germany had not lost the war but had been 'stabbed in the back' by the same pack of traitors now ruling in Berlin.[24] This simmering resentment of being cheated by the Allies pervaded the city and lingered with many of its people.

Meanwhile, Rosa Luxemburg and her comrade Karl Liebknecht headed the Spartacus League (Spartakusbund), a fledgling communist party named after Spartacus, the famous leader of a slave uprising against the Roman Republic in 73 BCE. They were fervently anti-war. The Spartacus League supported the 1917 Russian Revolution but did not support the brutal methods of the Bolsheviks, their campaign of Red Terror or their centralised systems. Luxemburg was a fierce critic of Lenin's governance and his theories, and an equally fierce critic of resurgent German nationalism after the war.

In November 1918, on Liebknecht's initiative, the Spartacus Group called for disarming the police and transferring power to workers' councils. Then in January 1919, the Spartacus League (now renamed the Communist Party of Germany, KPD) began the revolution. Workers armed with guns seized control of Berlin, and Karl Liebknecht declared the Ebert government deposed.

The Freikorps retaliated savagely. They had trained soldiers, better weapons and a clear strategy. Immediately, they set to slaughtering Spartacus workers in what is now called the Spartacus Week. Along with Luxemburg, Liebknecht was battered and shot, his corpse dumped on the steps of a mortuary. More leftist rebellions were totally crushed by the Freikorps. Luxemburg would go on to become a socialist martyr.

M.N. Roy observed all this from his cautious perch as a new and shaky convert to communism. He was in the city waiting for permission to enter Russia. Only three years earlier, he had been keen to visit Berlin, the city of revolution and activism. But now he thought differently because he was no longer in search of arms. Now he wanted a proper revolution that would take place across the world, not merely an insurrection. But what form would the revolution take? He was unsure. As he said, 'The old order collapsed like a house of cards; everybody seemed to have lost faith in it. But nothing new was filling up the vacuum.'

Meanwhile, the sorry state of Berlin was a warning to everyone about the dangers of war and the enduring message of the Spartakusbund. The city was filled with starving people looking for food, but there was no sugar, no coffee, no butter. As Roy put it, a 'whole generation of children had grown up without even the sight of milk'. Indeed, as he concluded, 'War certainly had done the majority of the German people no good. They had more than enough reason to be embittered by the experience.' But elsewhere, the streets were lined with luxury shops and posh cafes patronised by smart uniformed men wearing their decorations as if Germany had won the war. It was a country deeply divided.

Roy needed to find his moorings in this dangerous and confusing city quickly. Most of the leaders he knew were in prison or hiding. His closest friend among the German communists was August Thalheimer, a nerdy mathematics professor, who was more academic than anarchist. Their friendship would endure for years and Roy would be mentored by him. Thalheimer was also reportedly an expert on the Sanskrit grammarian Panini.

Most of the German communists were surprised that colonial countries also had people interested in communism. Another long-lasting friendship that Roy developed was with the Dutch communist Henk Sneevliet who introduced him to the leaders of the Indonesian revolutionary movement. However, Sneevliet came to a sad end, shot by the Nazis in 1942. Roy decided to ally with communists who respected Rosa Luxemburg but did not approve of her strong hatred of Lenin and the Bolsheviks. He believed that for communism to take root in India, the communist party would have to be built as a mass organisation because till then it existed only in tiny pockets outside India.

Roy, as we saw earlier, did not have a great opinion of the Indian revolutionaries who made up the Berlin Committee. He agreed that they had done well to acquire the support of the Germans, but believed that the 'deceitfulness of the German propaganda department created an atmosphere of unreality. The committee was completely isolated from India and could do little in Europe which promoted the cause of Indian independence.'[25] Nevertheless, he tried to meet some of them. The Berlin Indians were in a state of disarray and tension, as described in the previous chapter, but Roy wanted to meet Chatto, whom he had previously heard about, and had described admiringly as a 'livewire' and a 'restless soul of indomitable energy and adventurous temperament who had the predominant position amongst the Indians in Berlin'.[26]

Chatto was in Stockholm at that time, so Roy met others from the group instead, including Har Dayal and Chempakaraman Pillai. He also met Chatto's brother-in-law A.C.N. Nambiar, who later wrote about Roy that he had expected to meet a person dressed like a revolutionary, but was surprised to see 'a person of genteel look, well groomed, meticulously dressed, who could be easily mistaken for a film star, a young entrepreneur, diplomat, or one of the sort'.[27] Nambiar was by no means the first or last person to be impressed by Roy's movie-star good looks.

Nambiar described the Roy of that time as reserved and formal, very unlike the gregarious Chatto, and a man of strict routine. 'He used to sit at this table, reading or writing from 9 in the morning till 13 o clock [sic], then have a cup of tea with fruit, and work again from 14 o clock to 18 o clock. At about seven in the evening, he went out for dinner and then played bridge and chess with friends. He was interested in literature, art and music.'[28]

In 1920, with his path smoothed by Borodin, Roy made his way to the Soviet Union, where Lenin was establishing a new world order with the Bolsheviks. It was the appropriate destination for a man seeking powerful, anti-imperialist friends. Over the next few years, he would go back and forth between Moscow and Berlin, making allies as best he could.

10

Live the Life of a Cabbage I Would Not!

It seemed to me that men could go anywhere, do anything, discover new worlds, but that women could only trail behind and sit at home having babies. Such a fate I rejected.

Agnes Smedley

A FIERY FLAME CAME INTO CHATTO'S LIFE IN 1920, ONE THAT WOULD burn intensely for eight years, then disappear as suddenly as it had come. The flame was a restless journalist, activist, radical and great admirer of Eastern cultures by the name of Agnes Smedley. The two were inexorably drawn to each other but would make each other miserable for years. It seemed Chatto had met his match, his equal, and some might even say, his superior.

As her biographer Ruth Price wrote, 'One measure of the size of Smedley's life, and the magnetism of her personality was the extraordinary roster of her friends who included Margaret Sanger ... Madame Sun Yat-Sen, Mao Tse-Tung, Jawaharlal Nehru, Langston Hughes, Carson McCullers, Harold Ickes, Edgar Snow, Theodore White and Katherine Anne Porter. The roster of her enemies was no less worthy, from J Edgar Hoover to Chiang Kai-Shek, Douglas McArthur, and Robert Lowell.'[1]

Indeed, Smedley 'cut a swathe through history' as newspaper headlines from around the world showed:[2]

> From 1918: Hold American Girl as India Plotter: Agnes Smedley accused of trying to cause uprisings against the British
> From 1937: American Woman aids Chinese Rising: Agnes Smedley, Author takes leading role as 250,000 men plot northwest red regime
> From 1950: Agnes Smedley's death linked to Red Spy Ring: Authoress was ready to testify.[3]

Smedley's upbringing was very different from Chatto's genteel and intellectual childhood. She was working class all the way, with almost no education, born in dire poverty on a Missouri farm on 23 February 1892 as what she called 'poor white trash'. Her father was an unskilled labourer who 'drank to forget his hopes', and her mother a washerwoman. When Smedley was sixteen, her mother died from 'hard labour, undernourishment and a disease that she had no money to cure'.[4] Her father fell on his knees and wept, but then immediately ransacked her mother's tin trunk. With the money he found, he got drunk. Smedley was left to act as a surrogate mother to her younger sister and two brothers, plus the child of an elder sister who had died in childbirth.

But she chose to escape because she did not want to follow in her mother's footsteps. Instead, Smedley embarked on a career of 'semi-vagabondage' which lasted her whole life. 'It seemed to me that men could go anywhere, do anything, discover new worlds, but that women could only trail behind and sit at home having babies. Such a fate I rejected.'[5]

Smedley took a number of temporary jobs: stenographer, secretary, magazine agent, teacher. In many of them she was sexually harassed and once she even had to even fight off rape. She entered into a short-lived and unhappy marriage which collapsed because of her dislike of sex at the time. Eventually, she ended up in New York, attending night classes at New York University, while doing low-paying jobs to support herself.

In Greenwich Village, Smedley fell in with a liberal, progressive crowd, and soon became friends with a group of bohemian women activists and suffragettes, the most prominent of whom was Margaret Sanger. Sanger was a controversial birth control activist, sex educator and writer who opened the first birth control clinic in the US, which later became the Planned Parenthood Federation of America. Later, Sanger would be criticised for her support of eugenics. Smedley and Sanger would remain close, lifelong friends.

In 1917, women won the right to vote in New York state, a development that encouraged many more women activists to enter political life. The same year, Smedley met a man who was to change her life. The man was not Chatto, but the magnetic Lala Lajpat Rai, whom Smedley met at around the same time that M.N. Roy did.

On 10 March 1917, Rai gave a speech at Columbia University on the subject of independence for India. He berated the audience. 'You, Americans, can you be at peace in your minds when your system, your leisure that created culture, rests upon the enslaved bodies of others? I have spoken to you of the freedom for which we Indians are working; can it be that you, like England, believe in freedom only for yourselves? Your war is for democracy, you say. I doubt it—your principles do not extend to Asia, although Asia is three-fourths of the human race.'[6]

These strong words had a deep impact on Smedley. Like most Westerners, she had never thought about freedom for the colonised people of Asia. It was a radical idea for the time. She ended up having a long talk with Rai and decided to train to become a teacher in India. Theirs was a platonic relationship, perhaps the first of Smedley's life. Rai became the father and teacher Smedley never had. She described him with intense feeling: 'A dark man with white in his hair, a man from India, ugly and severe. There was a scar down one side of his face and one eye was blind. He stood for a brief hour upon the threshold of my life, and I think he always had a touch of scorn for me. Why he concerned himself with me at all is still inexplicable. Perhaps he was lonely in exile, or perhaps my need for affection, for someone to love, for someone to take the place of a father was strong, and when I found a person who seemed to promise this, I did not lightly release my grip.'[7]

Smedley began working as a secretary for Rai in the day, while attending classes in the afternoon. It was Rai who showed Smedley that fledgling Indian nationalism was a part of an international struggle, not just India's problem. Her world suddenly became larger, her horizon expanded. Rai's younger associates also convinced her that India could not progress until it was independent of British rule, just as America had progressed with its own revolution.

But Smedley soon moved on from Rai and became entangled with the young revolutionaries of the Ghadar movement, a more radical bunch. She idolised Sailendra Nath Ghose, a twenty-three-year-old Bengali who had freshly arrived in the States. Smedley also met M.N. Roy years before she would meet Chatto. Roy and his then wife Evelyn Trent introduced Smedley to more extreme, anarchist ideas. Some biographers later claimed she had an affair with Roy, though it is hard to say for certain. In any case, she became close to both Roy and Evelyn.[8]

By 1917, Smedley had become a kind of liaison for the young men of the Ghadar movement, keeping their letters, their addresses and lists of names safe. The two men she was especially close to were Sailendra Nath Ghose and Taraknath Das, who were working to smuggle guns and men into India to overthrow the British rule.

Smedley's friends thought she was ridiculous to work for people so distant, so wholly unrelated to her. Besides, she was working class, while most Indian nationalists were from the educated upper classes, so her closeness to the latter was considered odd. She would explain her love for Indian nationalists in her novel, *Daughter of Earth*. One of her socialist friends argued that India must 'shake off not only the English, but also the Indian capitalists and feudal landlords who only help to step into the shoes of the present rulers'. Smedley asked if that was a good reason for not trying to get the British out. No, replied her friend, but she should be clear about it. After all, he said, 'Only a nut could work for such a distant thing, and with such people.'[9]

But Smedley thought she was clear about it. 'I do not see that the idea is distant. I have no country ... my countrymen are the men and women who work against oppression–it does not matter who or where they are.' She attempted to convince her friends that without Asia being free, Europe or America could not be free either. After all, explained Smedley, Russia was almost as distant as India and yet the eyes of American socialists were following the Russian Revolution.

But it would be Smedley's fate to be forever intrigued by Indian revolutionaries, to forever respect and idolise them, but to never quite gain that same respect for herself. In that macho world, Smedley, without a marriage to give her respectability, was regarded by many as a 'loose woman'. Throughout her life, Smedley would need and long for the warmth of human affection. Not 'sex love', as she called it, but 'warmth, an intimate closeness that was not just sex, a gentleness'.[10] She never found it, despite searching for it ceaselessly.

Smedley's idealism and her lonely childhood may have blinded her to the fact that many in the Ghadar movement were no different from the wolves that had assaulted her so far. Only the gentle and avuncular Lala Lajpat Rai treated her with respect and give her the friendship she deserved. The rest of the revolutionaries ended up using and abusing her.

One of these men, whose identity she would never reveal, came late one night to Smedley's apartment and raped her. In her novel, Smedley invented a rapist called Juan Diaz. Her biographer Ruth Price claimed Diaz was a composite of M.N. Roy and another agitator called Herambalal Gupta. The book showed how her sympathy for the Indian cause muddled her reactions.

'"Let me go!... Do you hear?" I jerked in blind fear, for I liked him and a yearning in my blood, long suppressed in shame, had begun to struggle with my mind. Quickly he whirled me into his arms and his big shoulders crushed me. Terror ... the outspread wings of a bird, swooping, and his body had hurled itself upon me.'

Leaving the apartment, the man told Smedley not to tell anyone about the attack and left her fifty dollars as the ultimate insult. A shattered and traumatised Smedley attempted to commit suicide with an open gas flame but was rescued by her landlady in the nick of time.

The rapist is likely to have been Herambalal Gupta as per Smedley's biographer Ruth Price. But as we shall see, Smedley was eventually brutally shamed by Roy as well, who likely saw her as easy prey because she was a single woman. (Other characters in *Daughter of Earth* were the noble Sardar who represented Lajpat Rai, Talwar who represented Ghose, and Anand–which means joy–who represented Chatto.)

By March 1918, things got even worse. Smedley was arrested for plotting to cause an uprising in India against British rule. Her arrest was reported in the *New York Times*. 'Important evidence bearing on a plot to cause uprisings in India against British rule has come into the possession of the government as the result of the arrest yesterday of Agnes Smedley, an American girl, also known as Agnes Brundin.' Ghose was named as the mastermind behind the plot.[11]

A notebook belonging to Smedley with the names and addresses of several Indian nationalists was discovered. Just as M.N. Roy had been, Smedley too was bullied and browbeaten by the examiners, who were baffled by this white girl helping 'Hindoos'. 'To what church do you belong?' they demanded, and 'Are you a yogi?' Smedley replied, 'I have no religion–except to help people who work for freedom.' The investigators went on to accuse Smedley of receiving money from Lala Lajpat Rai for 'services' and of helping 'yellow dogs', the term they used for Asian people. Both Smedley and Ghose were jailed for attempting to stir up rebellion against British rule in India. Bail was set at a whopping $10,000 for Smedley and $20,000 for Ghose. Luckily for Smedley, her liberal friends, headed by the indefatigable Margaret Sanger, sprang to her rescue. They raised bail and, in the summer of 1918, Smedley was released.

By this time, Taraknath Das and other Indian nationalists had decided it was time to leave the country. They were looking for a contact in Europe and with the authorities constantly pursuing Smedley, it seemed like the right time for her too to leave for Germany. On 17 December 1919, she set sail for Danzig, working as a stewardess on a Polish American freighter. She was travelling as 'Alice Bird' and carrying a suitcase full of documents sent by Taraknath Das to be delivered to Chatto. But she had no clear aim in mind, except to find the Indian exiles in Germany. 'Whatever might result from this venture, I would at least see something of the earth on which I had been born. But live the life of a cabbage I would not.'[12]

Her life in Germany would be far from cabbage-like. Smedley would fall in love with Chatto straight away, although he was nearly twenty years older than her. She would describe him as 'thin and dark, with a mass of black hair turning grey at the temples, and a face that had something fierce about it. He might easily have been taken for a Southern European, a Turk, or a Persian. To me he seemed something like thunder, lightning and rain. His hatred for the islanders who subjugated his country knew no bounds.'[13]

Chatto and Smedley lived in an uneasy union for the next eight years. Their relationship was tumultuous, tender, abusive and ultimately destructive. They never legally married because of

Chatto's previous marriage to a Catholic woman, which had yet to be annulled. Smedley wrote that Chatto's previous wife had become a nun who had fled to a convent and refused to annul the marriage. Smedley and Chatto lived gloriously and unapologetically in sin. Once, Smedley blithely explained the relationship to an American consular official in China: 'My husband was married to a Catholic nun and for this reason could not marry me. You may call me a concubine if you will, but not a British subject.' The official threw up his hands in despair.[14]

By now, Gandhi's cult of non-violence was gaining massive support in India and abroad. Smedley was very taken by Gandhi, but Chatto despised him. 'He is unclear socially and knows nothing of economics. He was trained in British constitutional law, and that is always a poison that works in the system of Indian leaders, causing them to betray our people time and again for the sake of British phrases.'[15]

But Chatto did have one thing in common with Gandhi: a spartan lifestyle and a deep disdain for worldly goods, which initially captivated Smedley. Smedley wrote fondly of Chatto, 'He never possessed more than one suit of clothing, which I was constantly darning, patching and pressing. When he had money, he gave it to anyone in need, so that we were forever in debt. Money was merely a means of working for the independence of his country.'[16]

But Smedley's fondness for Chatto's generosity soon wore thin. He would invite every Indian in Berlin to their home even when they barely had enough to feed themselves. Their home became a joint family, patterned on Aghorenath's welcoming household but without the wealth and numerous servants. A joint family was fine for Chatto, who had grown up in one. But not so for Smedley, who was the one forced to feed the visitors, to wash, clean, scrub and iron. 'In the manner of India, no man could be turned away hungry.'[17]

But she had not travelled across the world to become a domestic drudge. A disillusioned Smedley realised soon enough that, while visiting revolutionaries talked at length about women's liberation, they were perfectly happy to treat her as a domestic slave and for her to go without food. 'The very walls of our home seemed to be permeated with the odour of curry.' Worse, Smedley was treated as Chatto's concubine. 'There were days when I did not have enough to eat because Indian hospitality demands that a man must be fed. But I had to cook for these men who were not idealists, who had never raised a hand to help free India. And I would sit and listen to them talk all night about how all European women were prostitutes.'[18] Money was a constant worry and eventually, Smedley was forced to sell her possessions.

Many visitors—once even Mohammad Ali Jinnah and his glamourous wife Ruttie—would gather in Smedley and Chatto's home. Chatto would hold court, surrounded by adoring Indian students. He was deeply contemptuous of Indians trying for British government posts. When told that one needed to earn money in order to live, he would answer sarcastically, in the words of Voltaire, 'I don't see the necessity.'[19] The irreligious Chatto would attack both the Hindu caste system and Muslim superstitions. He would eat pork in front of Muslims and beef in front of Hindus, often taunting Hinduism as being a 'cow dung religion'.

In 1922, Smedley and Chatto's difficult home life was interrupted by a visit from Chatto's sister Suhasini Chattopadhyay. Chatto had never seen Suhasini because she had been born after he had left India. On the other hand, Suhasini had grown up on stories and lullabies about her exiled brother, with incidents of her dolls being disembowelled and her possessions being searched by British police looking for evidence of Chatto's letters.

Smedley describes Suhasini as a woman of 'striking beauty and noble bearing'. The reunion was emotional. 'When she stood before her brother for the first time, neither spoke, and I saw

Suhasini trembling. Viren's face was tense with inner struggle; it was the first time in a quarter of a century that one of his family had come to share his life.'[20]

In 1921, Chatto and Smedley travelled to Moscow along with fourteen other Indian delegates to discuss the Indian nationalist movement and map out the way ahead. But when they reached Moscow, they found they had been pre-empted by M.N. Roy and Abani Mukherji, who by now led the Communist Party of Tashkent, a rival organisation to the Berlin Indians.

The two groups, one led by Chatto and the other by Roy, had deep differences. At the time, for Chatto, Smedley and their associates, independence for India was a priority and they were willing to ally with others, including the Congress, to get it. They were sympathetic towards communism but were not yet members of the Comintern. On the other hand, Roy and his associates were hard core communists first, who argued that India should first organise the proletariat and then aim for independence, because otherwise India would be taken over by rich industrialists and businessmen, many of whom were disciples of Gandhi.

Accounts of this meeting vary wildly. According to Smedley, Roy led an amazingly vicious campaign against her, calling her an 'evil temptress' and a possible British spy. Roy did not acknowledge an affair with Smedley in his memoirs but wrote scathingly of her. 'Ever since we met in the United States, she seemed to have a grudge against me. She was a fanatical hero-worshipper. When she espoused the Indian cause, she seemed to believe that to fall in love with famous Indian revolutionaries would be the expression of her loyalty to India. As a lonesome old man, Lajpatrai was reported to have played the first Indian hero worshipped by Agnes Smedley.'[21]

Roy also wrote that Smedley then transferred her affections to an unnamed 'young Indian' who had worked with Roy in New York and had then joined him in Mexico. This seems likely to have been Sailendra Nath Ghose. 'I felt that the infatuation of a young man for a woman much older than himself would do no good. But I could not persuade him to remain in Mexico. Eventually, he left, with a considerable amount of money under a false pretence. On his return to the United States, together with Agnes Smedley, he set up an organisation called "The Friends of Freedom for India", with headquarters in Washington. Soon both of them were arrested for the pretension of being diplomatic representatives of a foreign country without due accreditation. I received frantic cables to send money for their defence. But I was not prepared to waste any to support a frivolous adventure. Eventually, the young Indian married another American girl, and Agnes Smedley had to look out for a new hero.'[22]

On Smedley's Berlin interlude, Roy wrote: 'It seems that she managed to poison Chatto's mind against me. In any case, she was the evil genius of the Indian revolutionary group which came to Moscow. But for her influence, Chatto, who was an intelligent and practical man, would have behaved differently. I learned in the course of time that she was heartily disliked by all the other members of the group because of her pretension to be a more passionate Indian patriot than the Indians themselves.'[23]

Roy and Smedley's deep dislike of each other might have occurred because of their past history and Roy's puritan disapproval of Smedley's sexual mores. But by then Chatto and Roy were also competing for funding from Lenin and the Bolsheviks, and therefore it is likely that Roy was looking for excuses to discredit Chatto in Lenin's eyes. Smedley made an easy target.

Smedley wrote an angry letter to her friend Florence Lennon. 'The Indians opposing our plan did such dirty work as to call me a British spy. Think of it—not even an American spy, but a British one! If I had not been a member of a large delegation, I suppose I would have been locked up.'[24] Chatto did get to meet Lenin but did not accomplish much since Roy had already got there ahead of him. Ultimately, Chatto and Smedley were forced to return to Berlin without meeting anyone of significance.

Meanwhile, Smedley's chequered past was catching up with her. To her great dismay and disappointment, Chatto's liberalism and modernity did not extend to women. He was jealous of her many past lovers, and despite his liberal pretensions as a revolutionary, he never overcame this basic jealousy. She wrote bitterly to a friend in 1923, 'He is fine in theory, our modern man. But in practice he is a walking lie. He still judges woman by her vagina. In fact, a woman is nothing but a walking vagina to him, and he is the sole owner of it ... If you ever get married or contemplate it, look the man in the eye beforehand, and say "I have had many love affairs, so have you. I respect your own right. You must respect mine and keep your hands out of affairs which do not concern you, and which have nothing to do with you."'[25]

Smedley followed her own advice and was brutally honest with Chatto. But even honesty did not work with the jealous Chatto, who had by now become abusive as well. In late 1923, Smedley wrote to her friend Florence Lennon, saying that Chatto had begun to accuse her of being a woman of weak character because she'd had relations with other men. Apparently, he felt that he had 'got the leavings' of other men.

Chatto had also begun to feel ashamed of Smedley, of her unfeminine ways, her tempestuous personality, her poor dress sense, her working-class origins, but above all, her sexual past. He was reluctant to introduce her to his friends. Soon he began to restrict her writing, which he thought was her simply showing off. Smedley even claimed Chatto choked and hit her.

Chatto's artistic brother Harindranath Chattopadhyay came to visit with his sophisticated and beautiful wife Kamaladevi. Smedley, who had never stopped feeling ashamed of her humble origins and unglamorous looks, felt patronised. To hold her own, she narrated horrific tales of her childhood, of times spent in the mines. Harindranath would later describe her as a 'plain looking, sickly, nervy woman who looked more like a working-class woman, as we came to know later'. But he did not mean to be disparaging. He explained that 'Agnes was proud of her birth, as she had every right to be.'[26]

He also described her as 'an ardent champion of woman and her neglected cause. The instant anybody suggested that women's intellect or capacity to build was inferior to that of man, she jumped up from her seat like a wounded lioness and almost clawed him red in the face.'[27] Harindranath went on to call Smedley brilliant and one of the rarest reporters the modern world had come across, referring to her books on China and her eyewitness accounts of the Red Army's struggle. He did claim though that it was Chatto who had tutored Smedley in attaining freedom from fear, which seems unlikely. Kamala was far less generous and made Smedley feel small.

Meanwhile, of all people, her likely rapist Herambalal Gupta too had arrived in Berlin and started spreading rumours about her. So did M.N. Roy, by now her enemy, in an attempt to seize control of the communist movement.

At a meeting of the Berlin India committee, Gupta challenged Smedley's presence, arguing that foreigners and wives had no right to be there. Smedley was livid with rage. She spat, 'Juan Diaz sprang to his feet. "I object to foreigners influencing our movement. Not only am I opposed to foreigners, but I object to women and to wives influencing our members." I was on my feet livid with rage. "Foreigners! You do not object to foreigners who help save the lives of your men. Wives! Don't you insult me, Juan Diaz. I am not here as a wife, but as a comrade and a co-worker, and I demand to be treated as such."'[28]

Smedley was trapped within the macho culture of the Indian nationalist movement, where men were men and women were either wives or whores. Meanwhile, the couple was also being persecuted by the German police on instructions from the British government. They had to flee from hotel to hotel and house to house, followed by what seemed to be British spies. Once, according to Smedley, Chatto was even poisoned in a restaurant, by what a physician later said was arsenic. He was ill for days, but luckily recovered.'[29]

By 1923, Germany was on its knees. Allied reparations for the war and restrictions on German trade had sent the mark plunging, ultimately leading to its collapse. Inflation raged and a week's worth of wages could buy only a bag of potatoes. People queued for hours to buy food. Tuberculosis and other diseases were rampant. Smedley wrote in distress, 'Today twelve milliards (the currency then) may buy a loaf of bread, but tomorrow it will only buy half a loaf, and next week it may not even buy one slice.' She wanted to escape. 'There is no happiness here,' she wrote, 'I don't know when I have heard a person laugh a really joyous laugh. The only time they laugh is when they have beer, and then their laugh is heavy and deadly. I am weary of Germany, just as one wearies of suffering, dullness and ugliness over a long period of time.'[30]

Beset on all sides, Smedley began to take refuge in her many women friends, an accomplished set of writers, academics and activists. One of them was the Danish writer Karin Michaelis, who would describe Smedley as 'one who had renounced everything for a great cause'.[31] But in real life, Agnes was getting weary of the cause.

By now, she had started to despise the institution of marriage in general. In great despair, she consulted a psychoanalyst and began therapy. She could not escape an inescapable fact. She had become what she most feared: her mother. As Ruth Price, one of her biographers, said, 'Agnes had become what she most dreaded and fought against: a domestic drudge, just like her mother, who had lost her own identity in the name of love and become submerged in another.' Could there be a worse fate for Smedley, who had fought so hard to become her own person?[32] Eventually, she abandoned therapy and spent several weeks vacationing with Michaelis in her summer home on the Danish Island of Thuro.

Smedley was also beginning to see Chatto for what he was: an anarchist who could not and would not live in peace. 'I have married an artist,' she explained to her friend Florence Lennon, 'a revolutionary in a dozen different ways, a man of truly fine frenzy, nervous as a cat, always moving, never at rest, indefatigable energy, a hundredfold more than I ever had, a thin man with much hair, a tongue like a razor and a brain on fire ... I have been consumed into ashes. And he is always raking up the ashes and setting them on fire again. He doesn't believe in ashes, only in fire ... and he is always smouldering.'[33] Nobody would ever know Chatto so well or describe him so perfectly.

But who could blame Smedley for despising the institution of marriage? Chatto and Smedley never married officially, but they were man and wife in every way that mattered. She fought hard for her independence, going back to writing for magazines and the Indian press. She wrote to Florence Lennon at that time, 'Marriage automatically crushes all the nobility in a man's soul. Not so in a woman. She is often more human than before marriage. But she throws herself to a wild beast when she marries.'[34] Chatto had become ever more controlling, and often demanded that she write anonymously and leave off her byline. For Smedley, this was deeply insulting.

Unhappy as Smedley was, it took her a while to extricate herself from her toxic relationship with Chatto. She embarked on a risky plan to travel to India, having become intrigued by the Akali Dal, a Sikh movement fighting for freedom. She was sick of Bengali intellectuals and upper-class activists. The Akali campaign, led by working class Punjabi farmers, appealed to her. But her imprisonment in the US, her articles in the Indian press and her relationship with Chatto had made her persona non grata, which led to the British authorities refusing to let her enter India.

Despondent, Smedley conceived of a hare-brained plan to raise enough money to be treated by Sigmund Freud himself, and therefore went to Switzerland to find work. Chatto followed her there and begged her to return. Smedley agreed, but demanded a room of her own, like Virginia Woolf. The two led separate lives under the same roof in Berlin, but she 'deadened' her heart to Chatto.

She began to feel time that was running out for her. Since she had started living with Chatto, she had written very little, spending most of her time looking after him and his hangers-on. Whatever money she earned had often gone into rescuing him. The magazine she worked for had collapsed, and the two had been forced to beg their landlord for charity. She had nursed Chatto's family as well, helping his sister Suhasini, who was visiting, and Sarojini Naidu's son Jayasuriya, who was living in Berlin, through bouts of pneumonia. But resentment had started burning deep within her at being forced to care for everyone but herself.

Smedley returned to psychotherapy under a female analyst, Elizabeth Naef, using money given to her by Florence Lennon. She wrote of this time, 'I am sick to death of the Indians and their eternal demands upon one. I am sick of Chatto ... not so sick so much as hate him—except when I see him in a gathering, and see how damnably interesting and attractive he is, both mentally and physically—and how lovably naïve, and a victim of any cunning person who comes along.'[35]

In December 1923, Smedley suffered a complete psychological breakdown, hallucinating that Chatto was trying to kill her. Once again, she took an overdose of sleeping pills, and once again, she was discovered and rescued by her landlady. She had come to realise through therapy that her traumatic childhood accounted for her constant confusion and her preference for male pursuits, interests and the company of men. And yet, once again, she found herself reduced to doing what women had done for centuries—putting herself last.

She began to draw boundaries with Chatto, and the balance of power in their home began to shift. In March 1923, the beleaguered couple moved into a larger apartment. But Smedley flatly refused to do the usual housework and cooking. She had become more confident of her journalistic abilities and 'refused absolutely' to do any more 'servants work'.

Smedley continued to receive large sums of money from her supportive women friends, including Margaret Sanger, who gave her fifty dollars a month as a gift. This money she finally had the good sense to hide from Chatto. She began to write more, go out more, and firmly refused to manage the household. Her newfound independence alarmed Chatto. By now, he was reluctantly—and comically—doing all the housework. He demanded that she stop therapy, but Smedley refused. She found her emancipation too delicious to give up. She also begun a string of casual affairs, beginning with a tryst with a professor at Berlin University. She even flirted with the husband of her Danish friend Karin Michaelis. Writing to Florence Lennon, she revelled in her new and bold role as a seducer and the one with the upper hand in the relationship. 'Men will love you through all eternity if you beat them or scorn them or turn on them a face filled with dislike or active anger.' A jealous Chatto seethed in silence.

Then came an even more improbable affair. In his usual manner, Chatto had generously invited two Indian students—both orphans—to stay with them, perhaps hoping to once more chain Smedley to housework. But the new Smedley was no drudge. Instead, she embarked on an affair with one of them—Bakar Ali Mirza, eight years her junior. The handsome Bakar demanded nothing of her and did not try to control her as Chatto had. Instead, they shared an odd relationship, sometimes that of a mother and child and sometimes a romantic one. Smedley would oddly describe Bakar to visitors as her son.

Ruth Price, one of Smedley's biographers, claims that the mismatched couple even went to a deeply hurt Chatto to ask for his blessing. Apparently, Bakar and Smedley did not consummate their relationship, but letter after letter from Bakar arrived declaring his passion for her. Smedley enjoyed gloating over this relationship and rubbing salt in Chatto's wounds. She even made Chatto enter psychoanalysis himself, which proved to be unsuccessful.

Smedley next moved out of the house, but Chatto pursued her, begging her to return and threatening to commit suicide if she didn't. He was too old to start over, he argued. But Smedley had had enough. She was willing to work and die for his cause, but not be his wife. She wrote to Karin Michaelis, 'If I had many lives to live, as the Hindus believe they have—I could perhaps afford to experiment with this one and wait for my ideal love in another. But I do not believe in that. This is my only life, and it is the most precious of all possessions. I will not sacrifice it.'[36]

Smedley stayed reluctantly in Germany for a few more months, scared that Chatto might commit suicide. But by August 1925, she'd had enough of her melancholy lover and once again left for Michaelis's island home in Thuro. She would never live with Chatto again.

Spending three months in Thuro, she finished her thinly fictionalised novel, *Daughter of Earth*. Her angry, frank book contained her final views on the trap she considered marriage. Her heroine Marie jeers in one passage, 'Marry? No, I would not marry. I have no desire to submit to the life that most women live—darning socks, cooking, cleaning, depending upon a man for my living—in other words just existing.'[37]

She went on to allude to Chatto's jealousy of her work and his demand that she should give up her bylines. Marie says, 'What kind of work could I do if I gave this up ... go back to taking down the thoughts of some man, then spend the day typing them? Should I have to sit at home, a wife, a housewife, doing nothing but the work I hated—a female at last?'[38]

By now Smedley's love affair with India had cooled considerably too, but in truth the feeling was entirely mutual. The Indian nationalists had begun to be embarrassed by her as well. Smedley, influenced by her long and enduring friendship with Margaret Sanger, was staunchly in favour of birth control. Indeed, she had helped set up a birth control clinic in Berlin. But Indian nationalists like Taraknath Das knew that supporting birth control in India was a minefield. Instead, the male Indian nationalists 'dodged the problem of birth control in India by writing abstractly about the geopolitical concerns of the issue, much to Smedley's chagrin'.[39]

An infuriated Smedley wrote to Sanger, 'India always seems to think human beings should breed like lice as long as they can feed themselves. India produces droves of weak slaves which are pulling the nation to the earth. We are far stronger in meeting our opponents if we agree to all India's evils and merely prove that we are the ones who recognize them and are willing to change them ...'[40]

Smedley's gradual contempt for Indian ways would soon antagonise her former friends. Writing patronisingly about India's customs and culture, including its lack of a birth control programme, turned her into a white saviour.

By mid-1927 Smedley had concluded that India would have to choose between the West and its continued colonial status or Russia, in which case, she argued, Indian nationalist leaders like Gandhi and Nehru would have to give up their upper-class status for a more equal world. In an article titled 'The Indian Revolutionary Movement Abroad', published in *The People* on 11 August 1927, Smedley flayed Indian leaders in India for their dependence on British thought. 'The Indian leaders in India are nearly all poisoned by their English education or their dependence upon an English interpretation of world events.'[41] She further argued that India should ally with China and Russia against the British. By now, Chatto had joined the German communist party and believed that only communism could truly liberate all of India.

Smedley's articles were not received well. Her old friend Lala Lajpat Rai now found her condescending and patronising. He hit out at her. 'Miss Smedley is mistaken if she thinks we are all babies and do not understand even elementary politics. Sitting in Berlin and writing from her point of vantage, she can call us traitors, cowards and fools. But we know that we are nothing of the kind. Only we realise what our power is and what our resources are and what we can do and what we cannot do ...'[42]

Smedley was also targeted by her old nemesis Kamaladevi Chattopadhyay, the wife of Chatto's younger brother Harindranath. Kamaladevi published a blistering letter in *The People* on 17 November 1928 on the subject of 'champagne socialism'. 'Indians abroad fail to see that these Communist friends are usually those who have either no opportunity of becoming capitalists, and thus convert a disadvantage into a virtue, or bourgeoisie who play the superficial role of the Communists as a sort of recreation or amusement.'[43]

Kamaladevi believed in the Gandhian ideals of peace, humanity, non-violence. She wrote, 'If everyone learns to read and write, and every stomach is fed, the world is not going to become a paradise. Happiness can begin when we learn to hold life sacred. Then alone can we say the movement brings comfort and relief to a grief-stricken world.'[44] The resolutely working-class Smedley thought these were pretty, fluffy, idealistic words that India's peasants and farmers could not afford to live by.

By 1928, she had even tired of the young Bakar, who had finished his studies and returned to India. She had also finally broken off her relationship with Chatto. She wrote wistfully, 'For me, he embodied the tragedy of a whole race. Had he been born English or American, I thought, his ability would have placed him among the great leaders of his age.'[45]

Though on her own now, Smedley had found a new Asian love: the stirring giant, China. She travelled to China, becoming the first Western journalist to cover the Chinese communists, marching with Mao and the Red Army, and making her way out of the story of India's freedom movement.

Smedley and Chatto would meet once again in Moscow in 1933, after Chatto left Germany for the Soviet Union, a wistful encounter for both. 'He was at last growing old, his body thin and frail, his hair rapidly turning white. The desire to return to India obsessed him, but the British would trust him only if he were dust on a funeral pyre. What happened to him after that I do not know.'[46]

Four years later, Chatto would be dead. But Smedley would not get to hear of his lonely, uncharted demise. By then, she would be involved in another risky love affair with another charismatic and dangerous man: Richard Sorge, a German journalist and Soviet spy in Japan. Sorge was passing secrets to Russia, including information about Hitler's plans to invade the Soviet Union. But he would shortly be arrested, tortured and executed by the Japanese, the second of Smedley's lovers after Chatto to meet such a terrible fate.

Smedley would die in 1950, while under investigation by the House Un-American Activities Committee (HUAC). Revolutionary and un-American to the last, she would be buried in what is now the Babaoshan Revolutionary Cemetery in Beijing, China's main resting place for its highest-ranking martyrs.

11

Lenin's Young Man

For the first time, brown and yellow men met white men who were not overbearing imperialists, but friends and comrades, eager to make amends for the evils of colonialism.

M.N. Roy

'YOU ARE SO YOUNG. I EXPECTED A GREY-BEARDED WISE MAN FROM the East,'[1] said Vladimir Lenin when he first met M.N. Roy in 1920. The meeting was memorable for both the man who had started a revolution and the man who was waiting to start his first one. Roy walked into a vast room and his attention was immediately attracted by 'the bald dome of a head stooping very low on the top of a big desk. Nearly a head shorter, he tilted his red goatee almost to a horizontal position to look at my face quizzically.'

Roy's exploits had reached the ears of Lenin through Mikhail Borodin. Lenin invited Roy to attend the 1920 Second World Congress of the Comintern being held in Moscow and Petrograd. This was a great honour for Roy and he was ecstatic to be in Moscow. Indeed, this chapter in his memoirs is titled 'In the Holy Land'. 'The idea that at last I was in Moscow was so overwhelming as to make me walk as if in a dream.'[2] The Russian revolution in October 1917—when the Bolsheviks overthrew the aristocracy and seemingly restored power to the people—had long enthralled and fascinated Indian revolutionaries, who dreamt of a day when they would do the same.

But Roy's elation was tempered by the chaos and disorder of post-revolution Moscow. Poverty was widespread, food was scarce and the city was not much different from the war-torn Berlin he had just escaped. Still holding the faith, he concluded that 'A new order could not be built overnight'.[3] Elsewhere, he would describe Moscow as 'a beleaguered city', but go on to add, 'Yet, half-starved and dilapidated, Moscow was already then throbbing as the heart of the world revolution, and everybody there felt the throb.'[4]

But Roy conveniently did not mention another bloody Russian campaign that had begun in 1918, which would continue till 1922: the Red Terror.

On 30 August 1918, less than two years before he met Roy, an assassination attempt on Lenin had left the communist leader seriously injured, with two bullets in his body and battling for his life. This would throw long shadows over the next few years.

The assassin, a doe-eyed twenty-eight-year-old woman called Fanny Kaplan, who looked more like a ballet dancer than a sharpshooter, considered Lenin a 'traitor to the Revolution'. Kaplan was interrogated by the Cheka—the Bolshevik secret police—and quickly executed. There were also attempts to assassinate Leon Trotsky, the second most powerful person in the party.

Meanwhile, Soviet Russia continued to be racked by civil war, with the Bolshevik Red Army having to battle the White Army made up of conservative pro-monarchy Russians opposed to the revolution and allied to foreign powers. In response, Lenin unleashed a campaign of repression and executions that was carried out by the Cheka. Historians disagree on the number of casualties from that time, but estimates range from fifty thousand to two hundred thousand people as the Red versus White Army played out like in *Alice in Wonderland*. Later accounts would even doubt that Kaplan had carried out the assassination attempt for which she was executed.

Thus, at the time of Roy's meeting with Lenin, the latter was recovering, struggling to heal and battling for control over the country. But he welcomed Roy as an equal. Roy felt at ease with him almost immediately, helped by Lenin's impish smile and twinkling eyes. Lenin was always punctual and did not share the usual Soviet disregard for time. Punctuality, Roy noted drolly of the Russians, 'seemed to be blacklisted as an abominable petit bourgeois prejudice'.[5] Roy wrote of Lenin's gait, 'He was not a dwarf, being above five feet, but he walked with a stoop, and did not raise his eyes to see what was ahead. The posture suggested that he was engrossed in thought even when walking.'[6]

Roy was housed in a magnificent suite of rooms that had been the former residence of Count Gutchkov, a nobleman known as the Sugar King of Russia due to his business interests in the sugar beet industry. Post the revolution, the Gutchkov mansion belonged to the state and the upper storey was reserved for foreign guests. The Moskva river flowed next to the house, and on its opposite bank, 'in a forest of proud minarets, and high church steeples, several huge golden domes glistened in the afternoon sun',[7] That was the Kremlin, now the glorious seat of the revolution. A poor and virtually uneducated Bengali boy who had spent years on the run was now a guest in the lavish, beautifully decorated former home of a Russian aristocrat! There could be no louder demonstration of the power of the proletariat for Roy.

The food, however, did not match up to the splendour of the surroundings. While served in a magnificent room, the meal was only cabbage soup, a slice of brown bread and kasha (a kind of dark grain). He was told by Borodin that the kasha was a luxury and the soup usually did not have meat. That was the standard government meal. Food scarcity in the days after the revolution was common as the peasants refused to send supplies to Moscow.

The Second World Congress of the Comintern in July 1920 was an incredible experience for many of the colonised people in attendance, and certainly so for Roy. As he put it, 'all roads led to Moscow' that year as delegates from across the world made their way to the city. Many delegates travelled illegally and were smuggled through the Baltic states. The Chinese and Japanese delegates came through Mongolia. As one historian put it, 'The Second Congress was a coming out party for international Communism.'[8]

Roy wrote excitedly, 'For the first time, brown and yellow men met white men who were not overbearing imperialists but friends and comrades, eager to make amends for the evils of colonialism.'[9] Lenin asked Roy to prepare a document on the mobilisation of the masses in Asia towards a gigantic revolutionary movement. That cemented their friendship even further, with Roy feeling accepted and welcomed by international revolutionaries for the first time.

Other delegates may not have felt quite so enthusiastic about the preachy efforts made to educate them, though perhaps none could resist the lure of the great Soviet experiment. Upon arriving in their hotel rooms in Petrograd, as one historian described, 'delegates received a copy of Lenin's latest effusion: a condescending pamphlet called "Left Wing Communism: An Infantile Disorder". The delegates were then shown the revolutionary sights, including the Tsarskoe Selo (former imperial residences) which had been transformed into proletarian children's homes for orphans. Back in Petrograd, the delegates were shown around the Smolny Institute—the Bolshevik headquarters. Red flags blustered in the wind atop the Winter Palace as warships on the Neva lit up the hammer and sickle with searchlights.'[10]

On May Day, Roy gave his first proper speech at a mass meeting. In his youth, as a revolutionary associated with the Anushilan Samiti in Bengal, public speeches had been frowned upon because they were considered bourgeoisie and a futile method of the establishment;[11] action was what mattered. He'd thus had little experience of public speaking, having made only a few speeches in his life before, mostly in the US and Mexico. This made him wary and inhibited. He was also intimidated by the venue–Roy was to address the crowds in the Red Square under the shadow of the Kremlin walls, which were crowned by a giant clock chiming the *Internationale*.

Meanwhile, Lenin stood on a high platform, his right hand raised to his cloth cap. He was flanked by most members of the political party, except for Leon Trotsky and Joseph Stalin, who were fighting wars elsewhere. The crowd swelled on account of the processions coming from various parts of the city: delegates to the Congress, soldiers and workers from numerous factories.

Roy was introduced by Grigory Zinoviev, an old Bolshevik. Even though he had prepared no speech and there was no loudspeaker, Roy overcame his stage fright and spoke as loudly as he could. Speaking in English, which hardly anyone understood, he introduced himself as 'a new convert to the Communist faith'. The few people who understood English applauded, and when the speech was translated into Russian just a few minutes later, it drew more applause. Roy ended the day feeling pleased and confident.

In the days that followed, the delegates to the Second World Congress were wined and dined. In the evenings they were treated to operas, ballets and plays to demonstrate that the Bolsheviks were not against culture if it was the right kind of culture. By now, Roy had become intrigued by the Russian way of life. He described it as 'matriarchal, with the Volga River being the matriarch'. But he believed that Bolshevism was 'inspired more by the native tradition of revolt against tyranny, with the Russians revolting against the Tartars', than by what he called the 'outlandish cult of Marxism'.[12]

Roy was largely a self-educated man, a magpie gleaning what he could from the world. Now he educated himself in ballet, theatre and music just as he had in educated himself in the culture of Mexico. Russian theatres, he noticed, stayed open even during the worst of times, even when starvation and war plagued the country. With the revolution, a new elite had emerged. Blocks of theatre seats were allotted to trade unions, the Communist Party, schools and others, including to the delegates. Every delegate chose the entertainment they preferred. 'There were Englishmen fascinated by the grandeur of Rymsky-Korsakov's operas and Italians who appreciated Tchekov's new interpretation of *Hamlet*. Frenchmen went to Beethoven concerts while Germans preferred the open-air variety shows.'[13]

Around this time, in the summer of 1920, Roy would meet Leon Trotsky and visit the Red Army at the front. The country was still being ravaged by civil war, with armies opposed to the Russian Revolution and supported by America and Japan holding out in various parts of Russia. Trotsky, by now recognised as an incredible orator who could talk for hours in three languages, was in charge of founding, organising and equipping the rag tag Red Army.

Roy wrote of the formidable army which years later would defeat the Nazis but at that time was still in its infancy. 'Any military expert would have refused to recognise it as an army. There were no drill sergeants to teach the soldiers to keep their brass buttons shining and boots polished. All the soldiers did not even have guns. Yet, there was no doubt on the part of anybody that the Army of the Revolution was going to be victorious!' He described Trotsky as 'a great man, but very eager that he should be recognised as such. In that eagerness, he only accentuated the faults from which all great men, conscious of their defects, usually suffer.'

At the Congress, Roy met a number of interesting characters, some of whom had witnessed history being made. One of them was the famous American communist John Reed, a fascinating writer-adventurer who was very like Roy and had also become Lenin's friend. Reed had shot to fame by being an eyewitness to the Russian Revolution and writing the riveting book *Ten Days That Shook the World*, which described his experience during the revolution. In his short life, he captured the imagination of the world and became an icon for radical intellectuals.

Born in 1887, in a wealthy family from Portland, Oregon, Reed studied at Harvard and began a career in journalism, in the course of which he covered labour strikes. Fascinated by revolution, he went to Mexico, and from there to Russia, where he became a part of the frenzied crowd that stormed the Winter Palace on 25 October 1917. The Winter Palace in St Petersburg was the official residence of Czar Nicholas and the Romanov dynasty and an enduring symbol of the might of Imperial Russia. Its storming marked the beginning of the Russian Revolution and the downfall of the aristocracy. Reed's thrilling account of the events spread through the world like wildfire. 'Like a black river, filling all the street, without song or cheer we poured through the Red Arch,' began his story. 'The man just ahead of me said in a low voice: "Look out comrades! Don't trust them. They will fire, surely!" In the open we began to run, stopping and bunching together.'

Reed described the looting of the palace, which he claimed was stopped by the Red Guards because stealing was not deemed worthy of the people's champions. 'Somebody cried: "Comrades! Don't touch anything! Don't take anything! This is the property of the People!"' He had a close call when foreign members of the mob were accused of looting the palace but was rescued by an officer of the Red Army, who cried, 'Comrades! These people are foreign comrades–from America. They have come here to be able to tell their countrymen about the bravery and the revolutionary discipline of the proletarian army.'[14]

Roy liked Reed immensely, and indeed, after their first meeting, he went on to say, 'I simply fell in love with him. Everybody did, even men.'[15] He described Reed as an 'overgrown boy—tall, powerfully built, with a handsome face, and extremely friendly manners.'

Reed would die of typhus in 1921 before he could start a proper communist party in the US. In fact, Roy had stolen Reed's thunder by organising the first Communist Party outside Russia, in Mexico, tiny though it was. But Reed would be one of only four foreigners to have the honour of being buried at the Kremlin.

In recent years, Reed has been savagely criticised for being a propagandist for the Bolsheviks or at least a biased reporter 'who saw only what he wanted to see'.[16] One modern historian calls *Ten Days That Shook the World* a blend of 'reporting and propaganda', and claims Reed was paid one million rubles by Lenin to write the book.[17] Whatever the truth of this, the magnetic Reed drew the world's attention and brought hope to millions of colonised peoples. He would be immortalised in film sixty years later in the 1981 movie *Reds*, where he was played by Warren Beatty.

Another memorable delegate at the Comintern was the nervy Sylvia Pankhurst, the daughter of Emmeline Pankhurst, the leader of the British suffragette movement. The suffragettes had successfully got the vote for women in Britain along with many other rights. Pankhurst was in her early thirties—sparsely built and of medium height. She was from a privileged background, but more proletarian than the proletariat. She despised parliamentary reform. As Roy put it, 'Sylvia had come to the Second World Congress to defend the infantile sickness of left-wing Communism against Lenin's "senile reformism".'

Pankhurst gave a passionate speech, pointing an accusing finger at Lenin. When her time ran out, she snapped at the speaker and said that she would speak for as long as she wanted to. She continued, her face flushed with excitement, her hair falling over her shoulders. But then, 'evidently on the verge of hysteria, she made a gesture of resignation and tumbled down the steps of the tribune'.[18] Lenin then rushed forward and escorted the exhausted Pankhurst out of the hall.

Sylvia left before the Congress ended, because even the Communist Party was not radical enough for her. Instead, as Roy put it, she preferred to be the leader of a small ineffectual sect which championed all sorts of lost causes. Ultimately, she sank into oblivion, still quite young. Roy himself was not going to make the mistake of being too idealist. 'I know of other equally passionate souls who came to Russia only to be disappointed and embittered; because they would not learn that Utopia could never be reached.'[19]

At the Comintern sessions of August 1920, Roy and Lenin were at odds. As befitted an idealistic young man, Roy believed that the Comintern should not support bourgeoise nationalist movements in India, such as the one led by the Indian National Congress. Instead, he believed that downtrodden Indian masses would be willing to join the revolution. He was considered over optimistic by many. Indeed, many observers believed that Roy 'greatly exaggerated both the numerical and ideological strength of the Indian proletariat'.[20]

Lenin, being older and wiser, did not share Roy's confidence in the strength of the Indian proletariat. His 'Indian thesis', as it came to be called, was radically different. He pointed out to Roy that it would take years before Indian workers and peasants could be effectively mobilised. Lenin believed that temporary relations needed to be established with other nationalist movements, even bourgeoise ones like that of the INC, if independence for India was to be achieved. Roy wanted to force the pace of change; to him, revolution from below was the way forward. Lenin, on the other hand, wanted revolution from above.

Roy would later change his views, but at that time he was an optimist, with Lenin playing the realist. Lenin admitted that he did not know much about India, but nevertheless, he considered Gandhi a revolutionary. Roy, by then an atheist, believed that Gandhi was a conservative reactionary socially and culturally, though he might be a revolutionary politically.[21]

The Comintern decided to accept both theses and arrived at an uneasy compromise, which was clarified by Lenin as, 'We Communists should and will support bourgeois liberation movements in the colonial countries only when these movements are really revolutionary, when the representatives of these movements do not hinder us in training and organising the peasants and the broad masses of the exploited in a revolutionary spirit.'

The Tashkent experiment

Meanwhile, new shoots of communism were blooming in India and across the world. The Berlin Indians, the Ghadar party in North America and labour activists in India were all flocking to the rising Soviet banner, attracted by Lenin's anti-imperialist leanings.

One such people were the 'muhajirs', the Muslim pilgrims who had left India during the First World War and arrived in Central Asia. The Balkan War between Britain and Turkey in 1912 and 1913 had mobilised anti-imperialist support for Turkey. Many Muslims saw the country as a driver of a new, modern, resurgent Islam.

By 1914, Lahore, a key centre for education and British colonialism, had become a hotbed of dissent. Colleges founded to further imperialism had ended up spawning anti-colonialism ideas. There were strikes, protests and meetings, all of which groomed the students for revolution.[22] In this environment, a brave student of the Lahore Government College, Khushi Mohammed, had formed a student group that held ideas such as setting the college premises on fire. By January 1915, Khushi Mohammed and his student group had decided to embark on a hijrat, the term for

Prophet Muhammad's flight from Mecca to Medina, which they reframed as a flight from British rule. The students were later called 'muhajirs', or those who performed hijrat. Most came from poor backgrounds. They fled to Afghanistan secretly and underwent a long and difficult journey, sheltering in mosques, walking for days and hiding from the British. In Afghanistan, they were welcomed by the locals. But the Afghani ruler Amir Habibullah wanted to be on the good side of the British, and so imposed restrictions on the muhajirs. The muhajirs became virtual prisoners in Afghanistan, confined to dirty and cramped quarters watched by guards, and living on very little. They attempted to form an army but were constantly foiled by the British and the Afghani governments.

In 1919, the British decided to invade Afghanistan, trying to capitalise on the chaos and uncertainty in government. But they were driven back by the Afghanis, aided by the muhajirs. Even so, the muhajirs realised that Muslim rulers were not prepared for a full holy war with the powerful British. An Anglo-Afghan peace treaty was signed, and with that the muhajirs decided to move to Central Asia where they could evade the British government's pursuit. They began to look for support to Russia, since the Bolsheviks were fighting their own war against the British.

Meanwhile, there was a similar exodus from Delhi. Following the Afghan victory, which thwarted the British invasion, a call for emigration to Afghanistan was given at a meeting in Delhi in April 1920 under the burgeoning Khilafat Movement, which held out new hope for Indian Muslims. Nearly forty thousand refugees, mostly poor peasants, women and children, crossed over to Afghanistan. Not all of them were motivated by anti-imperialistic concerns. Some simply wanted to escape poverty and oppression in India and believed that Afghanistan, ruled by a Muslim monarch, would be a haven of dignity and prosperity for them. Others were tired of being used as cheap soldiers in the Punjab army. Many of the weaker refugees died on the long and hard journey. Contrary to what the migrants had imagined, Kabul did not welcome them with open arms—the country did not have enough to sustain such a huge influx of refugees. The locals were resentful and unwelcoming and soon began to attack the migrants.

About two hundred of these migrants fled to Turkestan in the latter half of 1920. Despite being dressed in rags, and surviving on crusts, they were warmly welcomed by a sea of humanity consisting of the Central Asian Turkomans, Uzbeks and Russians, who greeted them with cheers and slogans of 'Long live the Indian revolution!', 'Long live the world revolution!' A military band played the *Internationale* and the *Red Flag* in their honour. In fact, Tirmiz (in present-day Uzbekistan) was a Bolshevik island, which governed itself through a committee of workers, peasants and students. There were no powerful landlords or aristocracy there.[23]

Meanwhile, the Comintern and Lenin sent M.N. Roy to the nearby city of Tashkent (capital of present-day Uzbekistan). His job was to provide military supplies and aid to the frontier tribes in order to stir up rebellion along India's borders with Afghanistan. Roy's procession into Tashkent must have made an incredible sight for the locals. He arrived like a modern-day Midas, dragging behind him two wagon-loads of gold coins, bullion and pound notes, as well as twenty-seven wagons of arms and ammunition, ten wagons of dismantled airplanes and the staff of a military training school.[24]

When Roy reached Tashkent, he found the muhajirs waiting. Most had come from Lahore, Amritsar and Peshawar. Soon they were joined by the Delhi refugees. Most were not educated or trained. Some were motivated by religion and wanted to join Mustafa Kemal's army in Turkey, but several also wanted to join the Indian revolutionary movement and were enamoured of the Bolsheviks. Roy began to winnow out the religious 'fanatics' from the rest to find the right people to train. Arms he had in plenty, but as he pointed out, 'What would most of them do with their guns, and whom would they fight, and for what ideal? Most were anti British but had no idea of what would happen when the British were driven out of India.'[25]

According to Roy, a committee was formed so that the muhajirs could manage their own affairs in a democratic manner. But soon there was a split within the group. Some wanted to follow the laws of their religion, while others were happy to embrace the 'atheist creed' of communism. Roy claimed that this atheist section pressured him to form a communist party, despite his insistence that there was no hurry. Thus, a small émigré communist party called the Indian Communist Party was formed in Tashkent in late October 1920. It had only seven members, and oddly, none were muhajirs.

The members were Roy and Evelyn, the Bengali communist Abani Mukherji and his Russian wife Rosa Fitingov, Chatto's erstwhile associate M.P.T. Acharya, Mohammad Ali (also known as Ahmad Hassan) and Mohammad Shafiq. Later, the veteran communist Muzaffar Ahmad would claim that Roy had grabbed power and seized Ahmad's chance to form a party. He also alleged that it was Roy and not the muhajirs who was the driving force behind the party. The party was called 'bogus' by some, mostly by those who supported Chatto.[26] Roy was described at this time as being 'self-important and ill-tempered in discussion, and often vehement in seeking to impose his opinions on others. But also, a courageous and determined man.'[27]

Amongst the many revolutionaries that Chatto and Roy associated with, the slippery Abani Mukherji stood out. He shared their penchant for living dangerously, associating with foreign women and eluding the secret service in several countries.

Abani's story began, like that of so many revolutionaries, in rural West Bengal. He was born in Jabalpore on 3 June 1891, but his family came from Khulna in West Bengal, which at the time was seething with militant nationalism. By the time he was fifteen, he was attending mass meetings in Calcutta, addressed by Tilak and other nationalists. The agenda of most of these meetings was to protest against the partition of Bengal.

In 1908, Abani set up an organisation of his own called United Bengal Home. By now he had moved on from protesting the partition of Bengal to calling for Indian independence. He got a job working as a weaving master, but then, exactly like M.N. Roy, he met Bagha Jatin. Jatin gave him the same advice he had given Roy: go to Japan and build revolutionary contacts in order to obtain arms. In Japan, Abani was known as something of a maverick. He was described as the 'madcap Abani Mukherji' who would force other Indian nationalists to 'parade even in winter, as a necessary preparatory step to organising revolutionary activities in India'.[28]

In 1912, Abani returned to India, where he began working in a mill. There, he first encouraged mill workers to form a union to protect themselves against exploitation and then to go on strike. Unfortunately, the strike turned violent and two Europeans ended up being assaulted. Abani had to flee and eventually reached Mathura, where he started working as a personal secretary.

In 1914, when the First World War broke out, Bagha Jatin once again asked Abani to go to Japan to get arms. In Japan, Abani met Lala Lajpat Rai, and like Agnes Smedley, started working as his secretary there. He also met Rashbehari Bose in Japan. But before Abani could do much, he was arrested in Penang, Malaysia, and then taken to Canning prison in Singapore.[29] There he spent several months doing hard labour, waiting to be court-martialled.

Every day, the prisoners were allowed to bathe in the sea under the vigilant eyes of armed guards. The area in front of the prison was frequented by small fishing boats. One morning Abani, who unlike most Indians was a good swimmer, slipped into the water, swam underneath and managed to hold on to a fishing boat. In the meantime, his German prison friends sang, swam and splashed loudly, distracting the guards. Abani's absence was unnoticed until over an hour had gone by. The prison authorities assumed he had been drowned or eaten by sharks.

The boat Abani had latched on to belonged to Japanese fishermen who detested the British. They took him to an island where he survived for some time on monkey nuts and water from a spring.[30] Eventually, he was rescued by Indonesian boatmen and ended up in Sumatra, where he started working as a labourer in the home of a Dutch planter. Abani assumed the name Dr Shaheer to pass off as Malay. During his time there, he became friendly with Indonesian socialists and Marxists. From Sumatra, Abani moved to Rotterdam, and then finally to Berlin, where he met M.N. Roy, Chatto and Bhupendranath Datta. Abani's daring escape from prison has been called too amazing to be true. However, it was corroborated by many people, including Roy, who was never Abani's biggest fan.

The Tashkent experiment in communism soon started to fail. Roy picked a fight with M.P.T. Acharya, calling him an anarchist. He suggested that Acharya return to India and organise a communist party there. Acharya was not prepared to do this because he feared arrest in India. In his turn, an annoyed Acharya suggested that Roy should be struck off the Communist Party rolls for his high-handedness. The dispute was eventually referred to Moscow, which came firmly down on the side of Roy as always. Acharya was forced to leave the Soviet Union, move around in Germany and other countries, and finally die in penury in India.

The Tashkent experiment eventually collapsed. Soviet Union decided not to ruin its relations with Britain for the sake of such an experimental project, and decided to disband the Central Asiatic Bureau of the Comintern. Nevertheless, the Tashkent committee will go down in history for having laid the foundation of what would subsequently become the Communist Party of India.

Roy, Abani Mukherji and the British Indian activist Clemens Palme Dutt wrote prolifically about India in journals on everything from communal riots to Gandhi's policies. The men would often be smuggled into India and helped form the thoughts of early Communists there. Some of the Tashkent émigrés, including Shaukat Usmani, returned to India and worked towards supplementing Roy's efforts. Eventually, the Tashkent Indians grew into the Communist Party of India. But in 1964 it split into two factions, the Communist Party of India (Marxist), which claimed that Roy and his Tashkent friends had founded Indian communism in 1920, and the Communist Party of India (CPI), which claimed that the party had actually been founded in Kanpur in 1925.

Roy also achieved one significant personal goal: outdoing his arch rival, Chatto. A decision was made by the Comintern to channel all communist activity in India through Roy rather than Chatto. Roy had destroyed all other claimants to the throne.

Meanwhile, twenty-two muhajirs were selected to be trained further in Moscow at the grandly named Communist University of the Toilers of the East, set up to train future communists from across the world. One of the foreign students studying at the university was Ho Chi Minh (born Nguyen Thanh), who years later would play a key role in the Vietnam war, become the first president of the Democratic Republic of Vietnam and have a city named after him. Ho Cho Minh had come to Moscow to learn the principles of communism, or as Roy put it, 'He was packed up and patted and passed on to Moscow as a leader of the revolt of the colonial peoples against imperialism'.[31]

In Moscow, Roy said, Ho Chi Minh threw himself into the café society, where 'he appealed not only to the revolutionary erotics of the communist girls, but also to the morbid romanticism of the down and out ladies of the old order'.[32] Nevertheless, as Roy pointed out, history had cast a role for the alumni of Moscow's Communist University, even if they were philanderers.

On the eve of his departure from Tashkent in 1921, Roy got a call from Abani Mukherji, who was terrified that he might be arrested for spying. Mukherji was much distrusted by most of the revolutionaries and had the reputation of being a troublemaker. Some sections thought he was a British spy. In fact, Roy apparently intervened to save him from being grabbed by some of Lenin's more bloodthirsty Bolshevik associates.[33]

On his return to Moscow from Tashkent, Roy learnt that a group of the Berlin Indians led by Chatto had arrived to seek support from Lenin. Among the fourteen-member delegation were Bhupendranath Datta, the brother of Swami Vivekananda, Agnes Smedley and Ghulam Luhani, all of whom would end up playing crucial roles in the tussle between the factions of Chatto and Roy. Roy later claimed that he had welcomed the Berlin Indians, but the newcomers had been immediately 'hostile'. The Berlin Indians it would seem, regarded the new Communist Party (Tashkent) as a challenge to their authority. Most of them, Roy complained peevishly, would not even speak to him.[34] Jealousy and dissension spread like wildfire. The Berlin Indians appeared suspicious of Roy and envious of his close relationship with Lenin, and Roy appeared rather contemptuous of their naivete and thin skin, by his own account.

Meanwhile, the Berlin Indians demanded an interview with Lenin. According to Roy, Lenin immediately called him and asked if it was necessary for him to see them. Roy apparently suggested that he should, but later, when Lenin met them, he was 'surprised' to hear that the revolutionaries were not well disposed towards Roy, his golden boy. Roy wrote in his memoir that he told Lenin that he did not represent anyone but himself. This, as the veteran communist Muzaffar Ahmad pointed out, was patently false, because Roy had represented the Mexican Communist party in the Second Congress of the Comintern and had always represented the émigré section of the Communist Party of India. Later, Roy would be elected to the Presidium of the Comintern as the Indian representative. One can only guess that Roy's seeming self-deprecation could have been a Machiavellian strategy to go under the radar and assume more power within the Comintern.[35]

Lenin had apparently asked Roy to select three representatives to speak to him, but Roy had asked him to contact them directly. That had caused a great flutter among the Berlin Indians on the matter of who should meet Lenin. Roy wrote that Agnes Smedley wanted to meet Lenin and was backed by Chatto but she was vetoed by the other Indians. Finally, Chatto and Bhupendranath Datta, along with a man named Kankhoje, were chosen to meet Lenin.

Lenin welcomed them, but to their great disappointment and anger, stated that the Soviet Union would not actively promote revolution in other countries. In order to assuage their feelings, Karl Radek, the general secretary of the Comintern, set up a small commission to hear the Indian delegation in more detail. Unfortunately for Chatto and the Berlin Indians, the commission consisted of the German communist August Thalheimer, Mikhail Borodin and Tom Quelch of the British communist party, all of whom were friends of Roy. Bhupendranath Datta gives an account of the disastrous meeting of the Berlin Indians with the commission in his book *Aprakashita Rajnaitik Itihas*.

As Chatto was a poor speaker, Ghulam Luhani spoke on his behalf before the commission, Smedley having been excluded once again. But all hell broke loose when Roy offered to be the guide for the Indian delegation in Moscow. According to Roy, Chatto sprang to his feet, and with great indignation interjected, 'We have nothing against you, but we cannot have anything to do with you, as long as you are associated with a known spy who has been responsible for the death of many revolutionaries in India'.[36]

He was referring to none other than the wily and slippery Abani Mukherji, whom the Berlin Indians believed to be a British spy. Chatto and his colleagues believed that he had not dramatically escaped from the Singapore prison but had been released because he had given the British information on the underground revolutionary movement in India. Roy was no friend of Abani's, but felt he could not penalise him without any evidence.

But this was not the only disagreement between the two factions. The Berlin Indian delegation did not approve of the formation of the Indian Communist Party in Tashkent and demanded its dissolution. Roy explained to them that he had been forced to form the party, but Chatto and the Berlin Indian delegation refused to accept this. They issued an ultimatum that they would leave Moscow if their demands were not accepted. There was also constant tension between Mikhail Borodin and Chatto, and Chatto even resolved to boycott the commission if Borodin remained a member.

Prior to the meeting with the commission, Chatto had sent his thesis to Lenin, and had received this frosty and terse reply:

> Dear Comrade Chattopadhyaya,
>
> I have read your thesis. I am in agreement with your views. We will have to destroy British imperialism.
>
> Signed,
>
> V.I. Lenin.

Bhupendranath Datta had also sent his thesis to Lenin, where he argued that a political revolution was needed first to free India from British rule, but a communist party should be organised immediately so that there could be a socialist revolution after the political one. Dutta got an even frostier reply from Lenin:

Dear Comrade Datta,

I have read your Thesis. We should not discuss about the Social Classes. I think we should abide by my Thesis on colonial question.

Lenin concluded by peremptorily ordering Dutta to gather statistical facts about the Peasants' League if it existed in India.

At the meeting, Roy's thesis was distributed, but when Dutta tried to read some of his thesis out loud to the commission, Dr Thalheimer replied, 'Our Indian comrades have read too much Karl Marx.' It was couched as a joke, but the insult was obvious. Finally, Agnes Smedley, while placing her comments before the commission, was asked pointedly, 'Comrade, being a member of IWW [International Workers of the World—a US trade union which also had a branch in the UK], how can you be such an English hater.' All in all, the Berlin Indians felt ignored and despised by their fellow Indians.

Eventually, after leaving the meeting in despair, Bhupendranath Datta went to meet Roy and Evelyn. Roy, after all his scheming, invited Dutta to stay in Moscow and said arrogantly, 'Do not feel sorry for my victory.' Datta replied, 'Roy, it is not true. Neither have you won, nor am I defeated. Now you make your career here, I make my career elsewhere.' Roy, always wanting the last word, replied cheekily, 'The world is big enough for everybody.'[37]

Roy had seemingly won. The Berlin Indians left Moscow by mid-1921, having accomplished nothing and leaving behind Roy as the uncontested darling of the Comintern and the confidante of Lenin. It was also in 1921 that Roy met Stalin, then a rising star in the party. He would have a lifelong blind spot for 'Koba', as Stalin was called by his inner circle, refusing to recognise Stalin's cult of personality and his tendencies towards dictatorship.

For some time, Stalin had been away from Moscow in the South of Russia defending the town of Tsaritsyn, which would later be called Stalingrad. On Stalin's return to Moscow, Lenin had asked Roy to meet the man to discuss colonial revolution and be directed by him. When Roy returned from Tashkent, he attempted to meet Stalin, but Koba at the time was dangerously ill. Defending Tsaritsyn had involved many hardships, including 'nine months of desperate fighting with no food except a meagre ration of dead horses' flesh'. Roy went to meet him anyway, accompanied by Borodin as a translator. Stalin struck Roy as a very sick and exhausted man, but 'his eyes shone penetratingly out of their sockets in the slightly pockmarked face'. The first question he asked was direct and blunt. 'So, you do not see the revolutionary significance of Pan-Islamism?'[38]

This question staggered Roy. He protested that he could not discuss politics with a man due to undergo an operation the next day. Their meeting was brief, but one significant incident marked it. Stalin had received a phone call during meeting and had whispered softly into the receiver in a commanding tone. Later Borodin told Roy that the call had been from the chief surgeon of the Kremlin who had explained that Stalin needed to have an empty stomach for the anaesthetic the next morning. But Stalin had replied, 'No anaesthetic for me. I must be conscious when my abdomen will be opened to see how it looks inside.' A major intestinal operation was thus performed with no anaesthetic.[39]

Roy and Stalin's paths crossed again in 1921 after Stalin had recovered his health. By then Stalin had been appointed to the powerful position of the People's Commissar of the Workers' and Peasants' Inspection, which marked the start of his meteoric rise in the Russian communist party. Stalin had also become the Chancellor of the Communist University of the Toilers of the East. 'I faced the memorable figure in the uniform of the Red Army soldiers, a cheerful grin on the pock-marked face, smoking a pipe which he filled with several cigarettes, crushed tobacco as well as paper. In his long Red Army soldier's coat and with the star marked peaked cap on, he looked taller than his five feet six inches,' wrote Roy later about their second meeting.[40]

At the time, Lenin and Roy held disparate views on colonial revolution. Roy believed that, if the nationalist movement succeeded under the leadership of the bourgeoisie INC, it would only mean transfer of power to the native ruling class. There would be no social revolution and things would go on very much the same as they had before, except that the peasants would have a different overlord. Lenin believed that the Comintern needed to support the INC at least initially so that India could achieve independence.

But Stalin won Roy over by agreeing that the nationalist movement led by the INC was immature and had no revolutionary ideology. Therefore, said Stalin, it must be strengthened by a well-trained revolutionary cadre, which could be trained at the Communist University for the Toilers of the East. This meeting with Stalin gave Roy confidence that the Bolsheviks might eventually come around to his point of view. Roy later wrote that Stalin was Machiavellian, aways appearing to agree with others, then amending his view without stating it baldly and then stating the result as a generally agreed upon opinion.

Roy went on to heap lavish praise on Stalin: 'His readiness to respect an independent judgement, provided that it did not amount to heresy against the common faith, raised my esteem for him.' Later, he even defended Stalin's tyrannical excesses, blaming them on his followers: 'Even today I believe that for the intellectual cowardice, the sordid desire to be on the bandwagon, and moral sycophancy on the part of his foremost followers in Russia as well as abroad, Stalin's leadership might not have degenerated into a disgusting cult of hero-worship.'[41] Roy would never come to see Stalin for what he truly was and would go to his death with a sneaking admiration for 'Uncle Joe', as Stalin was called by his fans.

By April 1922, Roy was regularly moving between Berlin and Moscow. He had also begun publishing and distributing a bi-monthly journal in India, called the *Vanguard of Indian Independence*, to spread communist insurgency. Important dailies like the *Amrita Bazar Patrika* and the *Independent* began echoing Roy's views.[42] The *Vanguard* called for the overthrow of foreign rule because it was obstructing national growth and making the Indian people backward. In the December 1922 issue of *Vanguard*, Roy rashly decried Gandhi's campaign for non-violence. 'We have repeatedly said that the premature resort to violent tactics may be playing into the hands of the enemy, but it is altogether erroneous to think there is such a thing as a non-violent revolution, no matter how peculiar and abnormal the situation in India may be.'[43] The *Vanguard* changed its name several times to avoid a clamp-down by the British. Roy and his wife Evelyn Trent filled the pages of *Vanguard* with calls to start a party for the poor working class, urging the INC to heed the call of the worker rather than that of the rich Gujarati businessmen who flocked to Gandhi.

As a result of Roy's efforts, small communist parties began to sprout across India, and a burgeoning labour movement took root. The INC had all but ignored the trade union movement in the past. In November 1922, the Comintern provided £70,000 for trade union work in India and £35,000 for party work.

A new crop of communists in India began to arise, the most committed of them being S.A. Dange from Mumbai. There was also Muzaffar Ahmad in Calcutta, M. Singaravelu Chettiar in Madras and Roy's old friend Shaukat Usmani, who had graduated from the Communist University of Toilers of the East. But the efforts of these communists remained scattered. To make a real difference, Roy needed to make inroads into the INC, which even the *Vanguard* acknowledged was 'the leader of the movement for national liberation'. But the *Vanguard* repeatedly emphasised that the party needed to work for the betterment of peasants and workers or it would become irrelevant.

Roy needed an ally in the INC. He found one in the form of Chittaranjan Das, a popular leader within the party, known as Deshbandhu or the 'friend of the nation'. Deshbandhu had socialist tendencies, and by getting arrested once for his links with the communists, had proved his mettle to Roy.

The 37th annual session of the Indian National Congress at Gaya convened in December 1922 was when Roy hoped to make his move. The session opened with clashes between Gandhi's followers and those of Das. Das gave a fiery speech in which he pronounced, 'I do not want that sort of Swaraj which will be for the middle-classes alone. I want Swaraj for the masses, not for the classes. I don't care for the bourgeoisie. How few are they?'[44] On the other hand, Gandhi wanted to call off the non-cooperation movement after the violent incidents that had taken place at Chauri Chaura, which was an unpopular decision. Gandhi also wanted the INC to boycott elections, while Das believed the party should contest.

In the end, at the Gaya session, the formation of an organisation of Indian labour 'with a view to improve and promote their well-being and secure them their just rights, and also to prevent the exploitation of Indian labour and Indian resources' was approved. But this was a meaningless sop, which amounted to nothing. The truth was that Das's and Roy's extreme views and Roy's tacit endorsement of violence had frightened the conservatives of the INC, who had branded them both Bolsheviks.

Later, in a blunt letter to C.R. Das, Roy urged him to start a third party inside the Congress, a 'party of workers and peasants, which will infuse vigour into the national struggle by means of revolutionary mass action'.[45] This Das did. On 9 January 1923, he formed the Swaraj Party along with Motilal Nehru, with the primary aim of contesting elections to the new Central Legislative Assembly. The party had initial success, but the sudden death of Das in 1925 led to its slow decay and eventual demise in 1935.

It was clear that Roy had overplayed his hand and frightened away most of the orthodox INC members with his anti-Gandhi stance, his emphasis on class struggle and his insistence on power to the peasants. His best opportunity to infiltrate the Congress had failed.

12

The Red Millionaire

It does not help matters much, by calling people with whom you may happen to disagree, little traitors and the like.

An angry Jawaharlal Nehru to Chatto in 1929

IN 1940, TWO FARMERS IN CAGNET IN SOUTHWESTERN FRANCE stumbled upon a grisly scene beneath an oak tree. They found the badly decomposed body of a man in his forties who had been garrotted with a noose. The official verdict of the French authorities was suicide. But many friends of the victim suspected it was murder.

The victim was Willi Munzenberg, a communist media mogul, agitator and propaganda 'tsar' for the Soviet Union. Munzenberg had deep impact across Europe and many friends in high places. In modern times, he might have been called an influencer.

One historian described his power thus: 'At the height of his influence, Munzenberg controlled from his Berlin headquarters a seemingly invincible network of Communist front organisations–charities, publishers, newspapers, magazines, and cinema houses, which stretched, on paper at least, from Buenos Aires to Tokyo. Many of the interwar period's most famous intellectuals–Albert Einstein, Bertolt Brecht, and John Dos Passos–came under his ever-expanding organisational spell.'[1]

When the Nazis came to power, their own propaganda head Joseph Goebbels immediately targeted Munzenberg. But Munzenberg was so powerful that he would also be tailed by Stalin's

NKVD (the Soviet Secret police). He would go down in history as a polarising figure. To his many fans in the liberal West, he was 'a hero whose fundraising campaigns built bridges between the ever fragile Soviet experiment in proletarian government and Western socialists. To his critics, Munzenberg was a dangerous media man who preyed on native fellow travelling sympathisers to reap a personal fortune: a Communist Hugenberg or a Red Millionaire.'[2]

Even his common law wife, Babette Gross, called him 'daemonic'. Gross, a writer and activist, wrote in her biography of him, 'Was he an adventurer who used whatever means he could find to satisfy his lust for power, or was he a political leader whom fate refused the fulfilment of his dreams? Was he the brilliant creator of the front organisations which carried the influence of Communism so far that an American senator once described him as a genius of organisation? All these conflicting verdicts have at some time or other been passed on Willi Munzenberg.'[3]

Whatever Munzenberg may have been, he and Chatto met in Berlin and found they had a common passion: a desire to set up an organisation which provided an alternative to the all-white, all-Western, mostly colonialistic League of Nations, founded in 1920 by the victorious allies of the First World War: Britain, France, Italy and Japan.

Enter the League Against Imperialism (LAI), the first alliance of nations that included colonised nations. There was considerable support for it from the Comintern. As early as 1913, in an editorial in *Pravda* titled 'Backward Europe and Advanced Asia', Lenin had supported the colonised nations of Asia. 'Everywhere in Asia a mighty democratic movement is growing, spreading and gaining in strength. Hundreds of millions of people are awakening to life, light and freedom. Young Asia has a reliable ally in the proletariat of all civilised countries.'[4] When the Soviets later took control of Russia in the October Revolution, they made public and then abrogated the secret treaties that Czar Nicholas had made with the other European powers to divide up the 'darker nations' among themselves.

Chatto and Munzenberg had wanted to hold a Congress on anti-imperialism in Berlin, but the then Weimar government had refused permission. They were also refused by the French government. Finally, the Belgian government allowed them to hold the Congress in Brussels. This was deeply ironic, given Belgium's terrible colonial record in the Congo where it had inflicted a number of atrocities on the native people. But Chatto and Munzenberg decided to go ahead with the venue anyway. Soon word began to pour in from across the colonies: India, Indonesia, Egypt, Arabia, Korea and China. The event was covertly funded in part by the Soviet Comintern, in part by the Chinese Kuomintang party and in part by the Mexican government of Plutarco Elias Calles. The first Congress on anti-imperialism took place on 10 February 1927 in the Palais d'Egmont, one of the many grand and ornate palaces scattered around Brussels.

Delegates from countries under colonial rule were in the majority—107 out of 175 total delegates were from countries such as India, China, Syria, Korea, Japan, South Africa and Arabia. They worked on resolutions to address various acts of injustices across the world, from the tragedy of the Indian farmer to that of racism in the United States, from the growth of Italian fascism to the danger of Japanese intervention in Korea.

Many subjects were discussed at the Congress, but British imperialism dominated the agenda. Nehru spoke on the opening day and took care to emphasise the international nature of India's fight for independence, saying that neighbouring countries like Afghanistan, Burma, Persia and Mesopotamia were also deprived of their independence by the English to safeguard India.[5] British delegates, including the anti-war activist Fenner Brockway, Harry Pollitt and George Lansbury spoke about the brutality of the British regime in India and China. Albert Einstein and Maxim Gorky sent letters of encouragement. On the last day of the Congress, Nehru tabled a resolution. It gave the INC support for the liberation of India and stated that the world could only be fully liberated if India were liberated. The resolution also expressed its hope that the Indian national movement would base its programme on the full emancipation of the peasants and workers of India, without which there could be no real freedom.[6] The resolution was passed. Nehru's early socialist and internationalist leanings were apparent.

In another joint statement, delegates from Britain, China and India agreed to a plan to fight for full emancipation along with national forces in oppressed countries to secure complete independence, to oppose all forms of coercion against the colonised and to aid the working class.[7] African matters were not discussed in detail, but a resolution was tabled on the 'Negro Question' which called for the liberation of the 'Negro Race'.[8]

At the end of the Congress, delegates voted to continue their work through the founding of a new organisation called the League Against Imperialism and for National Independence (LAI).

Many delegates from the colonies would go on to say how deeply influenced and moved they were by this first Congress. Nehru, who attended as a representative of the INC, was one such delegate. Another was the Indonesian leader Mohammed Hatta, who would be influenced by his experiences in Brussels to argue for independence from the Dutch colonial regime. Hatta would be arrested and imprisoned by the Dutch in 1927. Later, he would become Indonesia's first vice president. At subsequent meetings of the LAI, many leaders of formerly colonised nations would refer to the Brussels event as a crucial foundation for the creation of solidarity across the borders of the colonised world, bringing together people who had never had a chance to meet before.

In spite of his admiration for the LAI, Nehru was a realist. He wrote to Gandhi later that he did not expect much support from the LAI and he was quite sure that none of the members of the league would help India if their interests conflicted. But he was also an internationalist. He did not think it was sensible for India to 'go it alone now or in the future'. He welcomed 'all legitimate methods of getting in touch with other countries and peoples so that we may be able to understand their viewpoint and world politics generally'.[9] Gandhi himself was not optimistic. He was suspicious of the Comintern's support of the LAI. He wrote to Nehru, 'I myself do not expect much from this league because its free activity depends upon the goodwill of the very powers that are partners in the exploitation of the oppressed nations.'[10]

Chatto held an important position at the International Secretariat of the LAI as the international political secretary. His job was to reorganise the LAI network with an emphasis on his individual contacts and to turn the LAI into a centre for anti-imperialist activists in Berlin and the rest of Europe. Organising the LAI and meeting anti-imperialists from all over the world would help Chatto feel less lonely in his forced exile, though only briefly. Chatto was the perfect man for this job because he had contacts with both the communists, through Munzenberg, and in India, through Nehru. His language skills were also useful. By now, he spoke French, German and Swedish, in addition to the other languages he already spoke.

Nehru was not very impressed by most of the Indian political exiles, a lot of whom had been mostly forgotten by those back home, though he admired their sacrifices. He would meet several of them, but the only ones who impressed him were Chatto and Roy.

In 1927, Nehru and his sister Krishna Hutheesing met Chatto for the first time in Brussels for the opening Congress on anti-imperialism. Nehru described Chatto as 'a very able and a very delightful person. He was always hard up, his clothes were very much the worse for wear, and often he found it difficult to raise the wherewithal for a meal. But his humour and light-heartedness never left him.' Nehru remarked on Chatto's homesickness and the pull of home that he still carried despite his ties with home being severed. 'No exile can escape the malady of his tribe, that consumption of the soul, as Mazzini called it.'[11]

Nehru was a staunch supporter of the league in its early years. He wrote numerous friendly letters to Chatto in 1928, discussing matters to do with the league. In a particularly poignant one, he counselled Chatto to not return home because he would likely be arrested. 'You write to say that you feel very tired and homesick. I can understand the feeling but I do not suppose you would feel happy if you were nearer home. Things are pretty dull here and it is extremely difficult to wake people up. And the feeling of being tired is common enough here too, the only difference being that it is not the result of work but of doing nothing.'[12]

In 1928, Nehru wrote a long and frank pro-labour foreword for a book in which he said, 'I have had the privilege of being associated with the League since its formation at the Congress held in Brussels in February 1927. I welcomed its formation because I felt that it supplied a common platform for the two great movements of revolt against the existing conditions which we have in the world today, the struggle of labour against the entrenched citadel of capital and the nationalist movements in countries under alien domination.'[13]

Nehru went on to argue that the independence of colonial countries was essential to their inhabitants obviously, but was equally necessary for the much-abused European working class because their lot would not be improved as long as the labour of colonial countries continued to be exploited. The LAI, he said, was the first group of nations which recognised the common cause of Western labour and colonised people. That alone, argued Nehru, was worth its formation. 'During the year of its existence it has already brought nearer together the various peoples of Asia and Africa struggling for freedom, and it has made them realise in some measure that there is a bond between them and the worker of the West. And gradually even national movements like the Indian National Congress, conservative in their social outlook, are beginning to look towards the socialist ideal of society,' wrote an optimistic Nehru. He went on to savagely criticise the British Labour party, which was in power at that time, for acting as 'full blooded imperialists indistinguishable from the more blatant variety belonging to the Tory Party'.[14]

Years later, Krishna and Nehru visited Berlin where they met the lonely Chatto again. By then, Chatto had been away from home for a quarter of a century, living a life of precarious poverty, constantly staying one step ahead of the law. He yearned for family, but he had only a string of disastrous affairs to look back on. Krishna writes that even the stoic Chatto—a man who had risked death for anarchy—had tears in his eyes as they parted. 'I remember the last smile on his lips which quivered though he tried not to show it. And so, we parted, leaving him a lonely, desolate figure on the platform—we to our home, comfort and security, and he back to his life of hardship, uncertainty and loneliness.'[15]

Nehru and Krishna would continue to hear from Chatto for a few more years, but then eventually the news would stop coming.[16]

Meanwhile, Berlin was also the scene of a long overdue family reunion for Chatto. He had last seen his youngest brother Harindranath when he had been only two years old. They likely met in November 1927 for the first time as adults. Harindranath wrote of the long overdue meeting: 'When my train arrived in Berlin ... the first question he asked was "You are Harin?". Then in Hindi he spoke to me "*Thum Hindi bol sakthey ho? Hindi mey bolo! Yahan ke log English se nafrat karte haen* (Do you speak Hindi? Speak in Hindi. The people here have a hatred for the English language)."'[17]

Harin described Chatto as a short, well-set, swarthy man, dressed in a suit which looked like it had not been ironed for months, the trousers which had long ago 'forgotten the idea of creases'. Harindranath tried to guess Chatto's thoughts behind his façade of good cheer. 'His face distinctly said "I am an exile, and forgive the loneliness in my face. I have tried to hide it under a constant smile of courage but sometimes the thought of being away from one's home, one's motherland, one's own people, becomes unbearable."'[18]

Chatto approved of Harindranath's young wife who accompanied him, the beautiful, aristocratic, and highly intellectual Kamaladevi Chattopadhyay. Kamaladevi would go on to become a prominent social reformer and a pioneer of Indian handlooms, handicrafts and theatre. Later, she would win a Padma Bhushan for her work.

But it was her exquisite looks that won Chatto over. Chatto made a comment that by today's standards would be highly distasteful but was taken as a compliment by Harindranath. He said, 'I am glad you have married a pretty person and brought her along with you. We need beautiful women from India to visit Europe. Usually, the ugliest women come out from India as students and visitors–women disappointed in love or cast away. The people here think that India has nothing to show.'[19]

Chatto also referred to Hagenbeck's zoo and the people it exhibited in dubious terms. 'A German showman paid handsomely and brought a number of the vilest specimens of men and women from Southern India and locked them up in cases, and exhibited them at a mighty exhibition in Berlin during the war. "Indian Zoo" it was labelled. We have got to counteract all the filthy propaganda which imperialism makes *(sic)* to lower our country in the estimation of the world.'[20]

Harindranath was invited to the celebrations of the tenth anniversary of the Russian Revolution. He wrote of how he composed a Hindi version of the *Internationale*, because India was the only country that had not contributed its version. 'I wrote it within half an hour. Virendranath gasped with excitement and said "Congratulations".'[21]

Harindranath heard Chatto's opinion of the chameleon-like Har Dayal, by now long gone to Sweden for refuge, who was apparently a 'veritable genius during the first half of every hour, and a pretty Polly prattling nonsense, a dull-as-ditch-water creature during the second half'. Har Dayal could apparently solve every political problem in the first half hour of conversation, but thereafter his brain would gradually 'dwindle like a dying ember'.[22]

Chatto took Harindranath around Berlin, and the two brothers got to know each other. By now, Chatto was something of an agent provocateur who enjoyed shocking people, especially newcomers to Berlin. One of Chatto's favourite hobbies, apparently, was to horrify Hindu visitors by recommending they drink beer and eat beef, otherwise they would not be able to fight or win freedom.

The irreverent Chatto also liked to criticise *Vande Mataram*, then the de facto national anthem. He would roll his eyes to heaven in assumed ecstasy, and then intone quite seriously 'Vande Mataram', drawing out the word 'Vande' as if chewing gum. Harindranath described him as saying, 'By the time you have finished with that whole length of agony, any conqueror could finish the whole lot of you Indians with one round of machine gunnery taking its own time to emit its bullets dipped in contempt of the whole nation and its mournful National Anthem.'[23]

When Harindranath and Kamala left Berlin, Chatto was in tears. His deep homesickness was finally apparent. He asked in a choked whisper, 'If I came back to India in disguise, would not my people hide me and give me protection?' Chatto argued desperately that if he could hide underground, he could 'drive out the British in a week'.[24] But Harindranath told him that India had traitors in every corner who would betray him, and persuaded him not to return.

As the train pulled out, Harindranath and Kamala could not speak for a long time, choked as they were with tears. That same year, Sarojini Naidu visited Berlin. She addressed Indian students at the Hindustan Association of Central Europe on 8 October

1927 and urged them to win independence on their own and not through foreign help.

A.C.N. Nambiar covered her speech in his column. 'Young India applauded. Only in her own family she finds opposition. Her son and her brother listened patiently, but one learnt afterward that they are not at all of the same opinion ... they await salvation from Moscow.'[25]

But Chatto and Sarojini must have patched up their disagreements because Chatto agreed to act as a local guardian for her son Jayasurya Naidu. In 1928, Sarojini visited Berlin again, ostensibly to supervise her son's studies at Humboldt University. The real reason was to work with Chatto, according to some authorities.[26]

Piecemeal efforts were made to further the LAI's reach in India. But India was a challenge for the LAI because of tough scrutiny and control by the British secret service. It was difficult to circulate money and propaganda in India. So, envoys from the Communist Party of Great Britain (CPGB) were sent. In September 1928, British journalist Lester Hutchinson, a member of the Communist Party of Britain, was sent to India to further LAI's interests. When he arrived in Bombay, he became the editor of the left-wing paper *New Spark* where he met Chatto's sister Suhasini, also a die-hard communist. Suhasini's husband A.C.N. Nambiar had by then left her and she had returned, distraught and lonely, to Bombay. According to some sources, Suhasini had an affair with the dashing Hutchinson.[27]

Chatto and Nambiar started the Berlin Indian Students Information Bureau, also called The Indian Bureau, in February 1929. The aim of the Indian Bureau was to recruit Indian anti-colonialists in Berlin. In 1930, Chatto sent a report to the Eastern Secretariat with the title 'Courses for Colonial Students in Berlin', where the bureau was described as 'extremely useful as a centre for recruiting students, for finding out the best and most reliable among them to take up the question of sending literature and also for obtaining journals, books and other literature on India, which are not directly available without payment by the League.'[28]

But by 1929, the LAI was sinking. Right from its messy beginning the organisation had been dogged by accusations, including some from socialists, of being too close to the Soviet Union and of being a communist front organisation. Indeed, one of its most savage critics, surprisingly, was Chatto's old friend and fellow anarchist, M.P.T. Acharya. Acharya thought the LAI 'was an organ bound to the Bolshevik state for its foreign propaganda purposes'.[29] He also believed the Bolsheviks were no friends to the Indian peasants. The Brussels Congress, Acharya thought, was a distraction from the independence movement in India. Instead, he believed leaders needed to work towards independence in their own countries without seeking foreign solidarity. He was not alone in this view. Acharya would eventually fall out with Chatto over this and other differences of opinion and move towards anarchism.

The second World Congress of the LAI took place in Frankfurt on 21 July 1929. Delegate after delegate attacked the British Labour government for its colonial policy in India, which would later make the British government take action against the LAI.

Meanwhile, relations between Chatto and Nehru were steadily deteriorating. Chatto wanted Nehru to support organisations outside the INC and to associate with workers' and peasants' organisations, trade unions and cooperatives, not just the upper classes and bourgeoisie represented in the INC. But this was not Nehru's plan. He wanted INC unity above all—not a separate organisation outside it. He was prepared to veer towards socialism, but that was as far as he would go.

Nehru began to feel badgered by the incessant demands from LAI and Chatto. By now, the LAI had transformed into a communist organisation and Chatto had started feeling a deep distrust of Gandhi, whom he considered a fence-sitter in every way and an enemy of the working class.

In October 1929, Lord Irwin, the then Viceroy of India, made a vague offer to grant India the status of a dominion and suggested convening a Round Table Conference to discuss the same. Dominion status would mean that India would retain the king of Britain as its constitutional head and the British parliament would continue to keep all political power in India. Nehru and Subhas Chandra Bose were against dominion status and were pushing for complete independence, but the cautious Gandhi and other moderates in the Congress were willing to negotiate a middle path. Gandhi had his way, and the Delhi Manifesto or Delhi Statement of 1929 was issued, pledging that the INC would attend a conference to discuss dominion status for India. Nehru accepted this for the sake of INC unity. But it was the kind of wishy-washy compromise that enraged Chatto, who would never be satisfied with anything less than complete independence.

In 1929, Nehru also agreed to preside over the Lahore session of the INC. A disappointed Chatto wrote to Nehru, 'In your new position of President elected on the initiative of Gandhi, your hands will be completely tied, and any action that you might have otherwise taken as a leader of the independence movement will be paralysed by the necessity of having to remain impartial inside the Congress.'[30]

Chatto's temper, never under the best of control, got away with him. He berated Nehru for surrendering to 'the traitors who are negotiating for their own class interests' and for not resigning from the Congress immediately. An immediate resignation, argued Chatto, would have rallied the workers and peasants to Nehru's side. 'It is a fundamental error to think that unity in the Congress is more important than the vital interests of the masses.' He went on to flay Nehru for his weakness and mental confusion, and called upon him to drive out moderates and the men who supported dominion status.[31]

Nehru was not going to be preached to by Chatto; he responded quickly and strongly. Ever the Congress man, he believed the Congress should remain united in its goals, even if he himself wanted complete independence. By now, he had serious misgivings about the labour movement in India and their intentions.

Nehru also had begun to feel that the revolutionaries abroad knew nothing of what was actually happening on the ground and of the often delicate negotiations taking place with the British government. He hit back, accusing Chatto of being out of touch with events in India and saying that cooperation with him would be difficult because they had fundamental differences. 'In any event, it does not help matters much by calling people with whom you may happen to disagree little traitors and the like. Perhaps if you came in personal contact with some of our most aggressive young men who pose as workers' leaders, you might change your opinion of them.'[32] Chatto had gone too far with his zeal.

Nehru then wrote bluntly to the LAI Secretariat, 'I am afraid you have not the least notion of conditions in India and yet you do not hesitate to lay down the law for us. The National Congress has welcomed your League and has agreed to cooperate with you, but it cannot tolerate outside interference of the kind you have been carrying on.'[33]

As it turned out, by December 1929, the INC would tire of the British government's excuses and pass a resolution at the Lahore Session demanding 'Purna Swaraj' or complete independence, bowing to popular sentiment. Gandhi would simultaneously launch his campaign of non-cooperation. But it seemed even this was not enough for Chatto.

Meanwhile, the LAI was having great difficulty in making inroads into India. In 1928, Nehru sent a message to the International Secretariat asking Chatto to send a delegate to the

INC conference in Calcutta. Munzenberg asked Chatto's advice on how to proceed, saying he did not have the time and energy to find a candidate in Berlin.[34] An American member of the Comintern, Jack W. Johnstone was told to travel to India as the LAI representative and to deliver a speech at the INC conference. As it turned out, this was a terrible move. Johnstone ended up being imprisoned for sixteen days right after his speech. He was then deported to Genoa, Italy, where he was again arrested. There was a global outcry. Johnstone was released eventually, but this only confirmed the LAI's difficulty in gaining traction in India, which was closely guarded by the British authorities. They could not do the simplest thing there: give speeches, organise meetings or hand out propaganda.

The LAI gradually began to sway towards the Comintern and so too did Chatto. He'd had communist sympathies for years, but they had been secondary to his nationalist and anarchist interests. But by now he was a full-fledged communist, probably because he had begun to see that collaboration with the Congress and Nehru was futile.[35] Being a keen observer of the increasing number of strikes in India, and the terrible conditions of Indian workers in textiles, railways and agriculture, he wrote, 'The only improvement in their lot is possible by the complete overthrow of imperialism and the establishment of a workers' and peasants' republic.'[36]

By the summer of 1930, Chatto had begun to see the Soviet Union as 'the only genuinely anti-imperialist state in the world'.[37] He had grown impatient with Congress leaders and what he saw as their obfuscation and cooperation with the British state.

By this time, his delicate relationship with his sister Sarojini had also collapsed. He did not hold back in his opinion of her. Chatto was scathing of Sarojini's friendship with Gandhi and called her a 'mere puppet placed in charge of the theatrical side of the campaign, while the wiser and cleverer heads are keeping their hands free for negotiations with the imperialist government'.[38]

Chatto also flayed Indian nationalist leaders for working with Japanese imperialists in spite of their brutal terror campaigns in Korea and China. He believed it was immoral for nationalists of one oppressed nation to betray the freedom of other oppressed nations by allying with any imperialist nation.

In April 1930, a stung and angry Nehru, tired of Chatto's preaching, instructed the INC to stop corresponding with the LAI. In retaliation, Nehru and several other non-communist members were expelled from the LAI in 1931. That was the year the Karachi session was held, where Chatto openly accused the INC of being in alliance with the British, despite its new demand for complete independence, adding that Gandhi was a traitor to the working class. 'The Karachi Congress represents the final and definite transition of the Indian bourgeoisie from the partial struggle against imperialism which they had carried on for a short while, into open alliance with British imperialism against the Indian revolution,'[39] he wrote in a fiery article, finally burning his bridges with the INC.

The Indonesian leader Mohammed Hatta would leave the LAI too, reducing the LAI's reach in Asia. Slowly, the LAI would lose its support in Europe as well, its position becoming increasingly wobbly as the Nazi party began to cast its dark shadow over the continent. In December 1931, its Berlin headquarters were raided by the police. In 1933, the LAI's international secretariat had to flee from Berlin to Paris and then to London, the last outpost against the Nazis. Even in Britain, members of the LAI were persecuted. Eventually, the LAI fell into obscurity. It was described as 'carrying through a very important function during a certain period, and like other organisations that outlive their usefulness, has passed into history'.[40]

Despite its short life, the LAI had a far-reaching impact. Nearly twenty-eight years later, Chatto and Munzenberg's anti-colonial vision was revived at the 1955 Afro-Asian conference held in Bandung, Indonesia. Nehru and the Indonesian president Sukarno were the chief organisers of the conference, and representatives from twenty-nine countries across Asia and Africa attended. By then, many of these countries had liberated themselves from colonialism, but the shadow of the Cold War loomed. It was the dawn of the global south. Those who attended included Premier Zhou En-Lai of China, President Gamal Abdel Nasser of Egypt and leaders from Liberia, Sudan, Jordan, Iran, Ceylon, Nepal, Pakistan and the Philippines. At the conference, Sukarno announced, 'I recognise that we are gathered here today as a result of sacrifices. I recall in this connection the Conference of the "League against Imperialism and Colonialism" which was held in Brussels almost thirty years ago.' The Bandung conference ended with a ten-point plan for the countries present to ally together in their own interests, very similar to the LAI's plan to fight colonialism. All this could be said to have been inspired by Chatto's initiative and hard work.

By 1961, Nehru would be one of the co-founders of the Non-Aligned Movement, along with Josip Broz Tito of Yugoslavia and Gamal Abdel Nasser of Egypt. Its chief aim was to abstain from allying with the US or the USSR in the prevailing Cold War and to join together to fight colonialism and imperialism. This was not much different from the LAI's main aim. Indeed, the NAM owed much to Chatto's early vision of an alliance of non-Western countries, but his contribution, of course, was long forgotten. The NAM would grow to include a hundred and fifteen countries.

In the ultimate irony, as Chatto's biographer Nirode Barooah later explained, M.N. Roy would eventually end up stealing Chatto's thunder. Chatto had always advocated for a united front against the British, but by 1930, he had started thinking of the INC as a petit bourgeois organisation that would not help the working class, and so he had distanced himself from both Nehru and the INC. In this vacuum, Roy swooped in to embrace Chatto's previous theories and announced that a united front was necessary to defeat the British, advising the communists to ally with Congress. The tussle with Nehru resulted in Chatto being elbowed out of Indian politics for his uncompromising views. But he would go to his death sticking to his convictions.

What of Munzenberg, the man who had co-founded the LAI? By 1939, Munzenberg had seen Stalin for what he was, a brutal tyrant. He came out openly against Stalin, calling him a traitor to the revolution. 'Soviet Russia is no more,' he announced. 'There is only a Russia which has announced its imperialist ambitions with fire and sword.'[41] He threw off his guise as a Russian propaganda tsar, denounced Stalin's great purge and attempted to break with his communist past.

But it would not be so easy for him to escape. Munzenberg's lonely death ten years later in 1940 would end up being one of the great enigmas of twentieth-century politics. By then, Stalin had already murdered many of Munzenberg's allies, so it seems likely that his secret police did away with Munzenberg too. But the murder of Munzenberg was never actually solved.

As one historian put it, 'Munzenberg, having latched so passionately onto the Bolshevik cause, was unable to sever the many cords that now linked his own fate with Bolshevism. He was in the end, a victim of the same ruthless revolutionary energy that had given meaning to his life.'[42] And like his close friend the charismatic Red Millionaire, Chatto too would be unable to break with the many ties and alliances that had dominated his chaotic life.

13

La Guillotine: The Downfall of M.N. Roy

For some time I have been standing before the sacred guillotine, the mad application of which is causing such a havoc to the International Communist movement. I have stood in that position for nearly a year, not shuddering with the fear for my head, but aghast at the incompetence of those who have usurped the leadership of the movement.

M.N. Roy

LENIN WAS DEAD. IT WAS 21 JANUARY 1924. THE GLORIOUS ICON OF the Russian revolution had finally succumbed to the long-drawn effects of the bullets dispatched into his body six years earlier by Fanny Kaplan. A series of strokes had weakened him, even though he was only fifty-four. His body was embalmed and placed in a gleaming red granite mausoleum at Red Square as millions wept across the world. His widow Nadezhda Krupskaya sat quietly by his side while masses of weeping workers filed by crying 'Ilyich!'

Lenin's prodigious brain had an even more gruesome fate. In an effort to understand the man's genius, it was sliced into thirty-one thousand wafer thin slivers, mounted on glass and stored behind three locked doors at the Moscow Brain Research Institute in large wooden cabinets. Years later, in 1993, after studying it in detail, the institute head would conclude that it was 'nothing special'. Lenin's brain, it appears, was just an ordinary brain.[1]

With Lenin's death began the fall of his bright young acolyte, M.N. Roy. By then, Roy had been elected a full member of the Comintern and had many close friendships with Russian leaders. But he was sucked into the factional struggle that began after Lenin's death. The tussle for power ended in Trotsky, Bukharin and many leaders of the old guard being eliminated, and Stalin battling his way to the top. Roy, as has been mentioned before, had a blind spot where Stalin was concerned and did not foresee the brutality that was to come.

The year 1924 was an annus horribilis for Roy. He had to draw upon all his resources to evade the British police. Roy's travails had begun even before Lenin's death, in the second half of 1923. In September 1923, he was forced to tour Europe looking for a safe place to print *Vanguard*, traipsing through Paris, Genoa and Amsterdam, eventually ending up in Zurich, where the Swiss were still famously neutral.

About a month after Lenin's death, Roy wrote a letter to the British prime minister Ramsay MacDonald pleading for amnesty for his previous terrorist acts in West Bengal when he had been a member of the Anushilan Samiti. He drew attention to the fact that his political views had changed radically and asked for permission to return to India. 'I suppose the declaration made by his Majesty the King Emperor in 1919 concerning Indian political offenders can be made applicable to me,' wrote Roy with his usual cheekiness.

The declaration that Roy was referring to granted royal amnesty to those who had been detained for political crimes and commuted the sentences of those who had less than a year to serve. It had been issued by King George V shortly after the government had scrapped the brutal Rowlatt Act and closed the notorious jail at the Andaman Islands where Veer Savarkar had been imprisoned for years. It was in effect an olive branch proffered to Indian revolutionaries.

Roy even asked if he could come to England while the issue was being decided. He never lacked in chutzpah. But before any decision could be taken, a slew of 'conspiracies' cooked up by the British government hit the fledgling Indian communist movement at its root. The first was the Peshawar conspiracy case, under which the British police arrested the muhajirs who had returned from Tashkent to Peshawar. From 1921 to 1927, five conspiracy cases were launched and a series of sham trials were held in Peshawar. Several muhajirs were arrested and sentenced to rigorous imprisonment.

Despite the British government's actions, communist activities began afresh in the big cities. In March 1924, the British government began another campaign targeting Roy. They arrested Roy's old friend Shaukat Usmani and the respected communist veteran Muzaffar Ahmad in Kanpur. Thus began the Cawnpore (now called Kanpur) conspiracy case, another sham cooked up by the British to contain communism in India. Several of Roy's associates were also arrested, including S.A. Dange, M. Singaravelu Chettiar, Nalini Gupta and Ghulam Hussain. Roy himself was accused, but could not be detained since he was in Germany at the time. The specific charge against them was that the communists had sought 'to deprive the King Emperor of his sovereignty of British India, by complete separation of India from Britain by a violent revolution'. Eventually, Muzaffar Ahmad, Shaukat Usmani, S.A. Dange and Nalini Gupta were punished with rigorous imprisonment for four years. Dange and Ahmad were released after a year because of illness.

The Cawnpore conspiracy case was also notable for the schisms it exposed within the fledgling communist movement. Dange and Gupta were accused of being British spies because they had written letters to the British government. Even forty years later, in 1964, Dange would continue to be accused of being a communist spy by opposing factions of Indian communists after the Communist Party of India split into the CPI and the CPI (M).

Some of the accusations against Roy in the Cawnpore conspiracy case were ridiculous. He was accused of conspiring to kill the unpopular Abani Mukherji because of a letter Roy had written that had been wrongly translated. This was a letter to Nalini Gupta in 1923 asking after Abani, who had by then returned to India and broken with Mukherji. The letter said, 'Where is that vagabond gone? Is he still in the country? If he comes here, I shall perform his Shradh (death ceremony). I shall not make any mistake this time.' This was actually a Bengali expression which meant 'taking one to task', but it was taken too literally by the translator. Roy was accused by British intelligence of plotting to kill Mukherji, while the wily Mukherji managed to return to the Soviet Union with the help of his wife Rosa, a Soviet citizen.[2]

The Cawnpore conspiracy case created rifts between the various communist groups. However, the communist movement also greatly benefited from the splashy newspaper headlines and press interest that the case generated. Roy himself wrote in November 1924 that the Kanpur case had increased the public's interest in communism. 'People have got used to hearing things which had simply terrified them before. We must prepare to begin the struggle for the legalisation of our party.'

By 1925, Roy was being constantly hunted by the British police. He even wrote to the then French President Gaston Doumergue, pleading for refuge. 'The British police have pursued me step by step, from one country to another, from Java to Japan, from China to Philippines, to America, to Mexico, and through most of the countries to Europe.'

Then came another blow in March 1929: the Meerut conspiracy case, the last in a long line of conspiracy cases that would prevent Roy from returning to India. Once again, Roy was accused and once again, his chief associates S.A. Dange and Muzaffar Ahmad were among those charged. The Meerut conspiracy case dragged on for four and a half years. Thirty-one people were charged, including the British communists and trade union leaders Philip Spratt, Lester Hutchinson (the alleged one-time lover of Suhasini Nambiar) and Benjamin Bradley. It was even thought that Nehru might be charged for his dealings with the communists.

The status of the Meerut conspiracy case hung precariously on the Assembly Letter, dated 30 December 1927, written by Roy in a secret code and dispatched to India through the British Indian communist Clemens Palme Dutt. It was called so because it had been read out in the Central Legislative Assembly on 10 September 1928.

In this controversial letter, Roy explained the need to form an 'illegal Communist party, a rallying ground of all exploited social elements'. But he also suggested another party, a Workers and Peasants Party (WPP) which could act as a legal distraction and evade the clutches of the law. According to British intelligence, the WPP was intended to 'throw dust in the eyes of the thinking public, lest the word communist should frighten people away'. This shadowy and disguised communist party was to be a much broader organisation.[3] The letter also said that the communist party in India must unquestionably be a section of the Comintern and follow their instructions. Roy, however, denied writing this letter.

The British government lost no time in cracking down. Roy and the other accused were immediately charged under Section 121 of the Indian Penal Code for 'conspiring to overthrow the sovereignty of King George V in India and attempting to establish a socialist state under the dictatorship of the proletariat and the supreme command of the Communist International'.[4]

Before the sessions court trying the Meerut conspiracy case, the question of whether the accused had intended to use violence came up and it was argued that he had. A number of cases were cited to show that members of the Communist Party of India supported violence. Philip Spratt had said at a conference in Malda in Bengal, 'We need not be careful to disguise the brutal, blood thirsty side of our proposal. We say these things are inevitable.' Dange had said in Bombay, 'Communism is this: if the state is based on violence, it cannot be overthrown but by violence.' And even the faraway Chatto's letter from Moscow to Nehru was cited as saying, 'But I hope this time there will be no sentimental nonsense about shedding a few litres of blood and that the revolutionary movement will be led on purely materialistic lines by trained Marxian revolutionaries.'[5]

That was all the evidence the British needed to proceed. The prosecutor for the case, Langford James, gave a biting, even darkly amusing speech where he flayed Marxism, Lenin and the Russian Revolution as a sham intended to benefit only the Bolsheviks and not the peasants. 'The Communist State has proved to be a practical impossibility,' thundered James. 'In spite of the fact that everybody now knows that the millennium can never be reached in practice and in fact, we have this monotonous bleating going on from Moscow in favour of the dictatorship of the proletariat, the betterment of the peasant, the betterment of the worker and so on ... I shall ask you to hold that all these slogans which they have sprinkled about so freely are not used to benefit the worker or the peasant but are used to push forward and foster this revolution upon which they have made up their minds.'

James went on to warn that, for the example of Russia to be followed in India, it was essential that the Government of the Majesty be smashed to pieces at the outset. 'There is no room for both of them,' he said. Roy, if he was reading, must have agreed with this at least. Clemens Palme Dutt wrote a scathing response in which he also criticised Nehru and the Congress for its token support of socialism, 'more often expressed as a vague ideal than connected with any concrete action on behalf of the class struggle', and as Dutt put it, 'a socialism in abstract'.[6]

After nearly four years waiting for trial in Meerut jail, most of the prisoners received very harsh sentences through a seven-hundred-page judgement of the sessions court. Muzaffar Ahmad received transportation for life, Philip Spratt imprisonment for twelve years, S.A. Dange for twelve years and Ben Bradley for ten years. There were widespread protests against these sentences in both India and Britain, especially among the trade unions. In appeal, most of the sentences were reduced by the Allahabad High Court to two or three years.

This case, like the Cawnpore conspiracy case before it, drew public attention to the cause and united British and Indian communists. They were now part of the rapidly growing communist movement worldwide.

But around this time, Roy's reputation in the communist movement began to be tarnished. British intelligence managed to start rumours that Roy was living a life of luxury in Europe while diverting much-needed funds meant for communists in India to himself. British intelligence lent credence to these allegations by intercepting some of the money Roy had sent to India. David Petrie, the head of British intelligence, admitted on record that £50 sent by Roy to India was intercepted.[7]

The result was that Roy's standing in the Indian communist movement was severely damaged. His standing with the British communist party was also low—it was still a very young party with fewer than four thousand members in 1924, and did not want to take on the responsibility of supporting the liberation of India.[8] As ever, the British had successfully used divide and rule to sow dissension.

Roy would gradually be eclipsed in the Indian communist movement by other leaders, mostly those from trade unions.

The China Syndrome

Meanwhile, far away in Soviet Russia, Roy was facing yet another set of difficulties. In 1924, he had been elected a full member of the Comintern, despite his backer Lenin's death.

Before the collapse of his reputation in India, Roy had been entrusted with an important mission in China by Joseph Stalin. From being Lenin's young man, he had now become Stalin's. Since the Russian revolution, the Soviets had been trying to increase their influence in China. China was not a Western colony, but it was under the control of Britain, USA, France and Japan, who had a hold on China's trade, customs duties and financial institutions.

China was governed by the Beiyang Army, an imperial army which would later get divided into various factions. The masses were led by the nationalist Kuomintang party (KMT) headed by Dr Sun Yat-Sen, whom Roy had already met and not been very impressed with. In 1921, the communist party of China too had been founded by Ch'ên Tu-Hsiu. The two parties entered into a precarious alliance to drive out the Beiyang warlords.

Roy's longtime mentor and friend Mikhail Borodin was sent to China in 1923 to increase Soviet standing there and had been instructed in no uncertain terms to be guided by the interests of the Chinese national liberation movement.[9] The Comintern's main aim at this point was to eliminate imperialism, especially British imperialism, rather than to promote communism. Therefore, it was happy to work with the KMT and hailed its victories.

To begin with, Borodin had some success in his work with Sun Yat-Sen. But in 1925, the KMT announced the formation of a national government. The British were horrified. The *Daily Mail* called Borodin a 'Leftist Jew out to destroy the British Empire' and another paper declared that 'Comrade Borodin was now dictator in Canton'.[10]

In the same year, the alliance between the KMT and the communists began to break down. The amiable Sun Yat-Sen died and Generalissimo Chiang Kai-shek took over. Chiang Kai-shek was a different prospect from Sun Yat-Sen, a hard, uncompromising military man who took no orders from anyone, and particularly not from Stalin.

To fix matters in China, Stalin hurriedly made Roy the head of a new delegation that included the British communists Tom Mann and Earl Browder and dispatched them in February 1927. Roy wrote that 'there were serious differences between Moscow on the one hand and the Chinese Communist Central Committee (CCP) the other'.

Moscow had by then decided that the Chinese Revolution ought to be developed into an agrarian revolution. But the leaders of the Chinese communist party, as Roy put it, were troubled by the thesis and extremely hesitant about unleashing a large-scale agrarian revolution over the countryside of China. Soon, 'the gap between Comintern's theory and Chinese practice became wider and wider'. Roy's task was thus almost impossible even before he had left for China.

The journey to China was immensely strenuous and terrifying. An airplane which was to have flown the delegation there broke down and the group had to travel overland in chairs carried by coolies. On the way to Hankow, Roy saw Chinese villagers hung from trees–villagers who had fought on the side of the CCP and then been massacred by the KMT.[11]

In Hankow, there was much talk of revolution and the air was thick with zeal. An independent observer described it thus: 'Hankow, then to sum up was a marvellous revolutionary spectacle. French communists, German communists, Hindoo communists, British IIP people, and numerous agitators responsible to the Comintern gave the place a fine mixed flavour of international revolt. The beautiful carved oak head of Manabendra Nath Roy, head of the Far Eastern section of the Comintern, could be seen across a restaurant table in effective contrast to the dishevelled pate of Jacques Doriot.'[12]

But many of the revolutionaries had feet of clay and there was huge dissent and confusion in the ranks of the Comintern section present in China. Borodin still wanted to support the KMT, but

Roy believed in disassociating from the KMT and supporting the agrarian revolution, establishing peasant power and creating an army of the CCP.

Roy eventually turned to Stalin for clarity. Stalin sent a message to Borodin and Roy, assuring the leftist KMT faction of his support. He wrote, 'Without an agrarian revolution victory is impossible. We are decidedly in favour of the land being seized by the masses from below. You must not sever yourself from the worker and peasant movement, but must assist it in every way. Otherwise, you will ruin the cause. Mobilize about 20,000 communists and about 50,000 revolutionary workers and peasants from Hunan and Hupeh, form several new army corps, utilize the students of the school for commanders, and organise your own reliable army before it is too late ... Punish officers who maintain contact with Chiang Kai-shek. The scoundrels must be punished. If the Kuomintangists do not learn to be revolutionary Jacobins, they would be lost both to the people and to the revolution.'[13]

The Soviet advisors and the CCP were shocked by this unrealistic advice and 'dumbfounded by this fairy tale from overseas'.[14] Even Borodin considered the instructions ludicrous. But Roy believed that Wang Ching-wei, the head of the left faction of the KMT government who was allied with Madame Sun, the widow of Sun Yat-Sen, could be persuaded to support the Comintern and opt for mass revolution. However, Wang and Madame Sun were terrified at the prospect of organising a mass revolution. In April 1927, Chiang Kai-shek savagely turned on his communist allies. He began a massacre of communists, leftists and workers in Shanghai in what came to be called the Shanghai Massacre. Thousands were killed and thousands more imprisoned. The KMT split into two, which further complicated matters. They started operating out of two capitals: the more leftist faction from Wuhan under Wang Ching-wei and the other from Nanchang (Nanking) where Chiang Kai-shek ruled.

A startled Borodin was overwhelmed by the task of supporting the CCP in the massive country that was China. He is reported to have had a breakdown. When comparing the Chinese and Russian revolutions he is said to have exclaimed, 'Our revolution was big, big but nothing compared to this. We work blindly, we lift the curtain, and are frightened by the immensity of the scene. This revolution will kill many a Borodin.'[15]

Borodin and Roy eventually had to flee for their lives. They made a desperate and ignominious dash from China, driving through the Gobi Desert in three hastily procured cars in August 1927. Roy made it to Baikal, where he took the Trans-Siberian Railway to Moscow. Madame Sun abandoned Hankow and fled to Shanghai. The Soviet Union cut off all ties with the KMT.

The debacle in China smashed Roy's reputation beyond repair. Even Mao Tse-Tung, then a rising star in China, would note the failure. Later, he would say in a frank interview with the American journalist Edward Snow, 'Roy was a fool, Borodin a blunderer and Chien Tu-Hsiu, the general secretary of the CCP at the time, an unconscious traitor.'[16] Mao went on, 'Roy, the Indian delegate of the Comintern, stood to the left of both Chien and Borodin, but he only stood. He could talk, and he talked too much, without offering any method of realisation.'[17]

The writer and observer John Sexton also wrote of Roy's endless plans that came to nothing: 'Roy liked to think of himself as a man of action, but all his actions failed—from his gun running in World War I, a rather adventurist 1920 scheme, endorsed by Lenin and Trotsky, to invade British India from Afghanistan, to his blunder in China. Indeed, he arrived in China knowing virtually nothing of the country, but convinced he knew all the answers. And while his bit part did not change anything fundamentally, it provided Stalin with another convenient scapegoat.'[18] Roy had overreached, but it was clear that Stalin's arrogance had played a huge part in the China debacle.

Around 1925, as Roy was deep in the midst of his China adventure, he and his faithful wife Evelyn Trent parted ways. Evelyn had spent nine years building her life around Roy. She had left her home, her family, fled several countries, assumed fake identities, worked with him as a co-author on *Vanguard,* co-written several books and moved from the US to Mexico, Mexico to Berlin, Berlin to Moscow and Moscow to Paris, Zurich, Annecy and Amsterdam. A talented writer and thinker herself, she willingly subsumed her personality to help Roy.

As Roy's biographer Sibnarayan Ray later put it, 'Evelyn's position was that of a competent and loyal comrade-wife who had perforce to live and work in her husband's shadow. More important was the fact that while Roy had become the centre of her universe—but for Roy India would probably have meant little or nothing to her—she was anything but the pivot of Roy's concernment.'[19]

Roy was completely obsessed with India's liberation. His personal life was secondary. He was a man of great charisma, and revolutionary women continued to buzz around him like moths to a flame. And he was only too happy to try free love and other partners, it seems.

Evelyn wrote a series of anguished letters to Henk Sneevliet, the Dutch communist politician who was a close friend of both Roy and herself. Her letters began to get ever more troubled as she complained about their 'roving and uncertain life', 'the precarious legality', her sense of alienation in Europe, Roy's marital cheating and of her growing conviction that she was tired of playing the doting wife.[20]

Roy made no attempt to persuade her to stay. By 17 August 1925, Evelyn was back in Chicago from where she wrote a long letter again to Sneevliet, complaining that she 'had given my whole self to India, because I must, if we were to live together, that being his whole life'. She accused Roy of betraying her, of shaming her, treating her as an appendage and tossing away their life 'lightly and scornfully', surmising that it was because someone who had been 'brought up in a patriarchal environment had been thrust too abruptly into a degenerate, post-revolutionary one'. Later, Evelyn wrote that she had received cold and hostile letters from Roy and revealed that she had been bluntly asked to leave, despite begging to remain (likely because Roy had found another lover). It was a wretched end for such an independent woman.

In 1926, Evelyn and Roy were divorced in spite of her offering several times to resume their relations and come with him to China. The request was icily refused by him. Evelyn wrote a ten-page-long goodbye letter to Roy in which she described their one-sided relationship in brutal terms: 'You had a definite goal and a fixed purpose in life. I was merely a side-issue who had become in time an impediment which had to be shaken off—whereas you were for me the end and goal, the very reason for my new mode of existence.' She bade him farewell, saying with no rancour, 'Such love will never come to either of us again. We know too much of life now ever to entertain so many illusions. Therefore, let us cherish the memory tenderly at its true worth ...'[21] Roy's reply, if he sent any at all, does not survive. Evelyn went on to find a job at the *San Francisco Chronicle*, giving up a life spent on the run. She would marry again but fade into obscurity, her talents never fully realised.

Roy went on to have an affair with a glamorous young woman called Louise Geissler, who was first his secretary and then became his lover. Louise, twelve years younger and besotted with the charismatic Roy, accompanied him to China. She too would later have her heart broken by him as he would move on to yet another young woman.

It was a season for break-ups and chaos for Roy, both on the personal and professional front. The time had come for him to pay for his numerous errors of judgement. On his return from China,

Stalin refused to see him, a dangerous sign that Roy was not slow to understand. He knew that those whom Stalin refused to see today would be history tomorrow.

The tussle between Roy and the Comintern got worse at the Sixth World Congress of the Communist International in 1928. Roy was ill and could not attend it. In his absence, the Comintern adopted a resolution which singled out the INC as the counter-revolutionary party of the bourgeoisie and advised Indian communists to denounce all nationalist leaders, including Jawaharlal Nehru, as agents of imperialism. The Indian communists, who were a part of the Comintern, accepted this resolution.

M.N. Roy thought this was pointless, performative rhetoric. He bided his time for a year or so, but then could not stay quiet any longer. He believed their acceptance of the INC as a counter-revolutionary party would isolate Indian communists from the national struggle. 'They could never be more than a small sect with no influence on the political life of the country. They gave out fantastic slogans and advocated absurd plans of action.'[22]

Roy was a pragmatist. Much as he despised some sections of the Congress, he realised that the communist movement in India was still far too undeveloped to fight the British on its own. As he put it, 'The young Indian proletariat being numerically weak, immature as a class, politically inexperienced, culturally backward, ideologically uneducated, cannot shoulder singlehandedly the task of overthrowing imperialism.'[23]

By now, Roy also disapproved of the steady vitriol of the communists against Jawaharlal Nehru and the INC. He had come round to Lenin's view and now reluctantly believed that only the INC could take India to independence because only they had the mass appeal. No longer the angry young revolutionary, Roy unwisely went on to praise the INC. 'It commands the confidence of the oppressed and exploited masses, that is to say of the forces of the democratic national revolution. It is a great mistake to look upon it as a political party of the bourgeoisie.' He acknowledged that there was always the danger that the party would be controlled by the bourgeoisie. 'As a matter of fact,' he said realistically, 'it has all along been more or less under their influence exercised directly or indirectly. The result has been that its objective revolutionary potentials have not been developed. But the potentialities remain.'[24]

Roy advised the Comintern to think again and be guided by reality. Their declaration, he explained, meant that not only was the urban lower middle class despised as counter-revolutionary, but the peasants supporting the INC across India were tarred as counter-revolutionaries too. But the Comintern would not accept this argument. They were firm in the belief that Indian communists should not join hands with the bourgeoisie Congress and were horrified by Roy's about turn on the 'India question' as it was called.

Meanwhile, Roy had made an enemy in the influential Finnish born Soviet official Otto Kuusinen, a member of the Comintern. Kuusinen accused him of being a British lackey and claimed that Roy had put forward the view that British imperialism would eventually liberate India. The charges were ludicrous and unfounded, but Roy began to realise that he was being made a convenient scapegoat before Stalin. The writing was on the wall.

Roy was called a 'renegade to Communism', 'traitor to the working class' and an 'agent of Imperialism'. Lenin's young man was no longer communist enough for the Comintern because he had deviated from the accepted party line.

He wrote an impassioned open letter titled 'My Crime', in which he defended himself against the charges of being a British spy and a bourgeoisie. 'For some time I have been standing before the sacred guillotine, the mad application of which is causing such a havoc to the International Communist movement. I have stood in that position for nearly a year, not shuddering with the fear for my head, but aghast at the incompetence of those who have usurped the leadership of the movement ... At the Tenth Plenum of the Executive Committee of the C. I. my humble head was demanded by the gentle Kuusinen in his characteristic manner of shirking responsibility. The prompted cry "a la guillotine" was raised from the obscure corner, and one connected with the Communist International nearly from its very foundation, active in the revolutionary movement for years previously, hitherto suspected of and criticised for alleged left deviation was placed automatically outside the pale of the Communist International.'[25]

As Roy pointed out, no evidence was produced to show how someone who had worked in the movement for nearly twenty years was now a renegade and a rightist. But his protests had come too late and found no takers. Roy was expelled from the Comintern in December 1929. His offence, as he said, 'was to lay claim to independent thinking'. It was an offence for which he would pay again and again in the future.

Leon Trotsky, Stalin's great rival, had already been expelled from the Comintern two years earlier and deported in 1929. The guillotine had fallen on Roy too. Like the outspoken Trotsky, Roy's life was now in danger.

14

The End of Virendranat Agornatovitch Chatopadaya

Death was ... random, the long-forgotten comment, the flirtation with the opposition, envy of another man's job, wife or house, vengeance or just plain coincidence brought the death and torture of entire families. Better too far than not far enough, Yezhov told his men.

Simon Sebag Montefiore on Stalin's Great Purge

IT WAS 4.30 P.M. ON 1 DECEMBER 1934 IN LENINGRAD, AND BOLSHEVIK supremo Sergei Kirov was looking forward to his dinner. Leningrad had strict rationing going on at the time and meals were usually spartan. Earlier that day, Kirov had turned to his wife Maria and asked, 'Say, Maria, when did I last have a birthday?' It was not his birthday, but he had wanted a good meal.

His wife replied, 'All right, my dear, you shall have cabbage dumplings tonight, and some especially strong tea; I'll brew it myself.' Kirov kissed her and said, 'You know, my dear, great things are afoot. Bread rationing is coming to an end, and then we can have a "birthday" every day.'[1]

The handsome, square-jawed Kirov was an appropriate match for his grand, magnificent office in the Smolny Institute: the headquarters of the Bolshevik party in Leningrad. Kirov was very popular within the Bolshevik party for his oratory, glowing war record, swashbuckling service to the communists and general all-round charisma. He had climbed the ranks of the party quickly, becoming a close friend and confidante of Joseph Stalin. He was also a close friend of Chatto's. The two friendships would intersect with tragic effect.

On that fateful day, Kirov never got to eat his cabbage dumplings. At 4.30 p.m., Leonid Nikolaev, a disgruntled party member, burst into the Smolny and shot Kirov in the back of the head. Kirov died instantly and thus was launched a 'great watershed at which the Stalinist regime, which had always been violent, toppled over into mass murder'.[2] Kirov's death gave Stalin the excuse to launch a nation-wide campaign of repression. Indeed, Stalin is still widely thought to have ordered the murder himself, both to get rid of his possible rival and to give him an excuse for the 'Great Purge'. The assassin was quickly executed without a proper trial.[3]

Kirov's unexpected assassination would signal the end for his friend and protégé Chatto too. Chatto had fled Berlin for the Soviet Union only three years earlier, in 1931. It would prove to be a foolish choice but in truth he'd not had much of an option. The Nazi party was on the rise in Germany and they were fanatically opposed to communism, especially foreign communists and even more so, foreign communists from Asia. The LAI headquarters had been moved to Paris and Chatto was banned from entering France, his other option. India had been out of the question for years, given the British clampdown on revolutionaries.

Hitler had a very poor view of Indian nationalists. As could be predicted for a Nazi, he did not believe in independence for India or indeed for any colonised peoples. As early as 1925, in *Mein Kampf*, Hitler had disdainfully called the Indian revolutionaries in Berlin 'mountebanks who put themselves forward as the champions of Indian freedom, then began to peregrinate throughout Europe, and succeeded in inspiring otherwise quite reasonable people with the fixed notion that the British World Empire was about to collapse in India'. With that phrasing, he could well have been speaking of Chatto. He did not believe that England would ever give up its domination over India, given that India was the jewel in its crown. He was no Kaiser Wilhelm II willing to aid Indians against the British. Indeed, he said bluntly, 'I as a German would far rather see India under British domination than under that of any other nation.'[4]

Chatto saw clearly that Berlin was no longer safe for him or for any people of colour, all of whom were classed together as spies. But what he failed to anticipate was that anti-foreigner sentiment was also rampant in the Soviet Union, which had been experiencing huge changes.

Joseph Stalin was gaining power and building his autocratic cult of personality. The collectivisation of the economy had begun in 1928 with the first Five Year Plan. Stalin wanted the Soviet Union to have more effective farms so it could be self-sufficient and resist the power of the West. Collective farms called kolkhozes were introduced, which would gradually replace the small holdings of peasants. Farm workers were expected to live and work together. To begin with, collectivisation was ignored by farmers, who continued with their small farms. But in 1931, the year Chatto arrived in Soviet Union, Stalin began to forcibly enforce collectivisation. There was fierce resistance from certain sections of the peasants called the Kulaks, who burnt crops and destroyed livestock. As punishment, the Kulaks were sent to the Gulag—Stalin's infamous system of forced camps—or forced to migrate to Siberia or work in lumber yards. In 1932, a catastrophic famine followed, with five million people dying in Soviet Ukraine. And yet, by the end of the 1930s, 99 per cent of farms had converted to kolkhozes.

This was the tumultuous country that Chatto arrived in, friendless, alone and unable to speak a word of Russian. The first year of Chatto's stay in the Soviet Union was an unhappy one. He was forced to do a number of odd jobs. British influence extended to the Soviet Union, and even here Chatto felt insecure and jittery. He started worked as an editor in the Foreign Workers Publishing House and later in the Indian section of the Byuro Kommunisticheskaya Akademii (Bureau of the Communist Academy).[5] But his work there was scattered and infrequent.

Then Chatto had a stroke of good luck. Or so he thought at the time. He became a sort of protégé of Kirov. Kirov was a close friend of Stalin at the time. Both Kirov and Stalin had grown up in poverty with abusive fathers. Kirov, apparently, was the only person allowed to see Stalin naked in his sauna. He was considered a moderate Bolshevik, though he had firmly supported collectivisation and had been content to look on when famine had struck as a result. Nevertheless, Kirov was the charismatic, genial foil to Stalin's dour Georgian personality. And in that difference lay his downfall. Stalin would gradually become envious of Kirov's popularity amongst the masses.

There is little information about how Chatto and Kirov met, but they were apparently good friends.[6] Kirov's influence eventually helped Chatto to get a position at the Institute of Anthropology and Ethnography (IAE) of the Academy of Sciences of the USSR. The IAE's aim was to popularise Marxism-Leninism in academic research. This Chatto did with enthusiasm. He learnt Russian quickly with his incredible talent for languages. He wrote for several journals on Leninist theory, and was perhaps happy and relatively content for the first time in his life. He was accepted and respected by his colleagues because of his hard work, scholarship and intelligence. And he was given a new Russian name: Virendranat Agornatovitch Chatopadaya.

In the Soviet Union, Chatto got a last chance at love and companionship. He met a Russian colleague, Lidiya Karunovskaya, who was about ten years younger than him. Karunovskaya was already married at the time, but unhappily so. Chatto began to live with her, her husband Andrey Danilin and an elderly relative in a small apartment in Leningrad. Unorthodox to the end, Chatto would write to Karunovskaya saying he always 'felt at home' at her place.[7]

Gradually, Karunovskaya became more and more drawn to Chatto, his kindness and his social conscience. She wrote of how he always had time to help the less fortunate, of whom there were many. 'Those were still very difficult years after the War. Many things, even the most essential ones, were not available for sale. On Chatto's desk he would find notes such as "My little son badly needs warm shoes. My mother has fallen ill, she needs butter badly. Do you have ten roubles to spare" etc. Chatto, not desiring to be different from his less fortunate co-workers, refused to use the coupons with which foreigners could buy essential items overriding control, but would take such coupons from his friends to buy the things asked for in the slips. As a result, he was often left without money to buy the most essential things for himself.'[8]

This was the overwhelming generosity that had annoyed Agnes Smedley, but Karunovskaya was impressed with it. By the end of 1933, she divorced her husband, and she and Chatto were married. They are also rumoured to have had a daughter, but no further information about her could be found.

But the happy times could not last for long. Kirov's assassination and Stalin's 'Great Purge' took Chatto by surprise, as it did many academics and intellectuals. M.N. Roy had managed to escape from Soviet Union in the nick of time, but Roy's unfortunate mentor Mikhail Borodin was imprisoned and died in a prison camp after years of torture and mistreatment.

The man helping Stalin with his 'Great Purge' was his henchman, the sinister Nikolai Ivanovich Yezhov, also called the Iron Fist. Indeed, nicknames for Yezhov were plenty. He was also called the Poison Dwarf because he was only four feet and eleven inches tall, and later Blackberry as well. Yezhov was the head of Stalin's notorious secret police, The People's Commissariat for Internal Affairs. In Russian, it was called Naródny Komissariát

Vnútrennih De, abbreviated to NKVD. At the time, he was the most powerful person in the country, apart from Stalin. As the historian Simon Sebag Montefiore has put it, 'Stalin was the mastermind but he was far from alone. Indeed, it is neither accurate nor helpful to blame the Terror on one man because systematic murder started soon after Lenin took power in 1917, and never stopped until Stalin's death.'[9]

Hitler's rise to power had caused many foreign communists to flee to the Soviet Union, including of course, Chatto. Yezhov's job was to check their backgrounds. By 1934, Yezhov was recommending careful verification of these immigrants, insinuating that many were spies. By 1936, the NKVD had arrested more than two thousand émigrés. A letter written by Yezhov indicated his belief that it was very easy for foreign powers to use political émigrés for espionage.[10] By March 1936, an ominous commission was set up to review political émigrés. All political émigrés were to be re-registered within three months, procedures for entrance were to be tightened and 'harmful people' were to be purged.[11]

The aim of the purge was to destroy all enemies of the Bolsheviks, but this term was defined so loosely that it could include almost everyone. On 30 July 1937, the bloodthirsty Yezhov suggested that 72,950 people should be shot and 259,450 arrested. Then the 'quota' was increased to another 70,000 between August and December. Ordering murder became natural.[12]

Yezhov's 'meatgrinder' chewed up a whole population, regardless of race, religion, nationality or gender, and for the smallest of reasons. As Sebag Montefiore has put it, 'Here, on the contrary, death was sometimes random, the long-forgotten comment, the flirtation with the opposition, envy of another man's job, wife or house, vengeance or just plain coincidence brought the death and torture of entire families. Better too far than not far enough, Yezhov told his men.'[13]

When Kirov was assassinated, Chatto apparently exclaimed, 'Well, now reprisals against foreigners will begin.' And so they did, very close to him. Chatto's very foreignness became the grounds for his arrest. The historian Robert Conquest explained, 'To have had anything to do with foreigners was one almost certain road to arrest. All direct contact with foreign consulates was likely to prove fatal.'

Most of the arrests were born out of a ridiculous paranoia. 'An opera singer who had danced longer than permitted with the Japanese ambassador at an official ball was sent to the camps. A Greek doctor was charged with espionage on the grounds that he had written to relatives in Salonika. Chinese were also arrested en bloc. One is reported as having been charged with taking a job as a tram driver in Kharkov, with the aim of crashing it into any car on the tracks in front of him which carried members of the Soviet Government.'[14] A crazy and murderous panic had taken hold of Stalin and his coterie.

In April 1937, a close friend of Chatto's, a German communist leader named Heinz Neumann, was arrested. Neumann might have been considered to be immune from persecution. He was a confidante of Stalin's from his younger days. Heinz and his vivacious young wife Margarete Buber-Neumann were members of the German communist party and passionate Leninists. In fact, Margarete was the sister of Babette Gross, the common law wife of Willi Munzenberg, of whom we read about earlier.

To begin with, the Neumanns were full of idealism and admiration for the Soviet way of life. Margarete wrote of Moscow, 'I did not fail to notice that the people on the street were poorly clad, or that begging children lay in wait, or that the comforts of life were noticeably absent. But what did it matter? Socialism was being built up, before long the country would enjoy its benefits, and good things would be available for everyone. I was only too willing to gloss over any doubts because I wanted to believe.'[15]

But gradually, the Neumanns stopped believing, and soon they started feeling bitterly, tragically disappointed. They would pay dearly for their naïveté, as would many others. In 1935, the Neumanns were ordered to come to Moscow by the Comintern. Heinz had been deposed as the head of the communist party in Germany and the Nazis had started pursuing him in Berlin. There was nowhere for them to go, so like Chatto they had come to Moscow in the hope of refuge.

From the day they had entered the country, they were watched like hawks by the NKVD. We know little about Chatto's life of that time, but we can get a picture of life under a crazed dictator from Margarete's detailed account of those days of terror, when thousands were summarily arrested and went missing, while their families waited for information.

Margarete herself was arrested a few months after her husband and ended up having one of the unluckiest experiences of the war, being imprisoned by not one, but two dictators. Cruel fate would make her a prisoner in Stalin's Gulag for two years, and then be traded to Hitler under the Stalin-Hitler Pact. She spent another five years in Ravensbrück, an infamous concentration camp for women. With her sheer iron will and determination, Margarete survived the Second World War. She would write a powerful book titled *Under Two Dictators*, in which she would describe both Hitler and Stalin as savage, sadistic dictators with not much difference between them. She would dedicate the rest of her life to campaigning against totalitarianism.

The Neumanns had lived in the Hotel Lux, where many other Comintern employees and foreign communists lived. Every day, a new person was dragged away from the hotel as the other residents looked on in terror. What had now become a den of fear and panic, was once something different. In the early days of the revolution, as M.N. Roy later described in his memoirs, the Lux had hosted midnight supper parties that lasted till the early morning hours, enlivened by singing and dancing and attended by members of the Russian communist party as well as the foreign members of the Comintern. Roy had, indeed, ended his memoirs with this loving ode to the Hotel Lux: 'Whoever had the opportunity of living in the Hotel Lux in those early days of the Revolution must cherish the memory as one of the richest experiences of his life. The Communist International had already developed its hierarchy. But in the Hotel Lux, they were all equals and in our midnight parties, we met like equals, all human beings with virtues which need not be magnified with artificial dignity, and frailties of which none need be ashamed.'[16]

But only a few years later, Hotel Lux had become Big Brother. As Margarete put it, 'No one could enter or leave the Lux without a special pass, and the name and particulars of everyone who did so were carefully noted down. All the telephones in the hotel were controlled by the GPU from the central switchboard. The fear of being spied on and listened to became so great that good friends would ask: "Have you carefully examined your room to make sure there isn't a microphone in it somewhere?" and have to be reassured before they would consent to visit you.'[17]

Far from being welcomed, foreign communists had started being viewed with deep suspicion, wrote Margarete. 'Communists who had been guilty of "deviations" were told to sign "a satisfactory declaration" admitting their political errors. After that they were to practise "Bolshevist watchfulness" and denounce any instance of criticism they noted amongst the people with whom they associated. Only if they did all this would the control authorities believe their protestations of loyalty and be prepared to use them for political work.'[18] In the two years that the Neumanns were in Moscow before Heinz's arrest, Heinz was summoned every day before the commissions that had been set up to investigate disloyalty. He was urged over and over to admit his political errors and confess to having made observations 'hostile to the party'.

On 27 April 1937, the Neumanns were woken up at 1 a.m. by a loud banging on their door. Three officials of the NKVD tramped in and shook Heinz roughly by the shoulder. 'I protest against my arrest,' he said firmly. 'You can do that later,' replied the leader of the three while he snapped at them to stop talking in German. Heinz was dragged away. Margarete clenched her fists, dug her nails into her flesh, and pressed her lips together trying not to cry. But when they embraced, 'the tears flowed'. Heinz pleaded, 'Don't cry. Don't cry.' But at the door, he turned and strode back and kissed her for the last time. 'Cry then,' he said. 'There's enough to cry about.'

Margarete spent the next few days looking for Heinz, going from one prison to another along with the other wives and children who had been left behind. In the day, she sold their meagre possessions to raise money. At night, she waited for her own arrest. Meanwhile, the children suffered even worse agonies. Margarete overheard one cruel conversation between children whose fathers had been arrested: 'Is your daddy arrested too?' 'No, my daddy is on holiday in the Caucasus,' replied the other. And then the eleven-year-old daughter of one of the arrested comrades had destroyed the child's illusion. 'Oh, he's in the Caucasus, is he? Well, why does your mother pay money into the prison, then? A fine Caucasus, that is!'

On 19 June 1938 Margarete too was arrested. She became prisoner No. 174,475 at the brutal Karaganda camp in Siberia, where she was forced to labour under harsh and filthy conditions. Then in 1940, she was handed over to the German SS and transported to the infamous Ravensbrück concentration camp for women, where she survived five years at the hands of the Nazis. She eventually escaped to Sweden and lived to testify in several trials in the post-war period. Her frank testimony convinced the world that Stalin's Gulag system was comparable to the horrors in Nazi concentration camps. Margarete died in 1989 but never learnt in her lifetime that Heinz had been executed years earlier, on 26 November 1937.

Chatto was arrested on 15 July 1937. When he said goodbye to his wife Karunovskaya, he whispered the name of a Comintern comrade and told her that she should take the news of his arrest to him. But she misheard the name and instead sent a telegram to Comintern about his arrest. Nothing was heard from them. In Moscow, Karunovskaya tried her best to trace Chatto, but at every turn she was misled by the authorities. In fact, Karunovskaya was lucky not to be arrested herself. She was dismissed from IAE two months later. The head of the IAE, Nikolay Maturin, had already been executed as a traitor in 1936.

It would take Karunovskaya nearly twenty years to find out anything of what happened to Chatto. She would have to wait till 1956, when the myth of the genial 'Uncle Joe' was finally debunked. On 15 September 1956, she was eventually given a certificate saying that the accusations against Chatopadaya Virendranat Agornatovitch had been checked by the Military Collegium of the Supreme Court of the USSR and that the verdict of 2 September 1937 had been lifted. Chatto had been officially pardoned. About two years later, she was handed a death certificate stating that Chatto had died on 6 April 1943. Neither the cause nor the place of death was mentioned.[19]

More information finally emerged when the KGB archives were revealed in 1991. The Russian historian–and a friend of India–Leonid Mitrokhin discovered that Chatto had been sentenced to death by the Military Collegium of the Supreme Court of the USSR on 2 September 1937, and was executed by firing squad the very same day. While in prison, Chatto had sent a book to Karunovskaya written in the Indonesian language, perhaps as a sign to her that he was alive, but it only reached her in 1941. Along with Chatto, the slippery Abani Mukherji and the unlucky Ghulam Luhani were also executed and just as quickly forgotten.[20] Abani had finally run out of luck. Luhani was simply in the wrong place at the wrong time.

In 1938, A.C.N. Nambiar wrote desperately to Jawaharlal Nehru, begging him to make enquiries. But Nehru did not want to anger Joseph Stalin at the time. In an India struggling for independence, it was important not to rock the boat. Chatto's disappearance was brushed under the carpet for over half a century as Stalin's murderous regime remained hidden from public gaze. He was, after all, just one insignificant man in a chaotic world. Nambiar did not live to see Mitrokhin's expose and he had come to believe that Chatto had died naturally. Indeed, he is known to have said with wry and somewhat unintended irony, 'I personally do not believe he was executed. Natural death is possible also in the Soviet Union.'[21]

But Chatto's death was probably far from gentle. His last days were likely unutterably grim. By 1937, prisoners were no longer being interrogated–that was taking too much time–but were instead being beaten and tortured with boots, fists and furniture. He was likely shot in the middle of the night and his body probably dumped anonymously at the Kommunarka mass grave, where up to fourteen thousand people are now estimated to have been shot and buried by the NKVD between 1937 and1941.[22]

Back home in India, the Congress and the Soviet Union were establishing new bonds. When on 22 June 1941, Hitler attacked the Soviet Union, the INC rushed to express its solidarity and sent its 'warm sympathy'.[23] So too did the Indian press. On 15 July 1941, Hitler approved the 'Plan of the Reorganisation of Germany's Land Forces after the End of the Eastern Campaign', which suggested the invasion of Iran, Turkey and India.[24] Indians could see Hitler's designs on India and knew that only Stalin's famous Red Army could hold back the Nazi surge. They needed Stalin, as did the rest of the world.

The Friends of the Soviet Union (FSU) was founded in India on 3 June 1944. In the ultimate irony, Sarojini Naidu became the president of the All India Society of Friends of the Soviet Union, even as her brother disappeared in that country. Writers, philosophers, activists, teachers and people from all walks of life eagerly supported it. The trade unions too rushed to support the Soviets, as did the Communist Party of India. Over the next few years, strong ties were built and India became ever closer to the Soviets in the hope of finding an ally against the British.

In 1943, Sarojini sent a gushing message for an exhibition of the FSU: 'The dream of Lenin swept like a fiery tempest across city and hamlet, steppe and mountains smiting back into a long-forgotten consciousness of their own human status vast multitudes of men and women whom generations of oppression had beaten down into a dreadful and fatalistic torpor akin to death. Whether, like me, they owe allegiance to the teaching of Mahatma Gandhi, or profess safer and more conventional social and political faiths, are there still people in the world today with a vestige of intelligence or integrity who dare withhold a just tribute of admiration for the magnitude of the Russian enterprise or the magnificence of its achievement?'[25]

Sarojini expressed the feelings of most Indians, who felt a deep kinship with the Soviets for having reclaimed their own land twice over, first from the aristocracy and then from the Nazis. They identified with Lenin and later Stalin's message of liberation, especially as the British government professed to be anti-Bolshevik. At the time, no one knew of the dark underbelly of the Soviet state.

In 1947, post Independence, Nehru's sister Vijayalakshmi Pandit, the then Indian ambassador to Moscow, had enquired about Chatto and his whereabouts. She was apparently told he had died of pneumonia.[26] Babette Gross, the wife of Willi Munzenberg, informed her that Chatto had left behind a mysterious German wife and three children, but there was no information about them.

Even the well-connected M.N. Roy did not come to know of Chatto's fate. He would write in his memoirs, 'The charge and counter-charge of betrayal and espionage is frequent amongst revolutionaries in exile. Indians were no exception. It is reported that in his last days Chattopadhyaya was also non-politically employed in Leningrad about the same time as Abani Mukherji. It would be a cruel irony of fate if ultimately they both were victimised by revolutionary hysteria. Chattopadhyaya certainly deserved a better fate.'

Karunovskaya would write sadly, years after Chatto's death, 'During the years of his wanderings in foreign countries, Chatto took from the West all the positive things which the West could give him, but he did not forfeit the stamp of special culture of his beautiful motherland. His intelligence, the warmth of his heart and his capacity to understand everybody were expressed in a charming smile which attracted people towards him.'[27]

Stalin's head of secret police, the terrifying Nikolai Yezhov, would eventually get what he deserved. By 1939, he had fallen out of Stalin's favour and was arrested, later admitting in a confession (that he subsequently claimed was given under torture) to having made 'unfounded arrests' during the Great Purge. He was executed in 1940, along with others who were made scapegoats for the purge. In fact, nearly all the members of the original Politburo who were present during the October Revolution or during Lenin's government were executed, exiled or assassinated or forced into suicide at this time.

Stalin died in 1953 after a series of strokes, but there has been speculation that he was actually poisoned. His thirty-year reign over the Soviet Union had ended in ignominy. But his iron cult of personality was so strong that his fans, including M.N. Roy, continued to affectionately call him Uncle Joe, though he had slaughtered an estimated 1.2 million people in the Gulag. Nikita Khruschev took over after a power struggle.

When India won independence on 15 August 1947, Harindranath wrote hopefully of his brother's possible return now that 'our country's banner with the Dharma Chakra centred amidst three colours is flying all over Hindustan'. He went on to wonder if 'our National Government will charter a special ship for the weary exiles yearning to return to the lap of the Ancient Mother?' But then a footnote added says baldly, 'Virendranath is no more. News has only just come that he passed away in the month of January 1941.' The gory circumstances of his death though, would remain unknown to his family.[28]

By 1955, shell-shocked and tortured prisoners from the Gulag had begun returning to their home, and they would tell appalling tales of abuse and torture. In February 1956, three years after Stalin's much-lamented death, a grim-faced Nikita Khrushchev revealed the terrible extent of the Great Purge in a speech before the Communist Party of Russia's 20th Party Congress meeting, damningly called 'On the Cult of Personality and Its Consequences'.

In a few hours, Khruschev demolished the myth of the kindly Uncle Joe who had saved the Soviet Union and the world from Nazi terror, all the while quietly conducting a terror campaign. Khruschev had gone along with the purge for reasons of his own, mostly to stay alive, but possibly to gather his own power.

Khrushchev said in what came to be called the 'Secret Speech', 'Stalin showed in a whole series of cases his intolerance, his brutality, and his abuse of power ... he often chose the path of repression and physical annihilation, not only against actual enemies but also against individuals who had not committed any crimes against the party or the Soviet Government'.[29] He savagely criticised the hero worship of Stalin as a kindly father figure, and denounced Stalin's cult of personality.

The speech did not remain secret for long. It spread like wildfire throughout the Soviet Union and then the world, where it changed the course of history. Bit by bit, Stalin's worshippers realised the truth of 'Koba's' long rule. And slowly, India did too, though Stalin would always have his fanatical worshippers in many corners of the world.

About forty years later, the path-breaking Mikhail Gorbachev would praise Khrushchev for his courage and for eventually becoming 'a moral man after all'.[30] And the once mighty Soviet Union would fall, partly because of the secret speech that changed the world. If Chatto had been there, he would likely have laughed bitterly at the collapse of his idyll.

15

The Twice-Born Heretic

Heralded as the salvation of the civilised world, communism in practice has come to be a spectre, terrifying not only the bourgeoisie, it is causing grave misgivings among the progressive forces of the modern world ...

M.N. Roy, explaining why he gave up on communism

IN 1930, A GROUP OF YOUNG STUDENTS AND TRADE UNION LEADERS in India received a mysterious message from a Dr Mahmud. It was somewhat pompously titled 'The Revolutionary Vanguard of the Toiling Masses of India'. But it contained much common sense. In the missive, the shadowy Dr Mahmud attacked the hardline Comintern position against the Congress and urged Indian communists to reject it. He said, 'The Communist Party cannot advocate that India will immediately be a Soviet Republic. That will be running after a Utopia.'[1] Instead, Mahmud suggested that Indian communists join with the INC and other nationalists to present a united front and defer their ultimate objective for a communist state until India achieved independence.

V.B. Karnik, a student leader who would become a top labour leader in Bombay, was one of the recipients of Dr Mahmud's message. Another was Maniben Kara, a Gujarati woman who would later lead the Bombay Municipal Workers Union. Charles Mascarenhas, secretary of the Bombay Seaman's Union and later a founding member of the Bombay Socialist Party, also received the message, and so did A.N. Shetty, founder of the Bombay

Transport and Dock Workers Union. But none of them knew that the mysterious Mahmud was actually M.N. Roy, forced to flee the Soviet Union and preparing the ground for his perilous journey back to India. Karnik would later write that the group was 'dazzled by the sweep and brilliance of his intelligence' and that he 'opened before them a clear path of revolution'.[2]

Roy had been convicted in absentia in 1924 in the Cawnpore conspiracy case for having conspired to organise a communist party with the object of overthrowing British rule. He could thus be arrested anywhere within the empire. His friends therefore tried to discourage him from returning to India.

Why then did Roy return to India in 1930, after being summarily expelled from the Comintern? It was mostly because he felt that Indian communists were struggling to form their identity. Unlike Chatto, he believed strongly that the communists in India needed to follow the nation rather than follow the directives of Comintern. He also believed that they should help to win independence for the nation before hoping for communism. This was a deeply unpopular stand amongst Indian communists. Indeed, it was the seed of a brand-new ideology that came to be called 'Royism'. Roy patterned his new ideology on the model of French Jacobinism. Indian communists believed in the creation of 'soviets' or workers' councils in India. Roy thought this was impractical. He urged the convening of a constituent assembly to draft a constitution for a free India. To do so, he was prepared to work with the INC.

He was roundly criticised for this by international communists, who believed the Congress was a bourgeois organisation. But Roy, as we saw earlier, had come to believe that Indian peasants and workers were too undeveloped to play an independent role in achieving the nation's independence, and that independence could only be achieved via the mass popularity of the INC. It was an immensely pragmatic viewpoint that would damn him completely in the eyes of both the communists and the INC.

The Royists put out huge quantities of pamphlets and journals. In fact, Maniben Kara later joked that she suspected she had been invited to join the Royists only because she owned a printing press.[3] But Roy's illusions about India were soon destroyed. He confided in a friend that he had overestimated the maturity of the Indian movement. He added, 'Strikes in India were an elementary revolt against intolerable living conditions rather than of revolutionary class consciousness.'[4] He did not find enough support for communism and was more than ever convinced of the need for the middle path: Royism.

Meanwhile, Roy also tried to build ties with existing INC leaders. But he was hampered by his cosmopolitanism and refusal to compromise. His years in Europe, where he had mingled with foreign activists of all stripes, had made him deeply suspicious of religion and convention. As an atheist and rationalist, he was repulsed by Gandhi's religious obsessions, his exploitation of Hindu traditions such as fasting, his mixing of religion and state and his wily politics of compromise. As Roy's biographer Sibnarayan Ray astutely put it, 'in his long political career, there were only two persons and a half who in his estimate, qualified to be his mentors: Jatin Mukherjee, Lenin and the half was Stalin whom he admired but also criticised'.[5]

Roy had more of an affinity with the Westernised rationalist Nehru, but also believed Nehru was totally under Gandhi's thumb. He felt that, secretly, Nehru was a modern, secular man who believed he needed Gandhi and his popularity to appeal to the masses. Roy had met Nehru in Moscow in 1927, when Nehru had been involved with the League Against Imperialism. Soon after returning to India, Roy met both Nehru and Subhas Chandra Bose at the Karachi session of the Indian National Congress in 1931. Indeed, he had been invited to attend by Nehru himself. But he was forced to attend in disguise, forsaking his usual Western garb for a kurta-pyjama and a Gandhi cap. So successful was the disguise that he managed to address the crowd from the stage, despite being hunted by the police.

The Karachi session of the Congress was notable for the dismay expressed at the Gandhi-Irwin Pact under which the civil disobedience movement had been suspended. Gandhi had also agreed to participate in the Round Table Conference. Even the faithful Nehru spoke out against Gandhi's capitulation: 'Was it for this,' he asked, 'that our people had behaved so gallantly for a year? Were all our brave words and deeds to end in this?'[6]

Only a few days before the Karachi conference, the fiery revolutionaries Bhagat Singh, Raj Guru and Sukh Dev had been hanged for the murder of an assistant superintendent of police in Lahore, despite Gandhi's desperate attempts to save them. A powerful wave of rage and grief was sweeping through the country. Bhagat Singh became a martyr and an icon of the freedom movement, while Gandhi was severely criticised for his wishy-washy compromise politics.

The Karachi delegates had assembled mainly to decide whether to endorse the Delhi Pact or to continue with civil disobedience. To avoid angry demonstrations Gandhi was forced to disembark early from the train on his way to the conference, where he encountered disillusioned and raging protesters.

Roy himself was opposed to the Delhi Pact. At the conference, he was represented by Tayab Sheik and labour leader Jamnadas Mehta, who spoke on his behalf since he was still hiding from the police. Roy described the Delhi Pact as a betrayal of India by the bourgeoisie. 'Independence,' added Mehta, voicing Roy's thoughts, 'had been given so many interpretations by Gandhi in the past several months from complete independence to the substance of independence and finally self-rule through self-control, that not even an Aristotle could now understand what exactly independence entailed.'[7]

Eventually Gandhi won as he always did. Nehru and Bose supported the Delhi Pact to maintain unity within the INC and to avoid strengthening the British side. Roy was left to lament: 'Any voice raised against Gandhi was doomed to be drowned in an indignant chorus of protest. There was not the ghost of a chance of overthrowing the god.'[8] Gandhi's decision was endorsed three hundred to two. A resolution was also passed on Bhagat Singh–in a sort of feeble compromise, his execution was condemned, but so were all acts of political violence.

Roy attempted to influence the bold resolution passed in the Karachi Session on issues of fundamental rights and the national economic programme. This resolution was the first time that the INC had committed to a socio-economic programme. It provided for state ownership of key industries and transport and labour and agrarian reform. There was a great deal of opposition to the resolution and it was watered down considerably before finally being passed.

Roy is often credited with inspiring the contents of this resolution and is reported to have discussed it extensively with Nehru. There is no doubt that there was a discussion with Nehru. But only a few months after the declaration, Roy called the resolution confused. He later called it an instrument of deception that had raised false hopes amongst INC left-wingers even as the INC had retreated from the path of the revolution.

In 1931, after a lifetime of escaping the police–sixteen years in fact–Roy's luck ran out. He was arrested in Bombay on 21 July 1931 and sent to Kanpur, where he was prosecuted for his part in the Cawnpore conspiracy case seven years earlier. No trial was held in open court and the proceedings were conducted inside the jail where Roy was held. Roy was neither allowed a trial by jury nor were any witnesses allowed to speak on his behalf. It was a kangaroo court.

He defended himself passionately inside the cloistered jail, admitting that he had instigated revolution but also using the arguments of the philosophers David Hume and Jeremy Bentham to defend his right to take up arms. In an eloquent piece of writing, Roy said as only he could: 'The oppressed people and exploited classes are not obliged to respect the moral philosophy of the ruling power. A despotic power is always overthrown by force. The force employed in this process is not criminal. On the contrary, the guns carried by the army of the British government are instruments of crime.'[9]

But the magistrate was not inclined to listen to the lofty words of Hume and Bentham and instead sarcastically urged Roy to consider the 'humble provisions of the Indian penal code'. Roy's defence was suppressed. But his supporters managed to get his statement smuggled out, and it was published as 'My Defence' in India and 'I Accuse' in the US.

Roy was taken to Bareilly central jail and ultimately served five years and four months in five different jails. The prison stint completely shattered his health. The conditions in Bareilly were harsh and unsanitary, and Roy found it particularly difficult to endure the blistering heat after having lived for so many years in Europe. He ended up with lasting damage to his heart, ears and lungs.

Out of his jail time emerged one of his most interesting books: *Fragments of a Prisoner's Diary*. One of the themes he explored was a possible renaissance of India, a movement away from religion, superstition, caste, community and obscurantism to rationalism and a more scientific temper.

He was allowed to write only one letter a month. That letter went to his new lady love, Ellen Gottschalk, a young German activist who would later become his second wife. His letters reveal a wide range of interests from music and food to European philosophy, science and the Renaissance. Roy, apparently, was a gourmet and greatly missed the pleasures of European food and wine when he was in jail. He wrote to Ellen, who shared his love of food and drink, 'How delightful it would be to see a bottle of 21 Rhine buried in a shining bucket of ice, or even a Krug of Mencheuner in Wilhelmshallen.' In another letter, he wrote, 'It is unfair to be mortifying the flesh with coarse woollen texture and not have a Benedictine and Chartreuse verti to drink as the jolly old monks used to.'[10]

Outside, the Royists had consolidated their position within the All India Trade Union Congress (AITUC). They had got nearly forty unions to affiliate themselves to the organisation, and had set up a permanent position in the country.

Life After Release

Roy was released on 20 November 1936 to general acclaim, except from the communist party. As his old comrade V.B. Karnik put it, 'He was an enemy to be fought against by any and every means, since he was not prepared as they were, to follow blindly and unquestioningly the instructions and mandates of the Communist International.'[11]

On the very day of his release, Roy confounded political observers by joining the INC. He had been corresponding with Jawaharlal Nehru during his imprisonment. He issued a statement explaining his about-turn: 'Real socialists or communists must realise that, if they wish to play a part in the struggle for freedom of the Indian masses, national independence is the immediate objective.' Roy believed that communists needed to demonstrate their solidarity with the rest of India. 'I am determined to show to the people of India that Communists are not alien elements within the body politics of India, but are the sons of the soil fighting as the vanguard of the army of National Freedom under the banner of the Indian National Congress.'[12]

But once again, he found himself out of place and struggling to be accepted. He was elected as delegate to the annual session of the

INC and became a member of the All India Congress Committee. Nehru welcomed Roy graciously in his address, saying, 'Comrade Roy though young, is an old and well-tried soldier in India's fight for freedom. He has come to us after a long and most distressing period in prison, but though shaken up in body, he comes with a fresh mind and heart.'[13]

Ranged against him were both the rightists and the leftists in the INC. Roy had made a statement urging political power to be given to workers and peasants and pleading for the INC leadership to be democratised. This had enraged the right-wing leaders in the INC. On the other hand, his about-turn had antagonised the leftists.

Roy was also not prepared to go along with Gandhism. In the Faizpur session of the Congress held in 1937, he met Gandhi for the first time, though of course he had by then spent years criticising Gandhi's policies. When they met, Gandhi patronisingly advised Roy to rest and avoid politics. Apparently, Gandhi had invited Roy to join him in the prayer ground at Faizpur. The atheist Roy, ever his own man even when it was inappropriate, declined, deeply annoying Gandhi who was used to getting his own way.

Later, when Roy was trying to raise funds for *Independent India*, the magazine he had started, Gandhi would write a terse message to him on a postcard, suggesting he 'render mute service in the cause of freedom'. When Roy wrote an article titled 'Science and Superstition', he was advised by someone very close to the inner circle of the Mahatma that he (Roy) had now been branded as Enemy Number One.[14]

The relationship between Roy and Gandhi was a complex one. In many ways, they were polar opposites. As Roy's close friend, the filmmaker J.B.H. Wadia, wrote, 'Gandhi was a puritan, Roy was a hedonist ... Roy was a rationalist–nay an atheist to boot, uncompromisingly opposed to bringing religion in politics–religion as it is generally understood with its rites, ceremonies, taboos and prayers.'[15]

Roy believed that Gandhi's approach to solving social evils and superstition by trying to bring about change within India's traditional social structure—and within the framework of Hinduism—was misplaced. How, he asked, would India improve if it continued to venerate religion? Roy made constant digs at Gandhi, which did not go unnoticed. In *Fragments of a Prisoner's Diary*, Roy refers to the fact that in jail he had learnt to 'play the divine spinning wheel with which Gandhiji proposes to save the world'. And he joked, 'The Mahatma has finally scored a point over me. If he only knew it.'[16]

Roy, true to his maverick nature, also managed to antagonise leftists because he wanted the socialists in the INC to either adopt the ways of the INC or adopt the 'plan of action and the organisational form of a Communist party'. Roy did not believe in compromise; he wanted the left-wingers to declare themselves as communist or leave the Congress. Meanwhile, the proper Communist Party continued to be deeply suspicious of Roy because he had been expelled from the Comintern and was still persona non grata in Moscow. They also had many differences of opinion with him on the organisation and tactics of peasants and workers. Essentially, Roy disagreed with everybody and was nobody's ally.

In Calcutta in May 1939, Roy formed a new party called the League of Radical Congressmen within the INC in a somewhat desperate bid to gain some foothold in the political process. This would be renamed the Radical Democratic Party a year later. By this time, the right-wingers in the INC had gained power. Gandhi had become supreme and Subhas Chandra Bose was embarking on his own path of military adventure. The Royists had no power within the INC.

When the Second World War broke out in September 1939, Gandhi and Nehru initially supported England and the allies in their war against the Nazis. But soon anti-British feeling grew in the country, made worse when Britain forced India into the war without consultation. The communist party was staunchly anti-British and believed that this was the one chance for India to seize its independence. Gandhi too wanted independence before India joined the war. But the viceroy and the British government refused to compromise and Gandhi launched the Quit India Movement.

Roy, as ever, found himself on the wrong side of public opinion when he opposed the Quit India Movement. He believed that the Nazis would engulf Soviet Russia and then the world, and thus Britain and its allies deserved the support of all freedom-loving people, even Indians. He put out a controversial statement on 6 September 1939: 'All freedom-loving people will congratulate the British government on the decision, even though much belated, to put an end to Hitlerism, which it has been encouraging all the time. Had the decision been taken earlier, the freedom of many European countries would have been saved.'[17]

Roy's views were considered heretical by the Congress.[18] He was widely denounced as an agent and lackey of the British, an ironic development for someone who had been fleeing the British secret service for most of his life and had already gone to jail for his defiance. Actually, he was in deep anguish. He did not love British or French colonialism, but he believed fascist Germany was a bigger enemy, which if allowed to win, would destroy Indian hopes for freedom as well. And unlike most of the INC, he actually had experience of fascist Germany. Rather than stay quiet, he suggested to the INC that a countrywide protest be held to express sympathy with France, which had just been invaded by the Nazis. That was the last straw. Roy was expelled from the INC. He had now managed to antagonise everybody.

By 1942, it became likely that the allies—Britain, France, the Soviet Union and the US—would win the war and Roy began to foresee freedom for India. He began to churn out a series of articles, drafts and proposals suggesting an economic structure for the country. In 1944, a group of eight industrialists, including

J.R.D. Tata and G.D. Birla, suggested the Bombay Plan, which would come to greatly influence India's Five-Year Plans. Some key suggestions were that future governments should protect Indian industries from competition, that government regulation and intervention in the industrial sector was essential and that critical industries ought to be reserved for the public sector.

In response, Roy suggested a People's Plan, which emphasised the development of agriculture. In December 1944, he released a draft constitution called the Constitution of Free India. It proposed the creation of a democratic state based on certain fundamental social principles. Most importantly, it called for organised democracy and the establishment of a relation between political rights and economic power. Several of these principles were adopted by Dr B.R. Ambedkar when he framed India's first Constitution a few years later.

With all this work, there was also time for play: friendships, food, fun and camaraderie. Immediately after his release from jail, the Roys had started living in a tiny flat in Empire Building opposite Charni Road Station in Bombay. In 1938, the Roys moved to Dehradun, a deliberate move away from mainstream politics. They set up court in a rented house at 13 Mohini Road, a house with a large garden planted by Ellen, full of flowers, fruits and vegetables.

They were surrounded by protégés including J.B. Wadia, V.B. Karnik, V.M. Tarkunde, G.D. Parikh and many others. Roy was a passionate cook, good at French, Russian, Mexican and Spanish dishes. In the Soviet Union, he had apparently even prepared a 'special soup for Stalin'.

The Roys loved cats, and Roy even wrote a book called *The Memoirs of a Cat*. Their various cats were called Muma, Divali, Totsy, Sooty, and Roy's favourite, Reddie. When lunch was ready, Roy would apparently ring the bell and announce, 'Mankind and animalkind, lunch is served.'[19]

In 1942, Roy did another unwise thing, which would smear his reputation. The British government gave Rs 13,000 per month to the Indian Federation of Labour, an organisation founded to propagate anti-fascist propaganda, which was led by B.R. Ambedkar, with Roy as his general secretary. Roy stupidly accepted the money, which resulted in him being then roundly vilified by both communists and Congressmen. Rumours were spread that Roy was travelling in a posh Rolls Royce and rolling in money.[20] The affair came to be called 'L'Affaire Rs 13,000', and Roy was called a British agent and spy.

Roy appeared to have admired Subhas Chandra Bose and his patriotism, but when Bose started the Indian National Army (INA) and allied with the Japanese, Roy had great misgivings. He believed India was more likely to get freedom under the British than under Japanese fascism. He told his friend Wadia that Netaji had sent an envoy personally asking Roy to join the INA. Roy had discussed the problem at length, then eventually refused. The envoy had threatened him, saying that when Netaji eventually won the war, Roy would be killed. Roy had thrown the envoy out by his neck, shouting, 'Thank your stars that I am not an informer. Or I would have handed you over to the police as a traitor to the cause of freedom.'[21]

In 1946, the Radical Democratic Party was completely defeated in elections, leaving Roy disillusioned and convinced about the venality of party politics. He had failed to see that his atheism had also isolated him from mainstream politics, where communal tension was on the rise. Roy declared that he was no longer satisfied with political activities and that RDP would be dissolved.

In September 1946, on the eve of independence for India, Roy founded the Indian Renaissance Institute. It was time for a new beginning and a new philosophy.

An Indian renaissance?

On 15 August 1947, as India awoke to life and freedom, Roy found himself in an introspective mood, looking back at his learnings over the years. He had fought for this moment all his life, but now that it had arrived, he was fearful of what India might become. The bloody savagery of Partition did not make him any more optimistic about an Indian renaissance.

Stalin's brutal dictatorship in Russia and the move towards tyranny even after the Nazis had been defeated had greatly disappointed Roy. On the day of India's independence, Roy wrote a manifesto of his new philosophy, which he called Radical or New Humanism. 'One hundred years have passed since the communist manifesto was issued to herald the age of the proletarian revolution,' he said reminding the public of Karl Marx's words.[22]

But he admitted that communism had failed the people. 'Heralded as the salvation of the civilised world, tortured and tormented by capitalist exploitation, communism in practice has come to be a spectre terrifying not only the bourgeoisie, it is causing grave misgivings among the progressive forces of the modern world ...' Roy went so far as to say that the proletarian revolution heralded by the Communist Manifesto and believed to have been actively inaugurated by the Russian Revolution had opened up an apocalyptic perspective rather than a higher civilisation. He had come a long way from being Lenin's young man.

What then did Roy suggest as an alternative? He now saw that the individual had been crushed by Stalin's move towards collectivism. So, he began to see individual freedom as all-important and began to formulate a new philosophy. Its basic principle was that man is essentially rational and man is the maker of this world. It went beyond the narrow confines of nationalism, religion and community—or at least it hoped to.

Roy explained his new philosophy with twenty-two theses, all based on the fundamental principle that *the individual was above society, and freedom can be enjoyed only by individuals. He completely rejected Soviet collectivism.* He wrote somewhat optimistically of a renaissance in India. 'Revolutions are heralded by iconoclastic ideas conceived by gifted individuals. A brotherhood of men attracted by the adventure of ideas, keenly conscious of the urge for freedom, fired with the vision of a free society of free men, and motivated by the will to remake the world so as to restore the individual in his position of primacy, and dignity, which show the way out of the contemporary crisis of modern civilisation.'[23]

Roy believed that a philosophical revolution would have to come before a social revolution. He was opposed to blind faith and superstition and supported rationalism. He was a physical realist, which meant he rejected the concepts of God, soul, karma and fatalism. His views were completely opposite to the Gandhian philosophy popular at the time. He wanted India to sever its link with religion and associate more closely with science.

No longer the angry young man, Roy now defined a revolutionary as 'one who has got the idea that the world can be remade, made better than it is today, that it was not created by a supernatural power, and therefore, could be remade by human efforts.'[24] Further, according to Roy, 'the idea of improving upon the creation of God can never occur to the God-fearing. We can conceive of the idea only when we know that all gods are our own creation, and we can depose whomsoever we have enthroned.'[25] One can imagine that this did not go down well with the Gandhians.

Roy was inspired by the philosophy of the ancient Indian saint Charvaka, long forgotten in modern India, who had been a rationalist, agnostic and sceptic. In contrast to Gandhi's nationalism and emphasis on the village, Roy believed India should be cosmopolitan and learn from other countries. Nehru was the only other Indian leader who had an international outlook, but Roy's philosophy was different from Nehru's too. Nehru believed that India's backwardness was due to foreign subjugation. Roy believed that it was India's backwardness that had led to subjugation. Nehru believed the difference between a poor India and a rich Europe was the Industrial Revolution. Roy laid more emphasis on Renaissance and the Enlightenment and sought a similar renaissance in India.

Politically, Roy supported the decentralisation of political and economic power and suggested a party-less democracy. The pyramidical structure of the state, he suggested, should be raised on the foundations of people's committees made of free individuals. He believed that 'a government for the people could never be fully of the people, and by the people'. He also argued that power should always be vested in the people, but they should be able to exercise their power effectively, not just periodically. Exercising their power to vote once in five years was not enough, according to Roy.

Instead, he argued, individual men ought to be recognised on merit and democracy and be placed above parties. He suggested that there ought to be a transition period during which a council of state made up of men of science, intelligence, integrity and wisdom drawn from professional groups of engineers, economists, historians, scientists and others engaged in intellectual pursuits would govern.

Economically, Roy was opposed to the centralisation of heavy industries. He believed that a cooperative system should be built up from the bottom, which would eliminate exploitation by big landowners.

Was Roy just an impractical, elitist idealist out of touch with reality? Many thought so then and many continue to think so now.

But radical humanism as preached by Roy was not that far removed from Gandhian philosophy. Gandhi's Sarvodaya movement—which meant the welfare of all—also believed in decentralisation and a party-less democracy, though Gandhi remained a spiritualist till the end. Gandhi did not believe in rapid industrialisation or state ownership of large enterprises like the Soviets. Neither did Roy.

In 1948, when Gandhi was assassinated by Nathuram Godse, all differences were set aside. Roy wrote a glowing tribute to Gandhi in the journal *Independent India*, saying simply, 'In death, there is no enmity.'[26] After Gandhi's assassination, it was Nehru's vision of socialism that came to dominate India. Neither Gandhi nor Roy would ever see their dreams come true.

These years spent in developing and refining radical humanism were perhaps the best years of Roy's life, though he continued to struggle with his health. In Dehradun, the Roys presided over a large, rambling house filled with cats for Roy, and flowers for Ellen, visited often by a string of disciples and acolytes. It was Roy's first house since he had left his father's home all those years ago and it would be his last. Many years earlier, he had told Ellen, 'I have been a homeless rover all my life; I want a place attached to my name.' From this house the two would put out a journal called *The Radical Humanist*.

Ellen was renowned for her devotion as a wife, and her Hindu friends apparently called her a reincarnation of Sita. She was, as one friend described her, a loving wife, a brilliant collaborator, an efficient secretary, a wonderful companion and hostess, and in the end, a dedicated nurse. Like Evelyn Trent before her, Ellen worshipped Roy, always putting herself in the shade and minimising her own very considerable contribution. 'There is no doubt that Roy was the original thinker, nor that it was Ellen's multilingual talents that added lucidity and coherence to his writing,'[27] wrote Sibnarayan Ray.

Maniben Kara, the trade unionist, also described Ellen as the 'ideal Hindu wife', shy in her ability to write and speak, but actually a fluent and convincing speaker and a competent organiser. But Ellen was remembered more fondly for her charming hospitality at 13 Mohini Road. As Roy's disciples flocked there and heated discussions took place, Ellen played hostess 'assuaging a vanquished critic, skilfully changing a topic when it developed into a controversy'. She arranged plants and flowers, found recipes, mixed drinks, came up with current news and small talk about men and events. As Kara put it, Ellen had 'made it into a place of pilgrimage which attracted seekers of truth and lovers of freedom'.[28]

The Roys both loved cooking, and the main meal at 13 Mohini Road was a huge brunch with eggs, bread, cakes, coffee, bacon and jam, a habit borrowed from their life in Europe. In a delightful piece called 'Cats, Brunches and the Open Society', the visiting Swami Agehananda Bharati—actually a former American professor of anthropology called Leopold Fischer—wrote of the atmosphere at Chez Roys. There were 'dozens of cats' all over, 'on the sofas, the chairs, the tables, in the kitchen, under cushions'. The Swami complained that he got quite ill because of the cats, but Ellen was impervious to suggestions that the cats be removed.[29]

Though a good hostess, Ellen did not suffer fools gladly. Neither for that matter did Roy. When Roy's brother and sister visited, they waited for dal bhaat (dal and rice) after the brunch, like good Bengalis, which they did not get. 'Ellen was not very polite, Roy withdrew to his writing, the junior Mrs Roy began crying, and the junior Roy couple left the next morning.'

Indeed, as the Swami noted astutely, 'If ever I attended an elitist house, it was 13 Mohini Road. Karl Marx did not like workers and people personally, though he wrote about them. Neither did Roy and Ellen.' But the Swami approvingly noted how Roy and Ellen were not in the least bit hypocritical. 'Not that they were uncomfortable with lowly people—far from it. They did not patronise servants and other folks, but they also did not humour them in any way. How different from the American counterculture crowd where the university professor tried so hard to identify with the underdog ... often pathetically.'

The Roys' domestic bliss was interrupted by a sudden illness. In June 1952, Roy took a trip to Mussoorie with Ellen, where he sustained a serious fall while walking in the hills. Bedridden for weeks with severe injuries and nursed devotedly by Ellen, Roy recovered well, and by May 1953, was planning a lecture tour in the United States. But in August, just a few months later, he had an attack of cerebral thrombosis. Despite Nehru's past quarrels with Roy, he visited him at his sickbed in December 1953 and said, 'Roy, I really want you to get well soon. We have much work to do together when you get well.' But he would not get well. Roy died on 25 January 1954, just before midnight.

Ellen was devastated. As Roy's disciple Sibnarayan Ray wrote, 'For seventeen years, he had been the centre of their life and now there was total emptiness.'[30] Ellen herself wrote sadly, a week after Roy's death, 'Perhaps it is not right to make a man the only point of reference of one's whole existence. In my earliest life, before I knew him, I could not have conceived of doing so. But with him it was different. His life and what he lived for were one. Living his life made mine bigger and better and very happy.'[31]

Ellen vowed to carry on the work of humanism and she did exactly that for several years, putting out issues of *The Radical Humanist*, collecting Roy's writings for a book and spreading his word, just as she always had.

But only six years later, in 1960, Ellen met a terrible fate. As some Royists pointed out, her fate was very similar to that of Leon Trotsky, who had been battered to death with an iron hammer. On 14 December, the sweeper and cook came in the morning to 13 Mohini Road and found blood on the veranda. They called for Ellen, but there was no response. Friends were called, who came and broke the door. Ellen Roy's body was found lying on the floor, with her head battered in. Her eyes and mouth were gagged with cloth and blood was everywhere.[32] Ellen was cremated in the same crematorium where Roy had been cremated seven years earlier. Condolences poured in, and President Dr Rajendra Prasad called her death 'a great loss'. The postmortem showed her death was due to five brutal head injuries and four broken ribs. The murder weapon had been an iron pestle.

The assassin was at large, but many in the Roy community of friends believed it to be a political murder committed by communists. Ellen had been a communist in her youth in Germany, but later, like Roy, had done an about-turn and become a savage critic of the Communist Party.

Eventually two teenagers, aged seventeen and nineteen, who appeared 'innocent eyed, timid and bewildered' were arrested on suspicion of murder. They were Basant Kumar and Suresh, poor school dropouts who were desperate for money and had likely never heard of communism. Both confessed to the murder before the police, but later retracted their confessions at trial, claiming that they were coerced by the police to confess. After protracted trials, they were released by the Supreme Court of India for lack of evidence–a sorry end to the whole violent saga. Ellen paid the ultimate price for the crime of loving a man to excess.

But the restless nomads Roy and Ellen had finally come to rest.

EPILOGUE

The Legacy of Chatto and Roy

WHAT IS THE LEGACY OF CHATTO AND ROY, THE TWO REVOLUTIONARY vagabonds? Mostly, they were forgotten, ignored and disrespected. Scarcely anyone remembers them today, except marginally as 'commies'. But they were so much more.

A waspish *Guardian* obituary published in 1954 began by describing M.N. Roy as 'having the most extraordinary career of a man of his generation in Asia. It was of interest out of proportion to his actual achievements.' The obituary then got even more savage. 'He had little skill in party manoeuvre' and 'Electorally, his party counted for nothing before or after Independence'.[1] But at least Roy got an obituary. Chatto did not.

Later historians were no less cruel about the Indian revolutionaries in general. As one wrote, 'The revolutionaries of the early twentieth century had little immediate impact in their own day, and failed to a considerable extent due to their own breathtaking incompetence. To modern nationalists, they are not an edifying example, while at the time their endeavours proved to the overwhelming majority of Indians that violence would do nothing to weaken the power of the Raj. In this sense, the revolutionaries' abysmal failure only served a purpose which they had never intended or wanted. It increased the popularity of MK Gandhi and his message of non-violent resistance.'[2]

Nehru, too, was never shy about sharing his scathing opinions of the Berlin Indians and their ilk. But, as we saw earlier, he believed Chatto and Roy to have been different from their brethren.

Some Indian historians were kinder, pointing out that though revolutionaries like Chatto and Roy failed to achieve their immediate aims, they did mould the long-term strategy of national leaders. 'These middle-class revolutionaries, were, after all, the first to demand complete independence from British rule. They refused to compromise with the halfway house of dominion status and other concessions that the colonial rulers were doling out, and which the then Congress leaders were willing to accept. In post-war India, widespread peasant uprisings, industrial strikes, the mutiny of the Royal Indian navy cadets, and the launching of the INA under Subash Chandra Bose, were in fact a continuation and extension of the legacy of the nationalist revolutionaries.'[3]

Part of their legacy which has remained unremarked is their often shoddy treatment of the women in their lives. Roy and Chatto had this in common among their many other similarities. If we are to believe Agnes Smedley—and there seems to be no reason not to—Chatto, for all his liberal ways, was insanely jealous of her past lovers, her work and her friends. He expected her to be a housewife and drudge while he played the part of a revolutionary. Smedley would manage to escape and find her own place in the world, but Roy's equally talented wives would not.

Evelyn Trent wrote poignantly of how Roy left her for the younger Louise Geissler and then moved on to Ellen Gottschalk, even though Evelyn had given up her life to follow him around the world, risked arrest, fled from secret police and acted as his unpaid secretary while her own skills had been ignored. She would accuse him of tossing away their life 'lightly and scornfully'. Ellen, who followed her and became the ultimate 'Hindu wife', would write wistfully, 'Perhaps it is not right to make a man the only point of reference of one's whole existence.'

Both men seemed to demand complete devotion from their wives, but did not return the favour. It was easy to be revolutionary in the world, but not where it counted: at home. However, Chatto seemed to have mended his ways by the time he married Lidiya Karunovskaya, who wrote fondly of him, 'I had the great good fortune to be the friend and wife of this astonishingly charming, beautiful man, to break his prolonged loneliness, to be together with him and to be useful to him.'[4]

Regardless of their personal faults, both men were ahead of their time in many ways. As one of his many biographers pointed out, 'Roy was not a successful man in the ordinary sense of the term. If he had acted differently from his ideas, he would have been an opportunist, and if he refused to revise his opinions, he would have been dogmatic and unrealistic. Yet, by the time he died in January 1954, he was a forgotten man. Perhaps no other Indian had dedicated his life in such totality to internationalism and received so little acknowledgement.'[5] The same might have been said of Chatto.

We speak today of internationalism, but these days internationalism has come to mean rampant consumerism. Meanwhile, India remains consumed by a petty, narrow, insecure nationalism. Chatto and Roy were true cosmopolitans, learning to take the best of what the West had to offer—rationalism, scientific temper, new thinking—and applying it to their theories. They fought against imperialism, but they never let nationalism dominate their lives. Only Nehru could match them in cosmopolitanism, but even he bowed to Gandhi's will. Chatto and Roy refused to bend to any will but their own.

Communism today is not fashionable and hasn't worked as Chatto and Roy had hoped it would. Roy himself admitted that communism had morphed into brutal tyranny and had thus moved to radical humanism. It's possible that, if Chatto had survived, he too would have denounced what communism eventually became in the Soviet Union, an Orwellian nightmare.

But is it correct to say that they were entirely misguided, when India's richest 1 per cent holds 40 per cent of its wealth? What

Roy predicted has come to pass. 'The Billionaire Raj headed by India's modern bourgeoisie is now more unequal than the British Raj headed by colonialist forces,' said a recent highly regarded study.[6] This makes India one of the most unequal societies in the world—exactly what Roy and Chatto warned against. The modern bourgeoisie have taken over, despite Nehru's efforts.

Roy's credo of radical humanism was impractical and utopian in many ways. A country governed by elitist people's committees made up of educated professionals, as he suggested, could never have worked in a country like India. We now acknowledge that universal suffrage for all, regardless of education and achievement, is crucial for proper democracy. Indeed, it is the poor and least educated who have often saved Indian democracy.

But who in modern day India—consumed by religious hatred, caste tensions, superstition and patriarchy—would not find some merit in Roy's goal? As Roy wrote, 'A critical examination of what is cherished as India's cultural heritage will enable the Indian people to cast off the chilly grip of a dead past. It will embolden them to face the ugly realities of a living present and look forward to a better, brighter and pleasanter future.'[7]

If Roy and Chatto became somewhat unimportant towards the end of their lives, it was not entirely their fault, but rather a credit to them. They both staunchly refused to use religion, division and their upper-caste status as a means to gain power, unlike many of their opportunistic peers. They certainly had little skill in party manoeuvring and petty horse-trading. They were of a different breed.

As another Samaren Roy pointed out, 'After 1947 and partition, Indian society was divided into castes and communities. Roy belonged to an insignificant minority of those who had outgrown those limitations. This minority was ineffective.'[8]

M.N. Roy predicted an India completely ruled by religion, caste, superstition and obscurantism, and that is exactly what we have in 2025. He wanted an India where party politics would not ban accomplished individuals from making their mark. It is a view that has been echoed by many.

What might have happened if Chatto and Roy had united in a common cause? Perhaps they could have learnt from each other and founded a more enduring party or ideology. Chatto might have been able to escape Stalin's purge, as Roy had. Perhaps they could have formed a party of enlightenment, as Roy had envisaged. Or perhaps that was too utopian, given the endless quarrels of the revolutionaries who did not join Gandhi. As with all of India, the communists' biggest weakness was their disunity, their quarrelling and their inability to compromise. In India's diversity also lies its great and enduring curse.

In 1967, fourteen years after his death, Roy's face made it to a postage stamp, as did the faces of Bhikaji Cama and Har Dayal. Chatto never even had a memorial, as far as I know, even as his sisters and brother were honoured and are remembered even today. Even his sister-in-law Kamaladevi Chattopadhyay made it to a stamp, but Chatto did not.

Roy's declaration in 'My Crime', his defence against the Comintern, was an apt obituary for both of them: 'My offence is that I lay claim to the right of independent thinking.'

There was no place for independent thinkers in their time—and perhaps there isn't in our time. Therein lies their tragedy and that of India's still. Forgetting their ideas, their sacrifices and above all, their great, enduring courage is our loss, and that of those who come after us.

Acknowledgements

THIS BOOK WOULD NOT HAVE BEEN WRITTEN WITHOUT A HOST OF people. Firstly, those historians and scholars that went before me. I am mainly indebted to Nirode K. Barooah's incredible biography of Chatto—*Chatto: The Life and Times of an Indian anti-imperialist in Europe* and Sibnarayan Ray's three volume biography of M.N Roy—*In Freedom's Quest: A study of the life and works of M.N Roy*. I have relied heavily on both, as well as on many others acknowledged in my footnotes.

I am also indebted to the staff at the British Library in London. In October 2023, the British Library was hacked and access to its computer systems remained restricted for over a year. In this time, the staff were generous with their help, despite being overworked and hampered. This book is dedicated to libraries and librarians, without whom I would be lost.

The Chattopadhyay family were unable to provide any letters or other memorabilia, but were kind and generous enough to allow me to write this book, for which I am grateful.

My agent and dear friend Jayapriya Vasudevan of Jacaranda Books was the first to believe in the promise and potential of this book, and has gone way beyond what most agents do.

My editors at Westland, V.K. Karthika and Ajitha G.S., continue to astonish me by publishing incredibly compelling books. I hope my book will be one of them.

I am especially thankful to Kushalrani Gulab and Pallavi Mohan, who edited this book with incredible dedication and meticulousness, and weeded out many mistakes. Any surviving errors are my own.

My online writing circle provided valuable feedback and kept me going with memes and jokes. You know who you are.

My wonderful family for providing support and encouragement. My father, as always.

And last but not least, the music of Fleetwood Mac that kept me going through several rounds of edits.

Notes

Introduction

1. Price, Ruth, *The Lives of Agnes Smedley*, Oxford University Press, 2005, p. 112.
2. Readers should note that the family generally spelt their name as Chattopadhyay, while Chatto added an extra 'a' to the family name.
3. Roy, M.N., *M.N. Roy's Memoirs*, Allied Publishers, Bombay, 1964, p. 488.
4. Ray, Sibnarayan, *In Freedom's Quest: A Study of the Life and Works of M.N. Roy 1887-1954*, Minerva Associates, Calcutta, 1998, p. 326.
5. Roy, Manabendra Nath, *Banglapedia*, www.banglapedia.org.
6. Roy, Samaren, *M.N. Roy: A Political Biography*, Sangam Books, London, 1997, p. vii.
7. Popplewell, Richard, J., *Intelligence and Imperial Defence: British Intelligence and the Defence of the Indian Empire: 1904-1924*, Frank Cass, London, 1995, p. 5.
8. Manjapra, Kris, *M.N. Roy: Marxism and Colonial Cosmopolitanism*, p. 14.
9. Barooah, Nirode K., *Chatto: The Life and Times of an Indian Anti-Imperialist in Europe*, Oxford University Press, New Delhi, 2004, p. 264.
10. Ibid., p. 271.
11. Haithcox, John Patrick, *Communism and Nationalism in India, M.N. Roy and Comintern Policy 1920-1939*, Princeton University Press, Princeton, 2015, p. 246.

1: The Magnificent Failure

1. Baig, Tara Ali, *Sarojini Naidu*, Publications Division, Ministry of Information and Broadcasting, New Delhi 1974, pp. 10–11.
2. Ibid.
3. Sengupta, Padmini, *Sarojini Naidu: A Biography*, Asia Publishing House, Bombay, 1966, p. 7.
4. Ibid.
5. Ibid.
6. Chattopadhyay, Harindranath, *Life and Myself*, Nalanda Publications, Bombay, 1948, p. 2.
7. Baig, Tara Ali, *Sarojini Naidu*, p. 7.
8. Ibid.
9. Chattopadhyay, Harindranath, *Life and Myself*, p. 15.
10. Ibid., p. 5.
11. Ibid., p. 20.
12. Ibid., p. 23.
13. Banerjee, Hasi, *Sarojini Naidu: The Traditional Feminist*, K.P. Bagchi and Company, Calcutta, 1998, p. 100.
14. Chattopadhyay, Harindranath, *Life and Myself*, p. 30.
15. Ibid., p. 35.
16. Ibid.
17. Sengupta, Padmini, *Sarojini Naidu: A Biography*, p. 9.
18. Ibid., p. 5.
19. Hyderabad Affairs, Supplementary Volume for 1886, p. 471, cited by Rao, Ramakrishna, *The Freedom Struggle in Hyderabad, Vol ii*, 1956, The Hyderabad State Committee, Hyderabad.
20. Ibid.
21. Ibid.
22. Ibid.
23. Barooah, Nirode K., *Chatto: The Life and Times of an Indian Anti-imperialist in Europe*, p. 9.

24. Chattopadhyay, Harindranath, *Life and Myself*, p. 118.
25. Ibid.
26. Ibid., p. 119.
27. Ibid.
28. Ibid., p. 120.

2: The Bomb Maker

1. Mukherjee, Prithwindra, *Bagha Jatin*, Dey's Publishing, Calcutta, 2003 (4th Edition), p/ 43.
2. Manjapra, Kris, *M.N. Roy: Marxism and Colonial Cosmopolitanism*, p. 26.
3. Roy, Samaren, *The Restless Brahmin: Early life of MN Roy*, Allied Publishers, New Delhi, 1970, p. 2.
4. Ibid.
5. Mukherjee, Prithwindra, *Undying Courage: The Story of Bagha Jatin*, Academic Publishers, Calcutta, 1992, p. 31.
6. Ibid., p. 39.
7. Ibid.
8. Roy, Samaren, *The Restless Brahmin: Early Life of M.N. Roy*, p. 26.
9. Ibid.
10. Ray, Sibnarayan, *In Freedom's Quest: A Study of the Life and Works of M.N. Roy*, Minerva Associates, Calcutta, 1998, p. 17.
11. Ibid., p. 28.
12. Ibid.
13. Popplewell, Richard, *Intelligence and Imperial Defence: British Intelligence and the Defence of the Indian Empire: 1904-1924*, p. 114.
14. Ibid., p. 115.
15. Ibid.
16. Ray, Sibnarayan, *In Freedom's Quest, A Study of the Life and Works of M.N. Roy*, p. 20.
17. Manjapra, Kris, *M.N Roy: Marxism and Colonial Cosmopolitanism*, p. 15.

3: India House: Dying for Dharma

1. Datta, V.N., *Madan Lal Dhingra and the Revolutionary Movement*, Vikas Publishing House, New Delhi, 1978, p. 18.
2. Mitrokhin, L.V., *Friends of the Soviet Union: India's Solidarity with the USSR During the Second World War 1941-1945*, Allied Publishers Private Ltd, New Delhi, p. 204.
3. Ker, J.C., *Political Trouble in India: 1907-1917*, Oriental Publishers, Calcutta, 1917, p. 407.
4. Barooah, Nirode K., *Chatto: The Life and Times of an Indian Anti-imperialist in Europe*, p. 11.
5. Bose, Arun Coomar, *Indian Revolutionaries Abroad*, Bhawani Bhavan, Patna, 1971, p. 20.
6. Barooah, Nirode K., *Chatto: The Life and Times of an Indian Anti-imperialist in Europe*, p. 14.
7. Popplewell, Richard, *Intelligence and Imperial Defence: British Intelligence and the Defence of the Indian Empire: 1904-1924*, p. 129.
8. Datta, V.N., *Madan Lal Dhingra and the Revolutionary Movement*, p. 19.
9. Owen, Nicholas, 'The Soft Heart of the British Empire: Indian revolutionaries in Edwardian London', *Past and Present*, Volume 220, Issue 1, August 2013, pp. 143–184.
10. Ibid.
11. Datta, V.N., *Madan Lal Dhingra and the Revolutionary Movement*, p. 19.
12. Gandhi, Mohandas K., *The Collected Works of Mahatma Gandhi*, Obscure Press, London, 2008, p. 30.
13. Ker, J.C., *Political Trouble in India*, p. 26.
14. Chattopadhyay, Harindranath, *Life and Myself*, p. 203.
15. Ibid., p. 205.
16. 'Indian Anarchism in England', *The Times*, 20 February 1909.
17. Ibid.
18. 'Indian Anarchism', *The Times*, 1 March 1909.

19. 'Indian Anarchism', *The Times*, 19 March 1909.
20. Ker, J.C., *Political Trouble in India*, p. 27.
21. Datta, V.N., *Madan Lal Dhingra and the Revolutionary Movement*, p. 19.
22. Sethna, Khorshed Adi, *Madame Bhikaji Rustom Cama*, Hind Swaraj, Builders of Modern India, Publications Division, Govt of India, 1987, p. 2.
23. Bose, A.C., *Indian Revolutionaries Abroad*, Northern Book Centre, New Delhi, 2002, p. 42.
24. Ibid.
25. Yadav, Bishamber, *MPT Acharya, Reminiscences of an Indian Revolutionary*, Anmol Publications New Delhi, 1991, p. 27.
26. 'Indian Anarchism', *The Times*, 10 March 1909.
27. Laursen, Ole-Birk, '"I have only One Country, it is the World": Madame Cama, Anticolonialism, and Indian-Russian Revolutionary Networks in Paris, 1907–17', *History Workshop Journal*, Vol. 90, Autumn 2020, pp. 96–114.
28. Ibid.
29. A speech delivered on 18 March 1934, quoted in Barooah, Nirode K., *Chatto: The Life and Times of an Indian Anti-imperialist in Europe*, p. 27.
30. Ibid.
31. Bose, A.C., *Indian Revolutionaries Abroad*, p. 42.
32. Ibid.
33. Ibid.
34. Ker, J.C., *Political Trouble in India*, p. 172.
35. Ibid., p. 175.
36. Ibid., p. 181.
37. Dustoor, P.E., *Sarojini Naidu*, Rao and Raghavan, Mysore, 1961, p. 4.
38. Baig, Tara Ali, *Sarojini Naidu*, p. 12.
39. Nehru, Jawaharlal, *An Autobiography*, OUP, New Delhi, 1936, p. 169.

4: In Search of the Golden Fleece

1. Hoover, Karl, 'The Hindu Conspiracy in California, 1913-1918', *German Studies Review*, 1985, 8 (2), German Studies Association: 245–261.
2. Roy, M.N., *M.N. Roy's Memoirs*, Allied Publishers, Bombay, 1964, pp. 3–12.
3. Ibid.
4. Ibid.
5. Ibid.
6. Ibid.
7. Ibid.
8. Ibid.
9. Mukherjee, Prithwindra, *Undying Courage: The Story of Bagha Jatin*, p. 180.
10. Ray, Sibnarayan, *In Freedom's Quest: A Study of the Life and Works of M.N. Roy*, p. 39.
11. Ibid.
12. Ibid.
13. Ibid.
14. Ibid., p. 40.
15. Roy, M.N., *M.N. Roy's Memoirs*, p. 12.
16. Ibid.
17. Ibid.

5: Archaeology and Jihad in Berlin

1. Gossman, Lionel, *The Passion of Max Von Oppenheim: Archaeology and Intrigue in the Middle East from Wilhelm II to Hitler*, Open Book Publishers, Milton Keynes, UK, p. 10.
2. Ibid., p. 31.
3. Ibid., p. 32.
4. Ibid.

5. Ibid., p. 33.
6. Ibid., p. 36.
7. Ibid., p. 38.
8. Ibid.
9. Ibid., p. 32.
10. Ibid., p. 41.
11. McKale, Donald M., 'The Kaiser's Spy: Max von Oppenheim and the Anglo-German Rivalry Before and During the First World War', *European History Quarterly*, 27 (1997): 199-219 (p. 203).
12. Schulz, Matthias, 'The Spectacular Life and Finds of Max von Oppenheim', *Spiegel International*, 28 January 2011.
13. Barooah, Nirode K, Chatto: *The Life and Times of an Indian Anti-imperialist in Europe*, p. 37.
14. Ibid., p. 39.
15. Ibid., p. 44.
16. Ibid.
17. Ibid., p. 90.
18. Roy, M.N., *M.N. Roy's Memoirs*, p. 286.
19. Nehru, Jawaharlal, *An Autobiography*, Digital Library India, 1936, p. 152.
20. Stuermer, Harry, *Zwei Kriegsjahre in Konstantinopel: Skizzendeutsch-jungtiirkischer Moral und Politik*, Payot, Lausanne, 1917. Quoted from the English translation *Two War Years in Constantinople: Sketches of German and Young Turkish Ethics and Politics*, George H. Doran, New York, 1917, pp. 152–53, 176–77.
21. Ibid.
22. Gossman, Lionel, *The Passion of Max Von Oppenheim*, p. 32.
23. Balachandran, Vappala, *A Life in Shadow: The Secret Story of ACN Nambiar: A Forgotten Anti-Colonial Warrior*, Roli Books, New Delhi, 2016, p. 39.
24. Ibid., p. 59.
25. Ibid., p. 35.

6: California Dreaming

1. Roy, M.N., *M.N. Roy's Memoirs*, Allied Publishers Private Limited, Bombay, 1964, p. 19.
2. Roy, Samaren, *M.N. Roy: A Political Biography*, Sangam Books, New Delhi, 1997, p. 15.
3. Ibid.
4. Roy, M.N., *M.N. Roy's Memoirs*, p. 22.
5. Ker, J.C., *Political Trouble in India*, pp 202.
6. Ray, Samaren, *The Restless Brahmin: The Early Life of* M.N. *Roy*, p. 25.
7. Roy, M.N., *M.N. Roy's Memoirs*, p. 24.
8. Ibid., p. 25.
9. Ibid.
10. US Military Intelligence File _F 5525, 27 April 1918, cited in Roy, Samaren, *M.N. Roy: A Political Biography*, p. 17.
11. Ray, Sibnarayan, *In Freedom's Quest, A Study of the Life and Works of M.N. Roy*, p. 49.
12. Ibid., p. 167.
13. Roy, Samaren, *M.N. Roy, A Political Biography*, p. 17.
14. Ibid.
15. Wadia, J.B.H., *M.N. Roy, the Man: An Incomplete Royana*, Popular Prakashan, Bombay, 1983, p. 26.
16. Roy, M.N., *M.N. Roy's Memoirs*, p. 27.
17. Ibid., p. 28.
18. Karnik, V.B., *M.N. Roy*, National Book Trust of India, New Delhi, 2005, p. 27.
19. Haithcox, John Patrick, *Communism and Nationalism in India*: M.N *Roy and Comintern Policy* 1920-1939, p. 8.
20. Roy, M.N., *M.N. Roy's Memoirs*, p. 30.
21. Ibid.
22. Ibid.
23. Ibid., p. 32.

24. *New York Times*, 24 April 1918.
25. Ibid.

7: A Dagger, a Revolver and a Bottle of Chloroform

1. Maugham, Somerset, *Ashenden: Or the British Agent*, Vintage Classics, London, 2010, p. 110.
2. Chattopadhyay, Harindranath, *Life and Myself*, p. 227.
3. Ibid.
4. Maugham, Somerset, *Ashenden: Or the British Agent*, p. 110.
5. Laursen, Ole-Birk, 'A Trustworthy Indian in Stockholm: A. Yusufali's Mission to Scandinavia, 1918', *Untold Lives*, British Library Blog.
6. Barooah, Nirode K., *Chatto: The Life and Times of an Indian Anti-imperialist in Europe*, p. 105.
7. Ibid., p. 113.
8. Ibid.
9. Ibid.
10. Sherif, M.A., *Searching for Solace, A Biography of Abdullah Yusuf Ali*, Islamic Book Trust, Kuala Lumpur, 1994, p. 24.
11. Ibid.
12. Ibid., p. 28.
13. Ibid.
14. Ibid., p. 44.
15. PRO: FO 395/190(1918), cited in Sherif, M.A., *Searching for Solace*, p. 52.
16. 'India's attitude to England, Answer by the Indian National Committee', *Stockholm Tidningen*, 2 May 1918, quoted in Barooah, Nirode K., *Chatto: The Life and Times of an Indian Anti-imperialist in Europe*, p. 128.
17. Laursen, Ole-Birk, 'A Trustworthy Indian in Stockholm: A. Yusufali's Mission to Scandinavia, 1918', *Untold Lives*, British Library Blog.
18. *Stockholm Tidningen*, 2 May 2018, quoted by Barooah, Nirode K., *Chatto: The Life and Times of an Indian Anti-imperialist in Europe*, p. 128.

19. Ibid.
20. Reuters report 'Bogus Indian Committee' in *The Times*, 11 May 1918, cited in Sherif, M.A., *Searching for Solace*, p. 55.
21. FO 395/190, cited in Sherif, M.A., *Searching for Solace*, p. 55.
22. Roy, Subodh, *Communism in India: Unpublished Documents 1919-1924*, National Book Agency, Kolkata, 1976, pp. 1–64.
23. Ibid.

8: Al Companero Indio: The Indian Comrade in Mexico

1. Roy, M.N., *M.N. Roy's Memoirs*, p. 51.
2. Ray, Sibnarayan, *In Freedom's Quest: A Study of the Life and Works of M.N Roy*, p. 68.
3. Roy, Samaren, *M.N. Roy: A Political Biography*, Sangam Books, 1997, p. 23.
4. Roy, M.N., *M.N. Roy's Memoirs*, p. 72.
5. Ibid.
6. Ibid., p. 73.
7. Gonzales, Michael, J., *The Mexican Revolution: 1910-1940*, University of New Mexico Press, Albuquerque, 2002, p. 11.
8. Roy, M.N., *M.N. Roy's Memoirs*, p. 70.
9. Ibid., p. 71.
10. Ibid., p. 78.
11. Remark by Wolfe, Bertram, an American radical socialist, quoted in Manjapra, Kris, *MN Roy: Marxism and Colonial Cosmopolitanism*, p. 37.
12. Roy, M.N., *M.N. Roy's Memoirs*, p. 143.
13. Ibid.
14. Ibid.
15. Sheridan, Claire, *Russian Portraits*, Jonathan Cape, London, 1921, p. 86.
16. Massie, Robert K., *The Fate of the Romanovs: The Final Chapter*, Random House, London, 1985.

17. Roy, M.N., *M.N. Roy's Memoirs*, p. 203.
18. Ibid.
19. Ibid., p. 217.
20. Ibid., p. 218.
21. Ibid.
22. Beals, Carleton, *Glass Houses: Ten Years of Freelancing*, Lippincott, Philadelphia, 1938, pp. 43–53.
23. Ibid.
24. Walker, Ian, 'Rosa Luxemburg, Death of a Revolutionary', *The New European*, 12 January 2019.
25. Roy, M.N., *M.N. Roy's Memoirs*, p. 286.
26. Ibid., p. 166.
27. Bose, A.C., *Indian Revolutionaries Abroad*, p. 399.
28. Ibid.

9: Live the Life of a Cabbage I Would Not!

1. Price, Ruth, *The Lives of Agnes Smedley*, OUP, New York, 2005, p. 3.
2. Ibid.
3. Ibid.
4. Smedley, Agnes, *China Correspondent*, Pandora Press, London, 1984, p. 11.
5. Ibid., p. 12.
6. Ibid., p. 35.
7. Ibid.
8. Price, Ruth, *The Lives of Agnes Smedley*, p. 4.
9. Smedley, Agnes, *Daughter of Earth*, The Feminist Press, New York, 1973, p. 276.
10. Ibid.
11. Mckinnon, Janice R., Stephen R., *Agnes Smedley: The Life and Times of an American Radical*, University of California Press, Berkeley, 1988, p. 45.

12. Smedley, Agnes, *Battle Hymn of China*, Victor Gollancz, 1944, New York, p. 16.
13. Ibid.
14. Ibid., p. 15.
15. Price, Ruth, *The Lives of Agnes Smedley*, p. 88.
16. Smedley, Agnes, *Battle Hymn of China*, p. 17.
17. Ibid.
18. McKinnon, Janice R., Stephen R., *The Life and Times of an American Radical*, Berkeley University of California Press, Berkeley, 1988, p. 81.
19. Smedley, Agnes, *Battle Hymn of China*, p. 19.
20. Ibid., p. 18.
21. Roy, M.N, *Memoirs of M.N. Roy*, p. 509.
22. Ibid., p. 510.
23. Ibid.
24. Mckinnon, Janice R., Stephen R., *The Life and Times of an American Radical*, p. 73.
25. Ibid., p. 87.
26. Chattopadhyay, Harindranath, *Life and Myself*, p. 217.
27. Ibid., p. 217.
28. Mckinnon, Janice R., Stephen R., *The Life and Times of an American Radical*, p. 75.
29. Price, Ruth, *The Lives of Agnes Smedley*, p. 112.
30. Ibid.
31. Ibid.
32. Ibid.
33. Ibid., p. 113.
34. Ibid., p. 114.
35. Ibid., p. 119.
36. Mckinnon, Janice R., Stephen R., *The Life and Times of an American Radical*, p. 103.
37. Smedley, Agnes, *Daughter of Earth*, p. 362.

38. Ibid.
39. Price, Ruth, *The Lives of Agnes Smedley*, p. 142.
40. Mckinnon, Janice., Stephen R., *The Life and Times of an American Radical*, pp. 122–124.
41. Ibid.
42. Ibid.
43. Ibid., p. 126.
44. Ibid.
45. Smedley, Agnes, *Battle Hymn of China*, p. 23.
46. Ibid.

10: Lenin's Young Man

1. Roy, M.N., *M.N. Roy's Memoirs*, p. 314.
2. Ibid.
3. Ibid., p. 315.
4. Roy, M.N., *Men I Met*, Lalvani Publishing House, Mumbai, 1968, p. 36.
5. Roy, M.N, *M.N Roy's Memoirs*, p. 341.
6. Ibid., p. 346.
7. Ibid.
8. Mcmeekin, Sean, *The Russian Revolution: A New History*, Profile Books Ltd, London, 2017, p. 371.
9. Roy, M.N., *M.N. Roy's Memoirs*, p. 349.
10. Mcmeekin, Sean, *The Russian Revolution: A New History*, p. 372.
11. Roy, M.N., *Memoirs of M.N Roy*, p. 350.
12. Ibid., p. 351.
13. Ibid., p. 363.
14. Reed, John, *Ten Days That Shook the World*, Boni and Liveright, 1919, p. 158.
15. Roy, M.N., *Memoirs of M.N. Roy*, p. 369.
16. Mcmeekin, Sean, *The Russian Revolution: A New History*, p. 372.

17. Ibid., p. 373.
18. Roy, M.N., M.N. *Roy's Memoirs*, p. 373.
19. Ibid., p. 373.
20. Haithcox, John Patrick, *Communism and Nationalism in India: MN Roy and Comintern Policy: 1920-1939*, Princeton University Press, New Jersey, 1971, p. 15.
21. Roy, Samaren, *M.N. Roy: A Political Biography*, p. 48.
22. Drawn from Chattopadhyay, Suchetana, 'Muhajirs to Bolsheviks: 1917 and Early Communists from Colonial India in Central Asia', paper presented at the Revolutionary Longings Conference, Eisenberg Institute for Historical Studies, University of Michigan, Ann Arbor, 8–10 March 2017.
23. Ibid.
24. Roy, M.N., M.N. *Roy's Memoirs*, p. 459.
25. Ibid., pp. 459–467.
26. Ahmad, Muzaffar, *Myself and the Communist Party of India*, 1920-1929, National Book Agency, Calcutta, 1970, pp. 45–46.
27. Khan, Abdul Qadir, 'The Road to Moscow', *The Times*, London, 25 February 1930.
28. Chattopadhyaya, Gautam, *Abani Mukherji, A Dauntless Revolutionary and Pioneering Communist*, People's Publishing House, New Delhi, 1976, p. 10.
29. Ghosh, Rakhal Chandra, *Biplabi Abani Mukherji*, Calcutta Press, Dacca, 1929, p. 32.
30. Ibid., p. 15.
31. Roy, M.N., M.N. *Roy's Memoirs*, p. 476.
32. Ibid.
33. Ibid., p. 477.
34. Ibid.
35. Ahmad, Muzaffar, *Myself and the Communist Party of India*, pp. 47–70.
36. Roy, M.N,, *Memoirs of M.N Roy*, p. 478.

37. Excerpts from *Aprakasita Rajnitik Itihash* quoted by Ahmad, Muzaffar in *Myself and the Communist Party of India*, p. 457.
38. Roy, M.N., *M.N. Roy's Memoirs*, p. 535.
39. Ibid.
40. Ibid.
41. Ibid.
42. Bose, A.C., *Indian Revolutionaries Abroad*, Northern Book Centre, New Delhi, 2002, p. 39.
43. Ibid.
44. Das, C.R., Speech at the thirty-seventh session of the Indian National Congress, 26 December 1922.
45. Roy, M.N., 'Open Letter to Chittaranjan Das and his Followers', Zurich, 23 February 1923.

11. The Red Millionaire

1. Mcmeekin, Sean, *The Red Millionaire: A Political Biography of Willy Munzenberg*, Yale University Press, 2004, pp. 1–2.
2. Ibid.
3. Gross, Babette, *Willi Munzenberg: A Political Biography*, Michigan State University Press, 1974, p. 5.
4. Lenin, V.I., *Pravda* 113, 18 May 1913.
5. Barooah, Nirode K., *Chatto: The Life and Times of an Indian Anti-imperialist in Europe*, p. 251.
6. Ibid.
7. Ibid., p. 252.
8. Jones, Jean, 'The League Against Imperialism', The Socialist History Society, London, 1996, p. 6.
9. Norman, Dorothy, *Nehru: The First Sixty Years*, The Bodley Head, London, 1965, p. 128.
10. Gandhi, Mohandas Karamchand, Nandi Hill, Mysore State, to Nehru, 25/5/1927, quoted in Petersson, Fredrik, *Willi Munzenberg, The League Against Imperialism and the Comintern*, p. 337.

11. Nehru, Jawaharlal, *An Autobiography*, OUP, New Delhi, 1936, p. 171.
12. Gopal, S., *Selected Works of Jawaharlal Nehru*, Jawaharlal Nehru Memorial Fund, New Delhi, p. 130.
13. Ibid.
14. Ibid.
15. Ibid.
16. Ibid., p. 41.
17. Chattopadhyay, Harindranath, *Life and Myself*, p. 197.
18. Ibid.
19. Ibid.
20. Ibid.
21. Ibid., p. 214.
22. Ibid., p. 215.
23. Ibid.
24. Ibid.
25. Balachandran, Vappala, *A Life in Shadow*, p. 67.
26. SAPMO-BA ZPA R1507/67113, 112, Resichskrommer: Vermerk, cited in Petersson, Fredrik, *Willi Munzenberg, The League Against Imperialism and the Comintern*, p. 468.
27. Papers of the Home Department, Government of India, folder RGASPI 542/1/25, pp 45-46, cited in Petersson, Fredrik, *Willi Munzenberg, The League Against Imperialism and the Comintern*, p. 469.
28. RGASPI 542/1/40, 119-123, 'Courses for Colonial Students in Berlin', 5 November 1930.
29. Acharya to the AITUC, 29 April 1928, box 2, 6.1.25, Horst Kruger Papers, ZMO, quoted by Laursen, Ole Birk, 'Anarchy of Chaos, MPT Acharya and the Indian Struggle for Freedom'.
30. Barooah, Nirode K., *Chatto: The Life and Times of an Indian Anti-imperialist in Europe*, p. 264.
31. Ibid.
32. Ibid., p. 265.
33. Ibid., p. 266.

34. RGASPI 542/1/25, 45-46, Letter from Munzenberg to Kuusinen, 12/11/1928, cited by Frederik Petersson, *Willi Munzenberg, The League Against Imperialism and the Comintern*, p. 473.
35. Barooah, Nirode K., *Chatto: The Life and Times of an Indian Anti-imperialist in Europe*, p. 268.
36. Chattopadhyaya, V., 'Unemployment in India', *Inprecor*, 6 March 1930.
37. Chattopadhyaya, V., 'India and the Second International', *The Pan Pacific Monthly* (San Francisco), No. 37, June-July 1930, p. 13.
38. Ibid., p. 15.
39. Chattopadhyaya, V., 'The Indian National Congress', *The Labour Monthly*, 13 May 1931, pp. 303–307.
40. Jones, Jean, *The League Against Imperialism*, p. 32.
41. Mcmeekin, Sean, *The Red Millionaire*, p. 302.
42. Ibid., p. 306.

12: La Guillotine: The Downfall of M.N. Roy

1. Higgins, Andrew, 'Lenin's Brain: They Took it out to Understand the Source of a Revolution They Now Reject', *The Independent*, 1 November 1993.
2. Taken from the account of Muzaffar Ahmad in his book, '*Myself and the Communist Party of India*, pp. 327–406.
3. Intelligence report of the Government of British India about the activities of communists in India, prior to institution of the Meerut Conspiracy Case, Intelligence Bureau, Home Department, Government of India, 1933, Chapter 14.
4. Ibid.
5. Roy, Subodh, *Communism in India: Unpublished Documents 1919-1924*, p. 58.
6. Ibid.
7. Petrie, David, *Communism in India*, 1924-1927, Editions Indian, Calcutta, 1972, p. 97.

8. Roy, Samaren, *M.N. Roy: A Political Biography*, p. 104.
9. Russian State Archive of Sociopolitical History, cited in Sexton, John, *Red Friends: Internationalists in China's Struggle for Liberation*, Verso Books, London, 2023, p/ 25.
10. Sexton, John, *Red Friends: Internationalists in China's Struggle for Liberation*, Verso Books, London 2023, p. 25.
11. Karnik, V.B., Epilogue, M.N. Roy's *Memoirs of M.N. Roy*, p. 578.
12. Sheean, Vincent, *Personal History*, The Modern Library, New York, 1940, p. 250.
13. North, Robert C., Eudin, Xenia J., *MN Roy's Mission to China*, University of California Press, Berkeley, 1963, p. 19.
14. Sexton, John, *Red Friends: Internationalists in China's Struggle for Liberation*, Verso Books, London 2023, p. 27.
15. Bennett, Milly, Grunfeld, Tom, *On her Own: Journalistic Adventures from San Francisco to the Chinese Revolution: 1917-1927*, Routledge, London, 2015, p. 221.
16. Haithcox, John Patrick, *Communism and Nationalism in India*: M.N. *Roy and Comintern Policy 1920-1939*, p. 73.
17. Snow, Edgar, *Red Star over China*: The Classic Account of the Birth of Chinese Communism, Grove Press UK, London, p. 161.
18. Sexton, John, *Red Friends: Internationalists in China's Struggle for Liberation*, Verso Books, London 2023, p. 32.
19. Ray, Sibnarayan, *In Freedom's Quest*: A Study of the Life and Works of M.N. Roy, p. 167.
20. Ibid., p. 169.
21. Ibid., p. 176.
22. Haithcox, John Patrick, *Communism and Nationalism in India:* M.N *Roy and Comintern Policy, 1920-1939*, p. 160.
23. Ibid.
24. Ibid.
25. Roy, M.N., 'Our Differences', Saraswaty Library, Calcutta, 1938, p. 1.

13: The End of Virendranat Agornatovitch Chatopadaya

1. From S.V. Krasnikov, Sergei Mironovich Kirov: 'Zhizn' i deiatel'nosti' (Moscow, 1964), quoted and translated in Borys Levytsky, comp., *The Stalinist Terror in the Thirties: Documentation from the Soviet Press*, Stanford, 1974, p. 38.
2. Johnson, Paul, 'Modern Times' quoted in the *Los Angeles Times*, 13 April 1988.
3. Popson, Nancy, *Who Killed Kirov? 'The Crime of the Century'*, Wilson Center, February 2000.
4. Hitler, Adolf, *Mein Kampf*, Ralph Manheim translation, Houghton Mifflin, New York, pp. 658–659.
5. Barooah, Nirode K., *Chatto: The Life and Times of an Indian Anti-imperialist in Europe*, p. 283.
6. Ibid., p. 324.
7. Ibid., p. 316.
8. Ibid.
9. Sebag Montefiore, Simon, *Stalin: The Court of the Red Tsar*, Weidenfeld and Nicholson, London, 2021, p. 233.
10. Getty, J., Arch, Naumov, Oleg V., *Yezhov, The Rise of Stalin's Iron Fist*, Yale University Press, New Haven, 2008, p. 183.
11. Ibid., p. 185.
12. Ibid., p. 233.
13. Ibid., p. 234.
14. Conquest, Robert, *The Great Terror, Stalin's Purge of the Thirties*, Penguin Books, London, 1968, pp. 404–405.
15. Buber-Neumann, Margarete, *Under Two Dictators: Prisoner of Stalin and Hitler*, Random House, New York, 2008, p. 12.
16. Roy, M.N., *M.N. Roy's Memoirs*, p. 362.
17. Buber-Neumann, Margarete, *Under Two Dictators*, p. 14.
18. Ibid., p. 15.
19. Barooah, Nirode K., *Chatto: The Life and Times of an Indian Anti-imperialist in Europe*, p. 323.

20. Mitrokhin, Leonid, 'A Triple Trap: Story of Three Indian Comintern Activists in the Years of Stalinist Terror', *Soviet Land*, No. 4, April 1991, pp 30, cited by Barooah, Nirode K., *Chatto: The Life and Times of an Indian Anti-imperialist in Europe*, p. 321.
21. Balachandran, Vappala, *A Life in Shadow*, p. 50.
22. 'Archeologists Find New Pits at Stalin-Era Moscow Mass Grave', *The Moscow Times*, 21 May 2021.
23. Mitrokhin, Leonard, *Friends of the Soviet Union: India's Solidarity with the USSR During the Second World War 1941-1945*, Allied Publishers, 1945, New Delhi, p. 11.
24. Ibid.
25. Ibid.
26. Gross, Babette, *Willi Munzenberg, A Political Biography*, p. 183.
27. Barooah, Nirode K., *Chatto: The Life and Times of an Indian Anti-imperialist in Europe*, p. 322.
28. Chattopadhyay, Harindranath, *Me and Myself*, p. 238.
29. Khrushchev's Secret Speech, 'On the Cult of Personality and Its Consequences', Delivered at the Twentieth Party Congress of the Communist Party of the Soviet Union, Wilson Center Digital Archive.
30. Ibid.

14: The Twice Born Heretic

1. Karnik, V.B., Epilogue, *M.N. Roy's Memoirs*, Allied Book Publishers, 1968, New Delhi, p. 588.
2. Ibid.
3. Interview with Maniben Kara, V.B. Karnik and J.B. Wadia, Bombay, 20 October 1961, quoted in *Communism and Nationalism in India: M.N. Roy and Comintern Policy, 1920-1939*, Haithcox, John Patrick, Princeton University Press, 1971, p. 177.
4. Haithcox, John Patrick, *Communism and Nationalism in India: M.N. Roy and Comintern Policy, 1920-1939*, p. 180.

5. Ray, Sibnarayan, *In Freedom's Quest: A Study of the Life and Works of M.N. Roy*, p. 320.
6. Haithcox, John Patrick, *Communism and Nationalism in India: M.N. Roy and Comintern Policy 1920-1938*, p. 187.
7. Radical Democratic Party, *The Radical Democratic party, An Introduction*, New Delhi, Radical Democratic Party, 1944, p. 10.
8. Ibid.
9. Roy, M.N., 'I Accuse', Roy Defence Committee of India, 1932.
10. Wadia, J.B.H, *An Incomplete Royana*, Popular Prakashan, Bombay, 1983, p. 27.
11. Karnik, V.B., Epilogue, M.N. *Roy's Memoirs*, p. 595.
12. Karnik, V.B., M.N. *Roy*, National Book Trust, New Delhi, 1980, p. 86.
13. Ibid.
14. Ray, Sibnarayan, *In Freedom's Quest: A Study of the Life and Works of M.N. Roy*, p. 326.
15. Ibid., p. 33.
16. Ibid p. 34.
17. Karnik, V.B., M.N. *Roy*, p. 93.
18. Ibid., p. 598.
19. Wadia, J.B.H., *MN Roy: An Incomplete Royana*, p. 62.
20. Ibid., p. 64.
21. Ibid., p. 31.
22. Roy, M.N., *New Humanism: A Manifesto*, Ajanta Publications, 1981, pp. 1–3.
23. Ibid.
24. Ibid.
25. Ibid.
26. Wadia, J.B.H., *An Incomplete Royana*, p. 35.
27. Martyn, Mady, quoted in *The World Her Village: The Selected Writings and Letters of Ellen Roy*, by Sibnarayan Ray, Ananda Publishers Private Ltd, 1979, p. 130.

28. Kara, Maniben, 'Ellen Roy, a Tribute', *Radical Humanist*, 25 January 1961.
29. Bharati, Agehananda, 'Cats, Brunches and the Open Society, Memories of Mohini Road', quoted by Ray, Sibnarayan in *The World, Her Village*, p. 101.
30. Ray, Sibnarayan, *The World Her Village*, p. 110.
31. *The Radical Humanist*, Vol 18, No. 8, 21 February 1954.
32. Ghosh, Tapan, *Caravan*, 1 May 1965, quoted by Ray, Sibnarayan in *The World Her Village*.

Epilogue

1. *The Guardian*, 26 January 1954, p. 12.
2. *Popplewell, Richard, Intelligence and Imperial Defence: British Intelligence and the Defence of the Indian Empire 1904-1924*, p. 4.
3. Mukhopadhyay, Ashoke Kumar, *Terrorism: A Colonial Construct: Select British Home Department Intelligence Reports on Indian Nationalist Revolutionary Activists 1907-1936*, Sahitya Samsad, Kolkata, 2009, p. xxxiii.
4. Barooah, Nirode K., *Chatto: The Life and Times of an Indian Anti-imperialist in Europe*, p. 322.
5. Roy, Samaren, *M.N. Roy: A Political Biography*, p. 138.
6. Bharti, Nitin Kumar, Chancel, Lucas, Piketty, Thomas, Somanchi, Anmol, *Income and Wealth Inequality in India: The Rise of the Billionaire Raj, 1922-2023*, World Inequality Lab, March 2024.
7. Roy, M.N., *New Humanism: A Manifesto*, pp. 12–15.
8. Roy, Samaren, *M.N. Roy: A Political Biography*, p. 139.